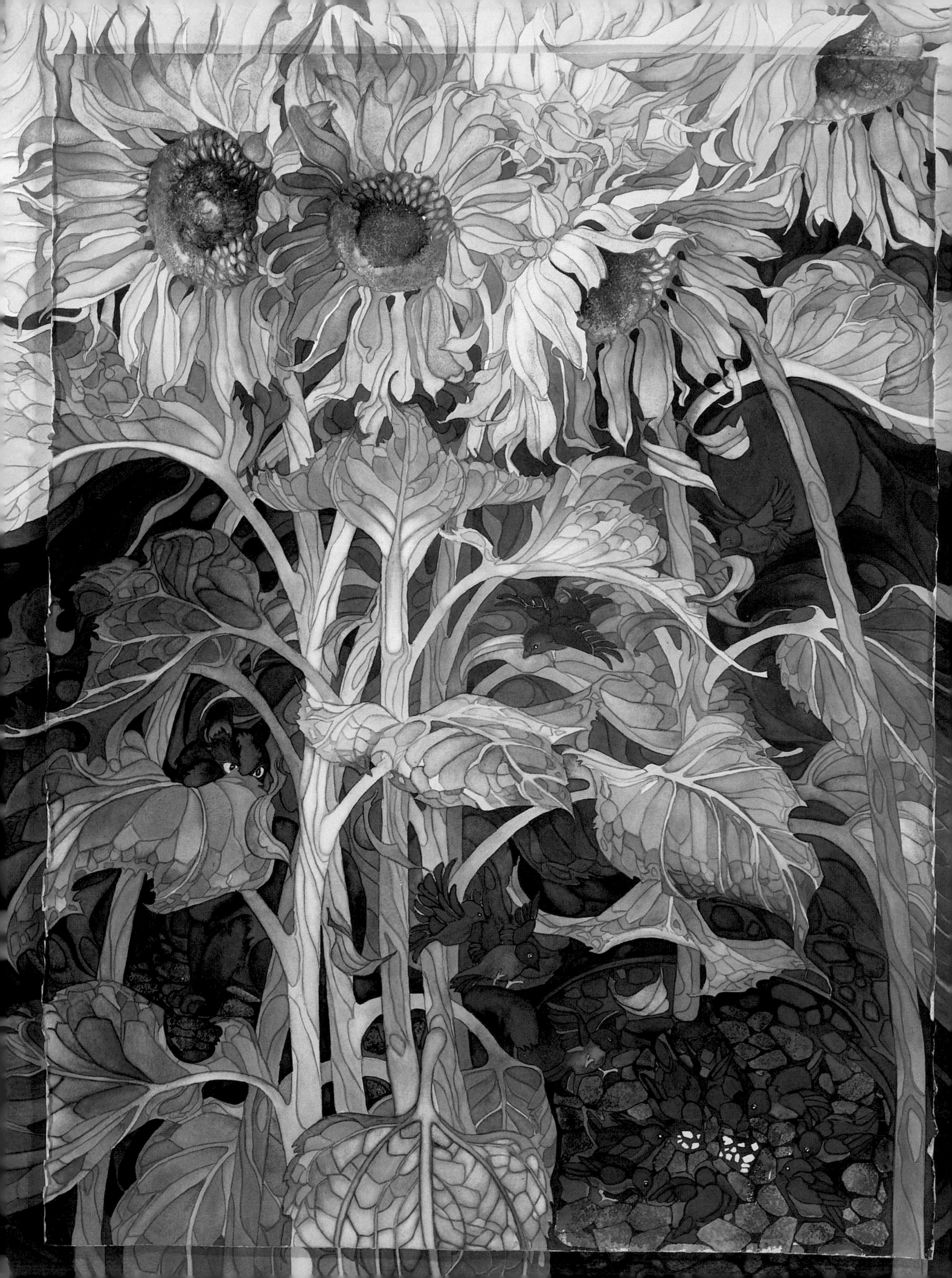

exploring
watercolor

Elizabeth Groves

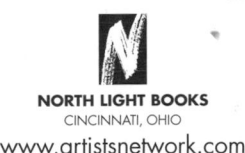

NORTH LIGHT BOOKS
CINCINNATI, OHIO
www.artistsnetwork.com

Exploring Watercolor. Copyright © 2012 by Elizabeth Groves. Manufactured in China. All rights reserved. No part of this book may be reproduced in any form or by any electronic or mechanical means including information storage and retrieval systems without permission in writing from the publisher, except by a reviewer who may quote brief passages in a review. Published by North Light Books, an imprint of F+W Media, Inc. 10151 Carver Road, Suite 200, Blue Ash, OH 45242. (800) 289-0963. First Paperback Edition 2012.

 Other fine North Light Books are available from your favorite bookstore, art supply store or online supplier. Visit our website at fwmedia.com.

16 15 14 13 12   5 4 3 2 1

DISTRIBUTED IN CANADA BY FRASER DIRECT
100 Armstrong Avenue
Georgetown, ON, Canada L7G 5S4
Tel: (905) 877-4411

DISTRIBUTED IN THE U.K. AND EUROPE
BY F&W MEDIA INTERNATIONAL LTD
Brunel House, Forde Close, Newton Abbot, TQ12 4PU, UK
Tel: (+44) 1626 323200, Fax: (+44) 1626 323319
Email: enquiries@fwmedia.com

DISTRIBUTED IN AUSTRALIA BY CAPRICORN LINK
P.O. Box 704, S. Windsor NSW, 2756 Australia
Tel: (02) 4577-3555

Edited by Jason Feldmann
Designed by Guy Kelly
Production coordinated by Matt Wagner

Library of Congress has cataloged hardcover edition as follows:
Groves, Elizabeth
  Exploring watercolor : creative exercises and techniques for watercolor and mixed media / Elizabeth Groves.
    p. cm.
  Includes index.
  ISBN 978-1-58180-874-2 (plc, concealed wire-o : alk. paper)
  1. Watercolor painting--Technique. 2. Mixed media painting--Technique. I. Title.
  ND2420.G76 2007
  751.42'2--dc22

                                         2007002663

ISBN: 978-1-4403-2476-5 (pbk. : alk paper)

Nocturne
26" × 34" (66cm × 86cm)

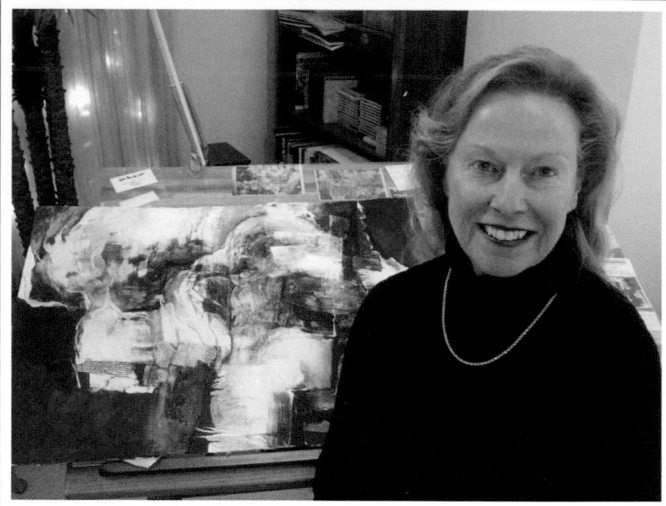

About the Author
Elizabeth Groves studied in post-graduate fine arts classes at the University of Colorado, followed by demonstrations and workshops conducted by nationally recognized artists in New York, San Diego, Pittsburgh, Houston and San Francisco. Her work has been exhibited in many juried shows and has won numerous awards. She has also attained signature membership in a number of national watercolor societies.

Her work can be found in many publications, including the North Light titles *Splash 4* (1998), *The Best of Flower Painting* (1998), *Splash 8* (2003) and *Splash 9* (2006). Elizabeth teaches oil and watercolor classes for senior citizens, adults and children in workshops, ongoing classes and private lessons.

METRIC CONVERSION CHART

To convert	to	multiply by
Inches	Centimeters	2.54
Centimeters	Inches	0.4
Feet	Centimeters	30.5
Centimeters	Feet	0.03
Yards	Meters	0.9
Meters	Yards	1.1

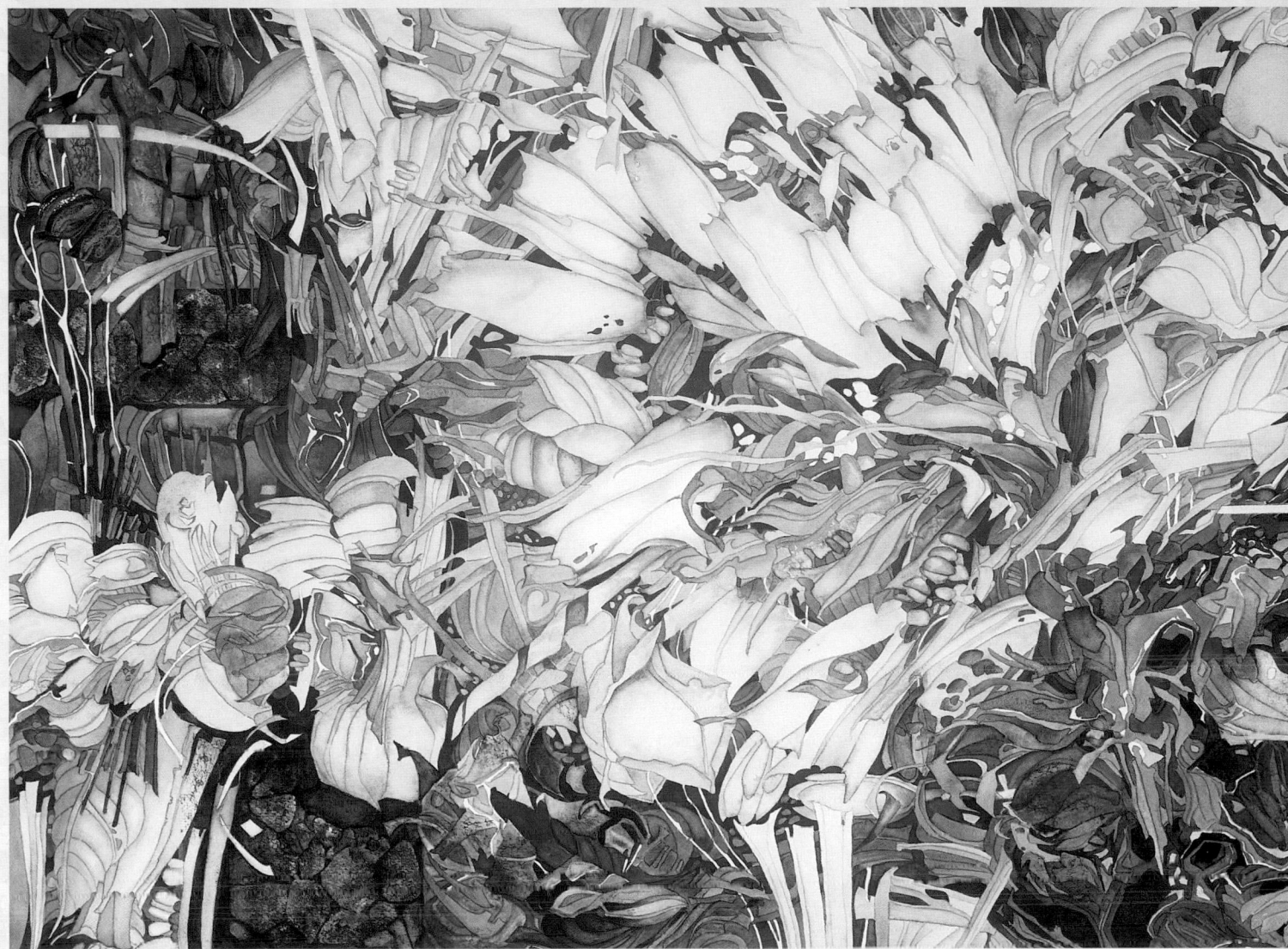

Entropy
22" × 30" (56cm × 76cm)

Acknowledgements

You wouldn't be reading this book if it weren't for the collaboration of several people. Thanks so much to North Light editorial director Jamie Markle, who believed this book was a good idea and who likened writing a book to sculpture. You start with a block of clay and whittle away at it until it resembles something. Sometimes it is similar to the idea you started out with, and sometimes quite different. Thanks to North Light editor Amy Jeynes, who got me started in the right direction, and North Light editor Jason Feldmann, who was with me chapter by chapter, line by line, word by word, and who created order out of chaos—which was the lion's share of the work.

My great appreciation goes to all the artists I have met and read about—they all have added to my store of knowledge so that I might pass it on to you, the reader. And of course, thanks to the students from whom I have learned so much, especially those who have an unerring instinct to be creative even if they don't think they do. I have thoroughly enjoyed working with each and every one of you.

Dedication

When I began this project a couple of years ago, I bought a roll of tungsten film to photograph my paintings. My husband, Tom, asked, "Why are you buying that film? It has thirty-six exposures on it and you will never use that many." Well, twenty-five rolls of film later he changed his mind and has since become my knight in shining armor. After months of "battle," his armor is still untarnished and without a dent. "Thanks" is not a big enough word for all the assistance and support he provided in being a computer wizard, a camera genius and a carrier of film back and forth to the camera store for endless developing. I am very lucky to have such a stalwart companion in arms.

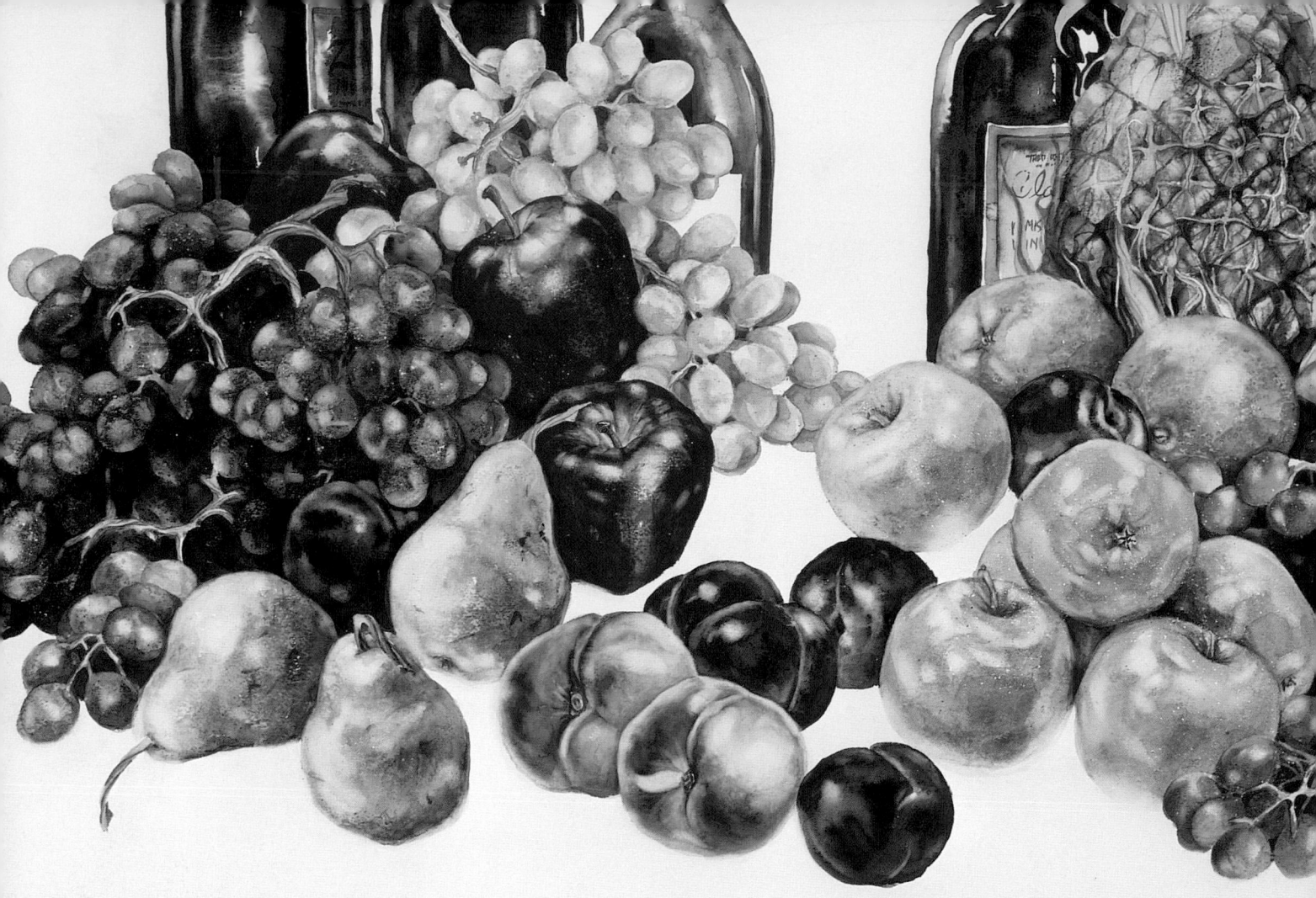

Grand Cru
22" × 30" (56cm × 76cm)

table of contents

Fisher Kings
22" × 30" (56cm × 76cm)

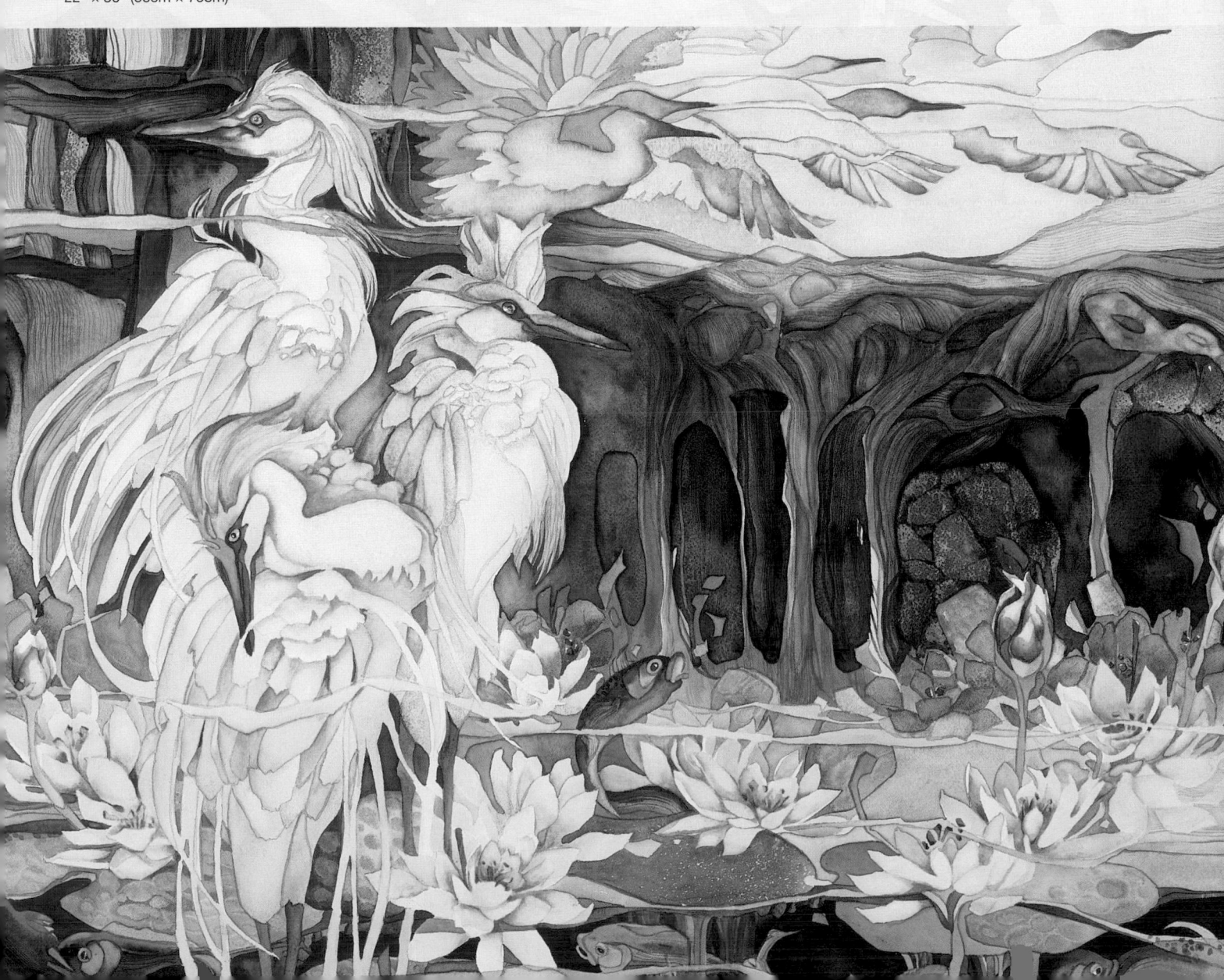

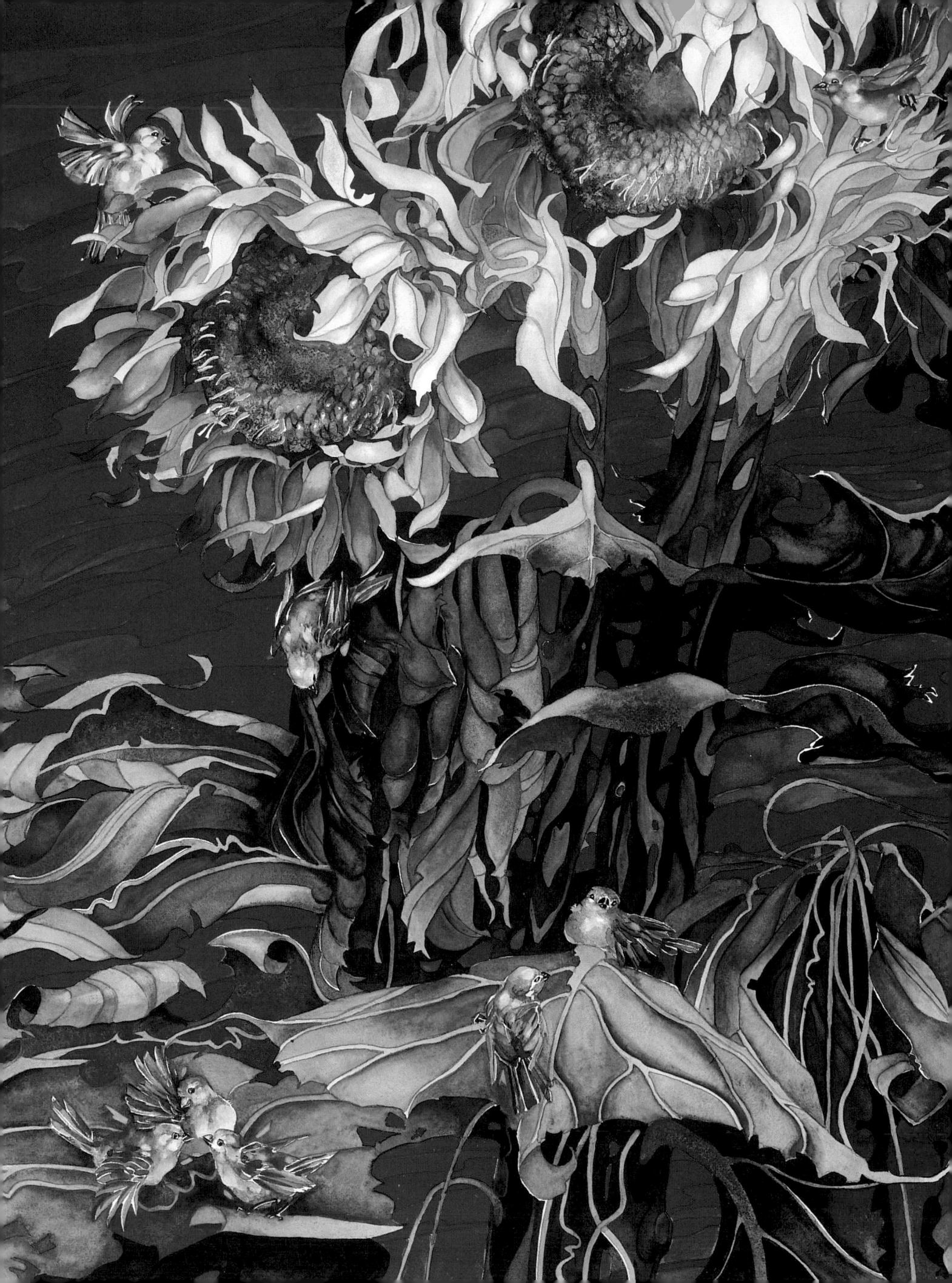

introduction

"The real voyage of discovery consists not in seeking new landscapes but in having new eyes."

— **Marcel Proust (1871-1922)**

Do you know how lucky we are—those of us who make art? We can explore every aspect of our imagination, add form and substance to our ideas and present to the world our individual interpretation of the reality that surrounds us. Art has been with us since the dawn of civilization and will continue throughout the centuries. As individuals, each of us can add our one small voice to art's grand tradition and thereby become, in a sense, immortal. By creating art, our lives become not temporal but timeless.

French author Anatole France wrote, "To know is nothing at all; to imagine is everything." Intellect must be enhanced by imagination. Imagination is what you alone can bring to the painting process in order to create a compelling expression that is lush, layered and rewarding to both the artist and viewer. It is imagination that gives breath and life and subjectivity to that which is objective. When your intellect, heart and soul become one with the painting process, that is when you hear the angels sing.

As artists we see reality as anyone else does, but through imagination we embellish and embroider upon that reality to create a richer tapestry. It is this envisioning of the world beyond the obvious that the artist shares with the viewer; that is the essence of painting. Each painting is a tiny attempt to enter into the depth of the human spirit. Therefore, it is not the product but the act of painting itself that is the soul of the creative endeavor. There is an old Chinese saying that the most beautiful paintings capture a scene between reality and imagination so never let reality stand in the way of imagination.

In theory, the philosophy of this book is to move from the reality of patterns in nature to the more imaginary interpretations that only come from aspects of the individual personality and are therefore unique. Your emphasis should be on the spirit of painting, rather than the technical aspects. Your mood should be upbeat and your attitude can-

do. Your colors should be bright and beautiful. Your goal should be to reach for a higher level of artistic achievement.

In practice, this book will provide you with a variety of hands-on practice exercises and over twenty step-by-step demonstrations (from basic to complex) that anyone can do.

In order to create memorable artwork, you must first arm yourself with different application techniques, then arrange the materials in a visually pleasing way that forms an interesting design. By abstracting certain shapes, you can create aesthetically pleasing compositions that push the viewer to see common things in a different way.

Creativity is the flow of the process involved in any painting. Give yourself permission to experiment on paper with little concern for the consequences. Value the process because we are at our most creative when enjoying the work.

Remember, to create art we must have:

- A thorough knowledge of the subject matter.
- A strong emotional response.
- An understanding of design principles and composition.
- Knowledge of craft and technique.
- Passion to create a personal and unique expression.

Your painting journey is, as Proust says, "a voyage of discovery." Over the years of your painting experience you may become a master of the craft and develop extraordinary technical expertise, but if you paint with your eyes only the result will be pale and shallow. Let what your eyes tell you be influenced by your unique individuality and by allowing your true heart and being into your work. Tap into your very essence and "see" with your soul. Paint what you feel, not what you see, and you will see the world in a different way.

In this book, you will be introduced to many different painting techniques that you can add to your growing repertoire. More importantly, I hope this book will embolden you to make your painting statements meaningful and memorable. Don't be afraid to put a piece of yourself into your work. Remember to see the world around you with new eyes. So come now, and let your own personal painting journey begin.

Elizabeth Groves

Windrush Blue
30" × 22" (76cm × 56cm)

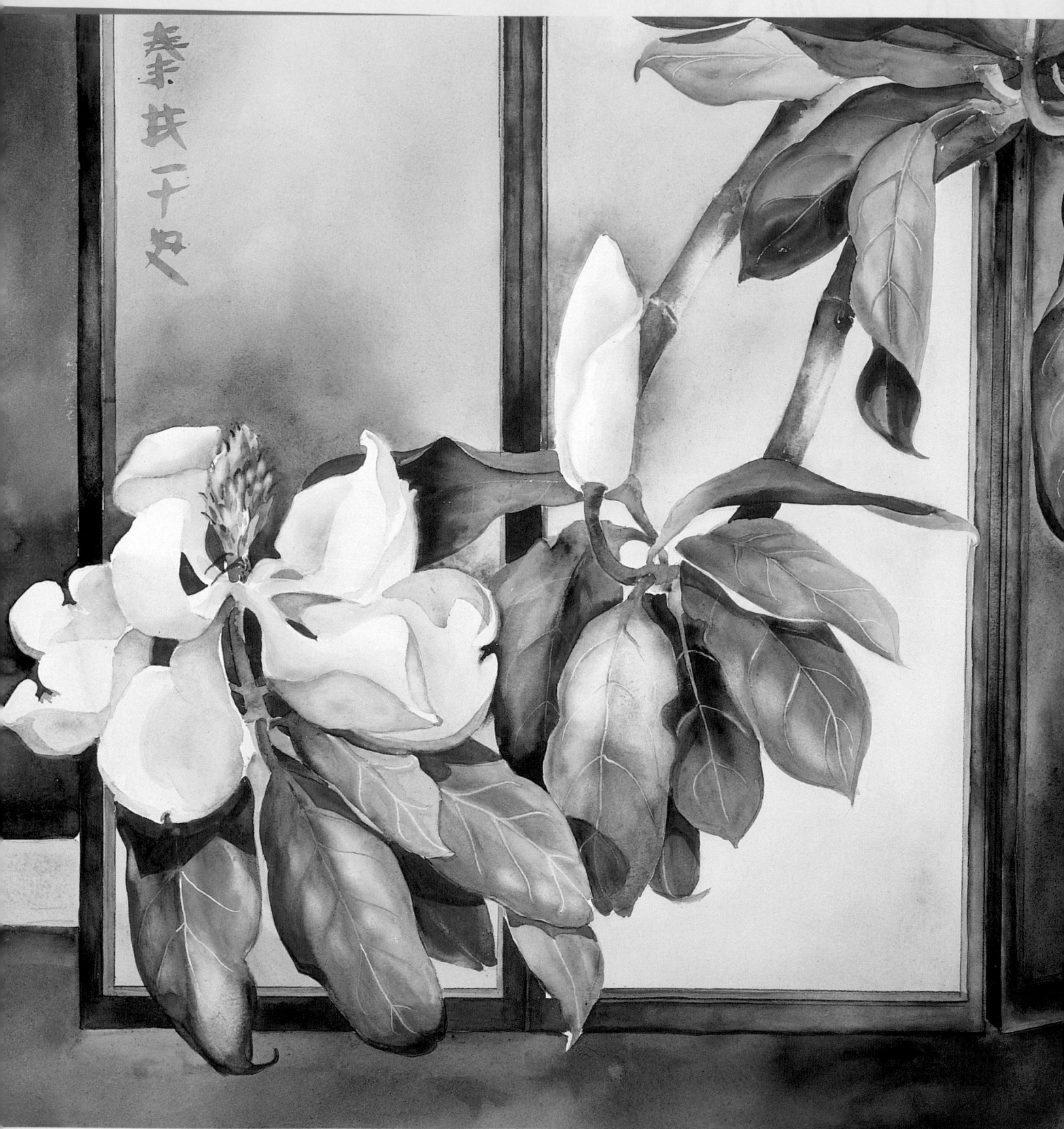

Toki Nihon No
22" × 30" (56cm × 76cm)

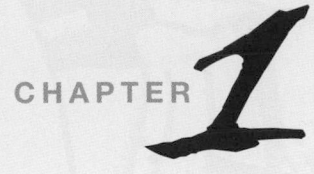
the painting process

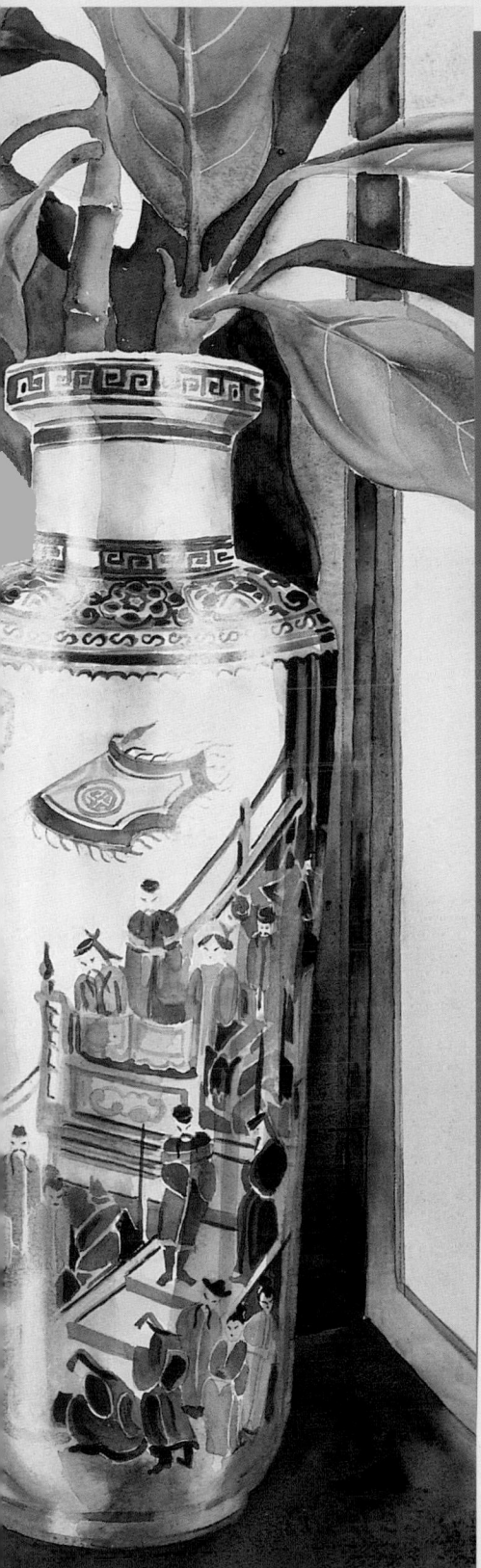

LONG AGO, THERE WAS AN OLD JAPANESE POT MAKER WHO was highly esteemed for the creative artwork of his exquisite pots. Before beginnning a new work, the pot maker would consider several questions: "Will this idea for a pot work?" "Will it crack inside the kiln?"

After asking these questions, he would put them from his mind. Only then was he able to concentrate on the making of the pot and not on his worries. He enjoyed the process and, therefore, was very successful.

Just as the pot maker must remove questions from his mind and not think about what can potentially go wrong in the process, so too must watercolorists disengage from these things and immerse themselves in the spirit and flow of the painting itself. Do not trouble yourself with questions such as: "Will this painting be successful?" or "Will someone want to buy it?"

Put aside these concerns. Only then will a painting truly succeed as it is meant to, ensuring the reward of a job well done. In the end, questions and concerns are secondary to the painting process itself. The process is the reward.

Over time, every artist develops an individual painting style, determined by a number of factors including personality type and how long the artist has been painting. Styles may change as artists experiment and adapt to new ideas and painting methods. Some people prefer to be highly organized and detailed during the preplanning process. Others prefer a free-flowing, spontaneous approach involving random color splashing.

This chapter will provide an overview of some methods for expressing yourself through painting: the tried-and-true traditional method, the adventurous experimental method and the two methods combined. Also in this chapter, we'll explore what to think about while immersed in this wonderful, creative process.

The object of painting is to evoke emotion in the viewer. A picture is not just something to look at; it elicits a feeling or train of thought.

The step-by-step process of painting—whether through the traditional, experimental or combined methods—begins with a wisp of an idea, which gestates in the back of the artist's mind, eventually growing into a distinct impression or vision.

An artist uses four different kinds of vision:

- Practical vision—seeing what you need to express.
- Curious vision—investigating what you actually see.
- Innovative vision—seeing something within what you actually see.
- Aesthetic vision—disregarding other apects to focus on color, shape and design.

An artist's vision is more than just the identification of the subject matter—it's what drew the artist to the subject in the first place. Think of it as painting the adjective instead of the noun. For instance, in a vineyard scene, you may be attracted to the rich, deep purples of the ripening grapes. Don't set out to paint grapes (the noun); paint rich, deep, purple and ripening (the adjectives). Paint what attracted you to the subject matter. Paint what you think best describes the subject so the viewer can understand what you see and feel about it.

This is the reason we paint.

This is the true joy of painting.

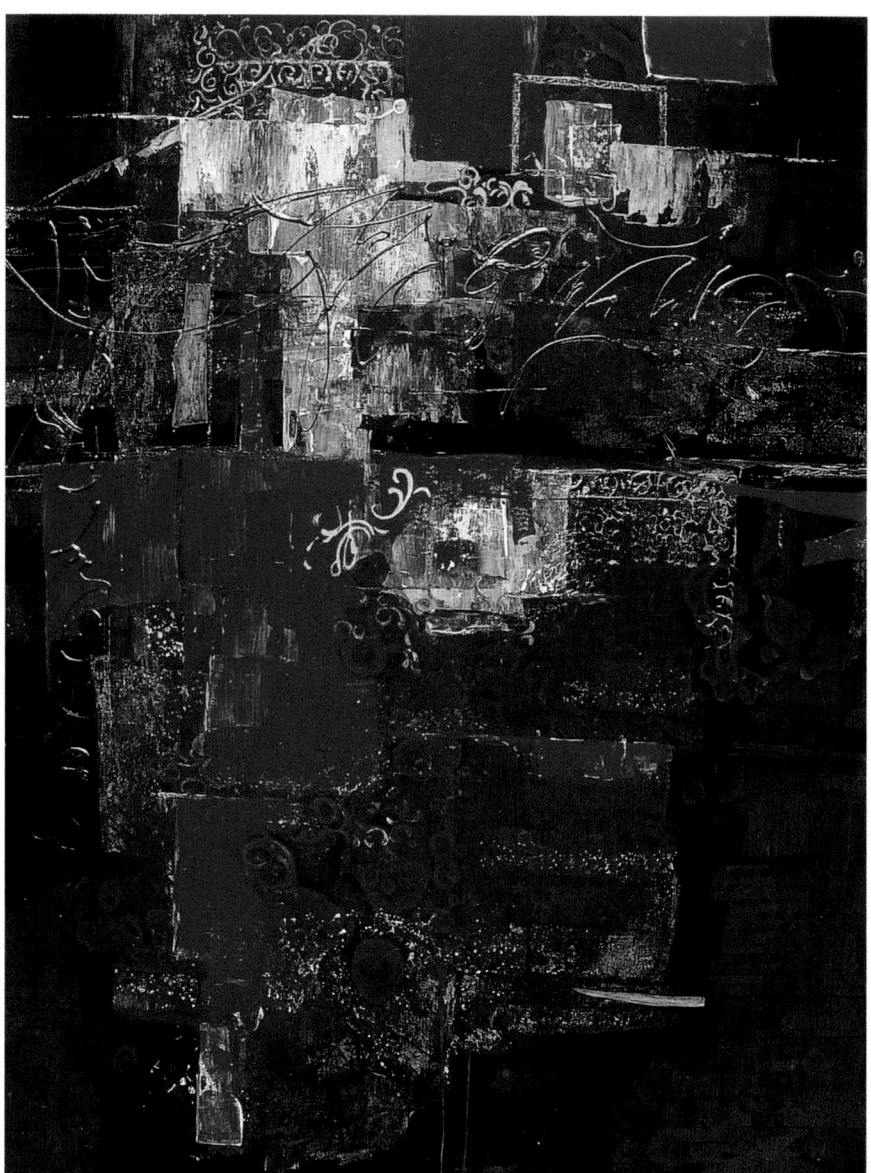

Curious Vision

Using curious vision, an artist examines different ways to express a personal interpretation of a subject. It is a "What if I tried ...?" type of approach to painting that allows for the exploration of innumerable artistic avenues. Anything goes when putting your own vision on paper! The inspiration for *Chinese Laundry* occurred when I was walking through the streets of Chinatown one day. Looking up, I saw rows and rows of colorful laundry strung between buildings. By layering on brilliant color, then scraping, repainting and trying out many texturing devices, I was gradually able to capture the scene's cheerful mood.

Chinese Laundry
30" × 22" (76cm × 56cm)

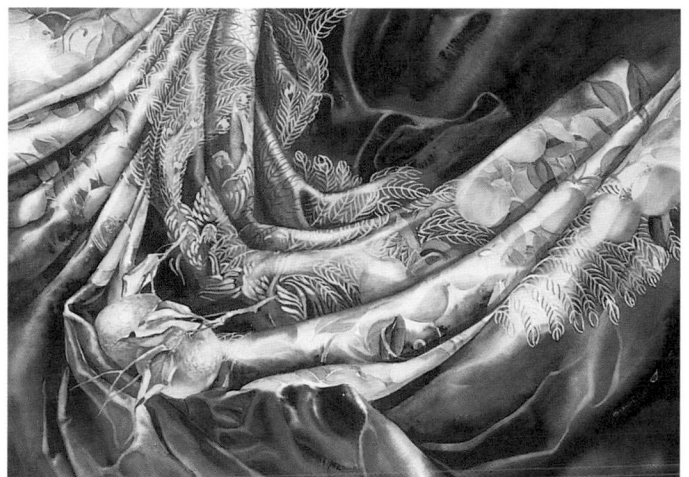

Practical Vision

The practical vision refers to a literal translation of the pictoral content done in the most expedient way rather than in a theoretical or ideal way using abstraction. *Tangerine Dreams* is a realistic interpretation of a still life with fruit and drapery done in a conventional manner.

Tangerine Dreams
22" × 30" (56cm × 76cm)

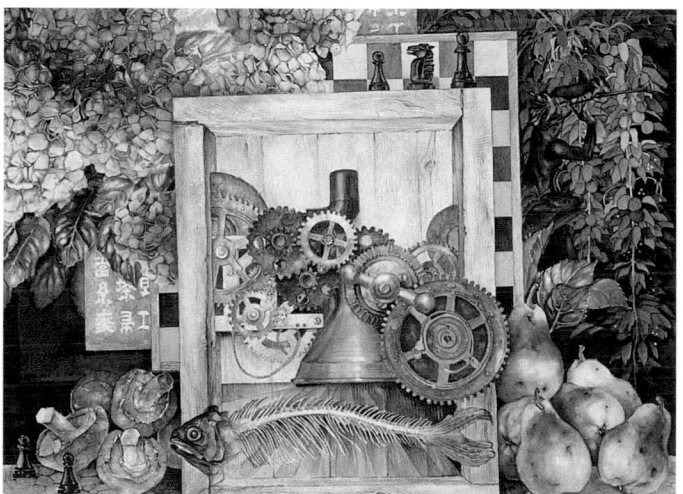

Innovative Vision

The innovative vision is used by artists wishing to express something new about what has been seen or done before. Use ordinary subjects, but arrange and combine elements in unique, even slightly off-beat, ways. In this type of vision, an artist sees the ordinary in a not-so-ordinary way. In *Pier's Paradox*, common items are used to build the composition in a realistic painting style. The uniqueness of the painting is that these elements are not usually associated with one another and are in no way related in real life, yet each one holds its own in the total composition because of their color and shape relationships.

Pier's Paradox
22" × 30" (56cm × 76cm)

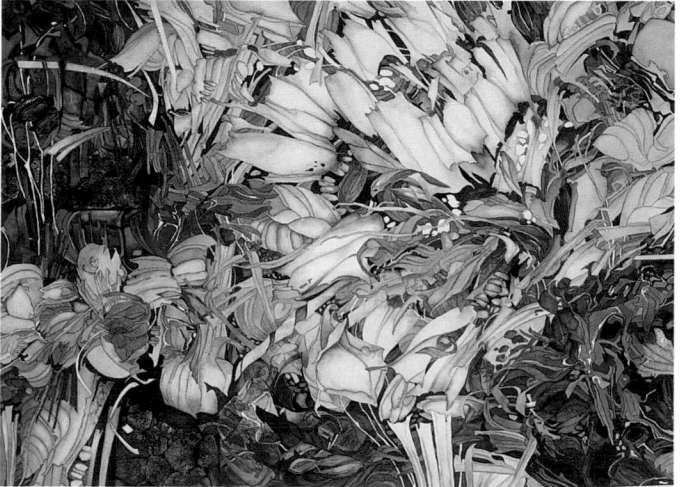

Aesthetic Vision

Sometimes even the most ordinary and overlooked things strike us at a certain moment as astonishingly beautiful. Using the aesthetic vision, an artist can capture this instant, surprising revelation in order to relate his excitement to others. One morning, while walking in my summer garden, I noticed a pile of leaves and fallen petals gathered in a corner by the wind and struck by sunlight. The beauty of this tiny scene lay in its chaos. The challenge in *Entropy* was to make order out of this disordered jumble of leaves, but retain the aesthetic value that was its orginal appeal.

Entropy
22" × 30" (56cm × 76cm)

The Traditional Method

The *traditional method* is an analytical and technical approach to watercolor painting. It is a time-honored, systematic series of steps that begins with an idea that advances from the reference subject to value sketches (or thumbnails) to precise line drawings and, finally, to the step-by-step painting process. It is a well-planned procedure that carefully incorporates all elements and principles of composition. This step-by-step approach ensures a successful painting by resolving as many problems as possible at the start.

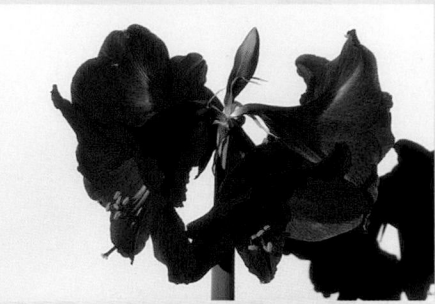

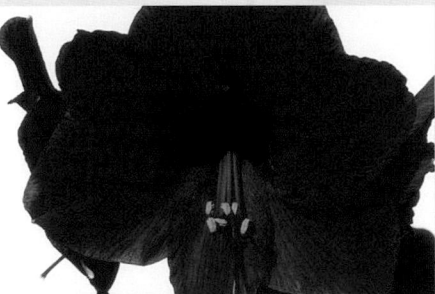

Reference photos

MATERIALS LIST

BRUSHES
Nos. 3, 6, 8 and 14 rounds

WATERCOLORS
Da Vinci: Permanent Red

Grumbacher: Burnt Umber, Cadmium Red Light, Cadmium Red Medium, Thalo Blue, Thalo Yellow Green

Holbein: Opera

M. Graham & Co.: Alizarin Crimson, Cadmium Yellow, Cadmium Yellow Light, Quinacridone Violet, Sap Green

Winsor & Newton: Winsor Red

SURFACE
¼ sheet (11" × 15" [28cm × 38cm]) 140-lb. (300gsm) Arches cold-pressed paper

ADDITIONAL SUPPLIES
Black marker, newsprint paper, pencil, reference photos, scrubber brush

1 Draw Thumbnail Sketches
Make several pencil sketches on scrap paper about 2" × 2½" (5cm × 6cm) using light, medium and dark values. Construct different, pleasing patterns and select your favorite.

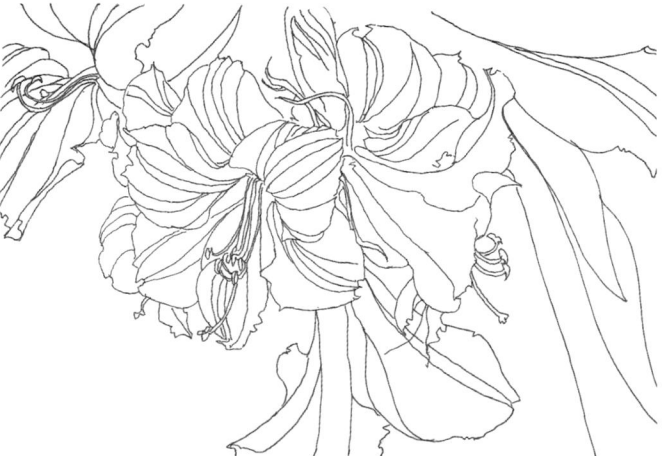

2 Create a Detailed Outline Drawing
On a half sheet of newsprint, make a detailed outline drawing in pencil using your favorite sketch from step 1 as a guide. Concentrate on interesting shapes and a fluid flow of lines across the page. Trace over the lines with a black marker and then lightly trace the results in pencil onto the watercolor paper. Don't use too much graphite or it will smear during the painting process.

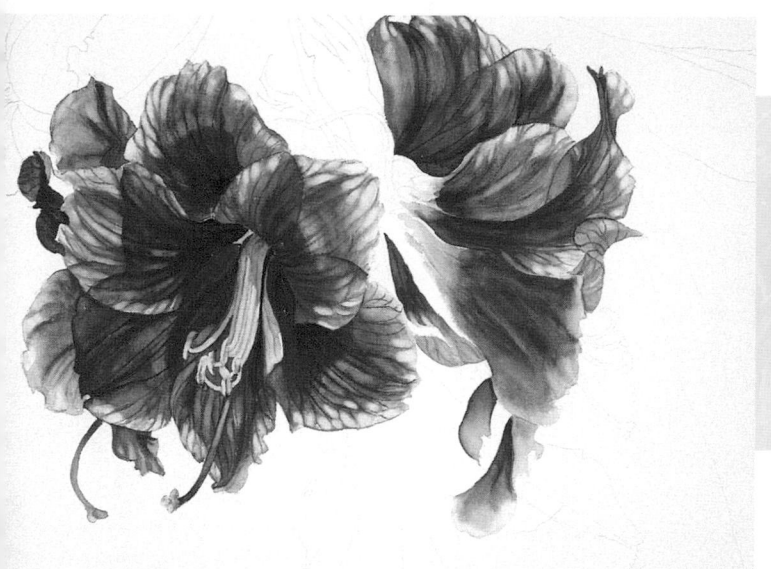

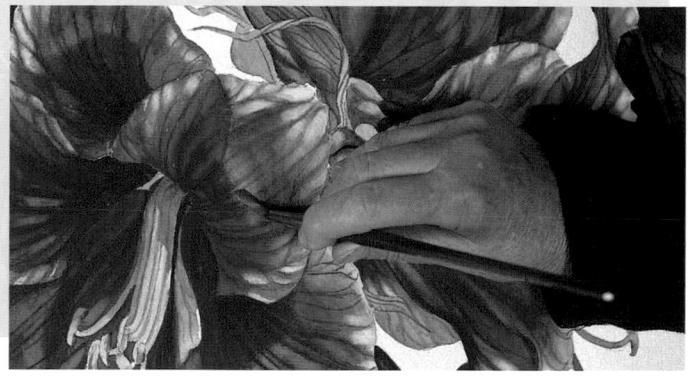

Detail: Lifting Highlights
Carefully lifting the paint to create highlights adds dimension and helps to model the form of the petal. (See page 63 for more on lifting.)

3 Paint the Petals, Lift Out Highlights

With the no. 8 and 14 rounds, paint the petal outlines with Cadmium Yellow. Charge in a mixture of Cadmium Yellow and Opera, then Cadmium Red Light, Cadmium Red Medium, Alizarin Crimson and a little Quinacridone Violet near the flower's center. Let the colors blend. While the paint is still wet, lift out highlights with an almost dry brush. Do several petals in succession.

With the paint slightly damp, use the no. 3 round to draw small lines for the petals' veins so the edges of the lines will be slightly fuzzy. Let dry, then add more hard edge lines. Using the scrubber brush, gently rub out highlights on the petal edges and some soft areas in the center of the petals where the light would hit. Continue working area by area to complete all the central flowers.

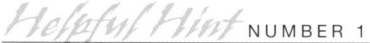

Helpful Hint NUMBER 1

When lifting paint (still slightly wet), dampen your brush and squeeze out the excess water. Then, without using any paint, slowly stroke through and lift the paint where you want highlights to appear. The brush will absorb paint like a sponge. You may have to repeat the process, depending on the dampness of your paper.

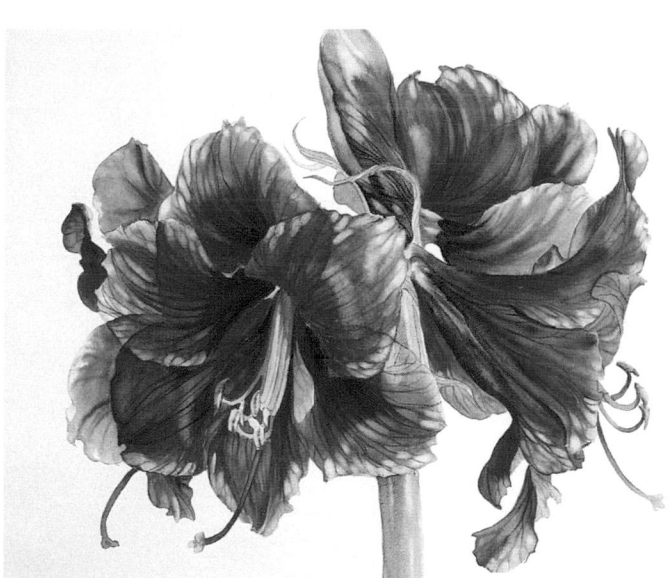

4 Add the Greens and Darks

Mix several green shades on your palette, ranging from yellowish to bluish. (Suggestion: Thalo Blue and Cadmium Yellow make beautiful greens.) With the no. 8 round, apply the greens to the stem and the beginning of the blossom where the greens blend into the reds. Add more dark reds into the greens at the base of the blossoms. Continue with the stem. Let everything dry, then add the darkest darks (like the flower centers) with Burnt Umber mixed with Alizarin Crimson.

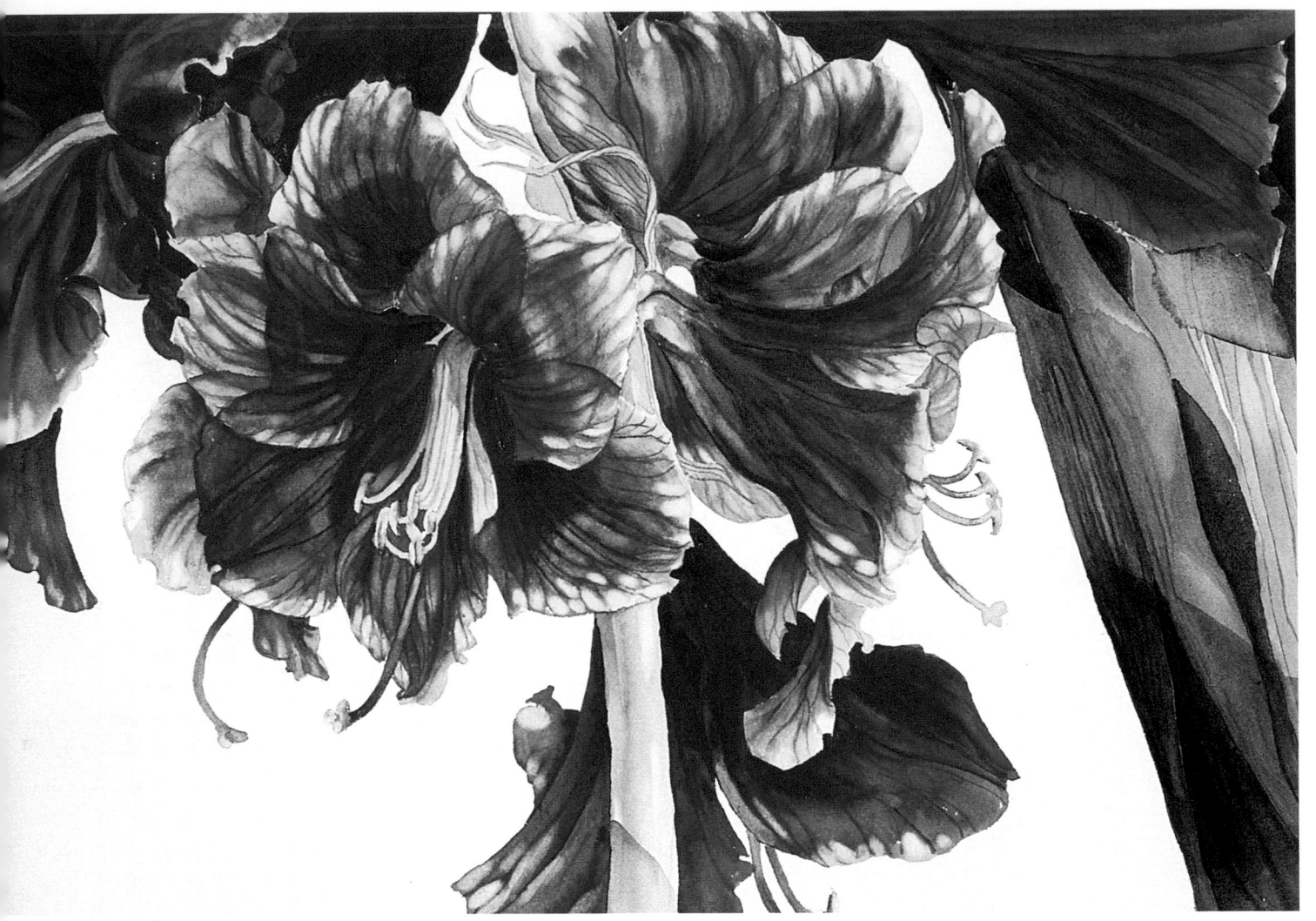

5 Develop the Darker Background Blossoms

Use your darker reds, such as a mix of Burnt Umber and Alizarin Crimson or Quina-cridone Violet and Winsor Red, to loosely swish in the petal areas at the top of the painting with the no. 14 round. Let dry and add detail, but not as much as the central flowers, because the background flowers should command less attention. Then, using your green mixes, wash in the leaves at the right and left edges of the painting. When dry, add veins, a few highlights and shadows under the petals with a darker green.

STOP OR CONTINUE?
I was tempted to stop at step 4 because the red against the stark white background is quite dramatic. Also, it would have been nice to crop the painting into a square format. But in the interest of a good and complete composition I decided to add the remaining darker shapes to draw attention to all sides of the format. Which version do you like the best?

Helpful Hint NUMBER 2

Watch out for diagonals! Diagonal lines are so powerful that they can instantly change your design for better or for worse. Think of the ocean on a calm, summer day where horizontal lines give a feeling of peace and serenity. Now, think of the ocean in a thunderstorm with lightning bolts crashing down over choppy waters. Diagonal lines in a painting create powerful movement and a sense of unrest, but they must be used carefully because they can dominate a painting, drawing the viewer's eye.

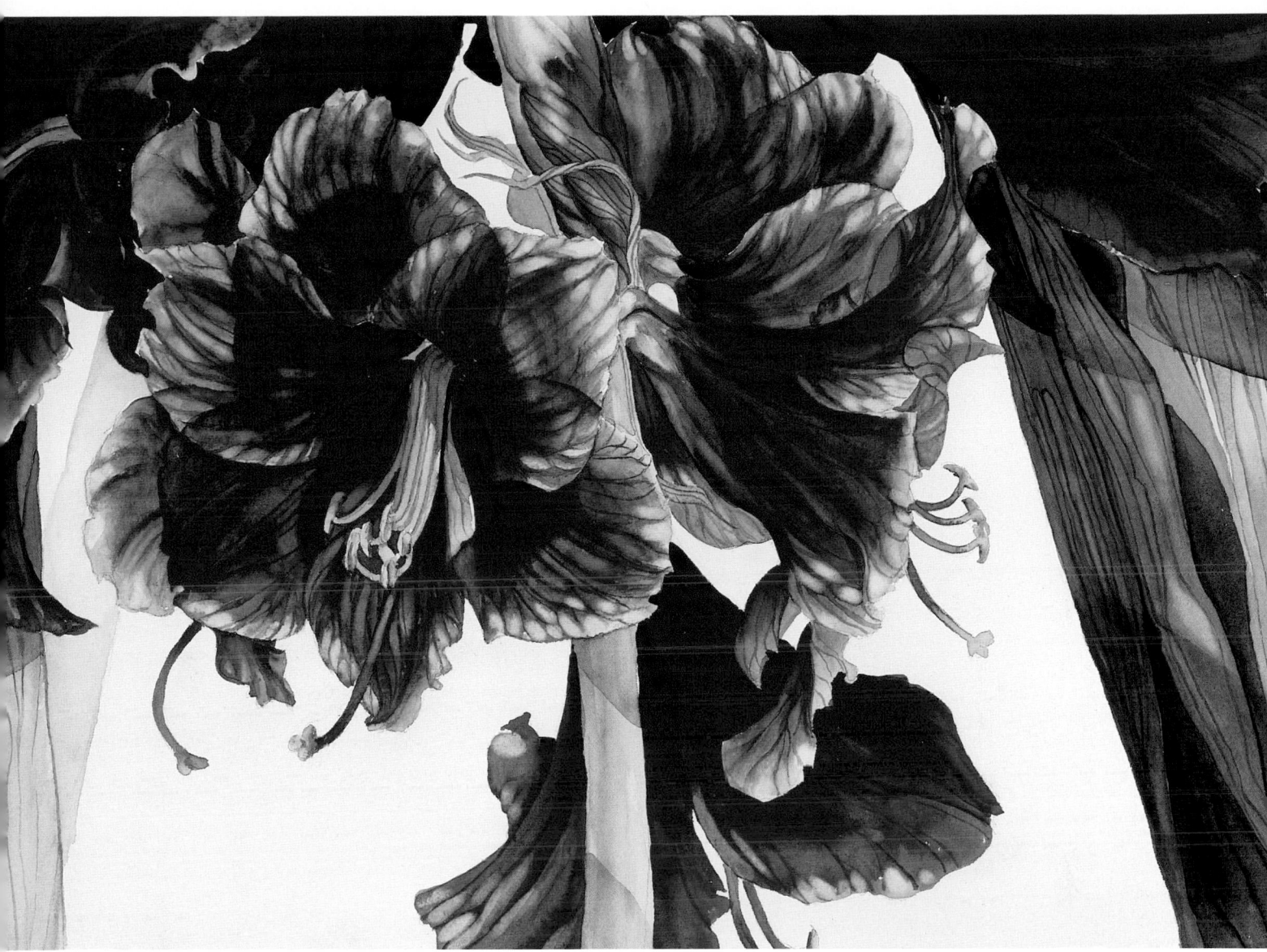

6 Make the Final Adjustments

Study the painting for color relationships and pleasing shapes. Put more leaves on the petals if that helps to make more interesting interlocking shapes. Add layers of color, darkening some areas to push them back into the painting, or add more color to brighten other areas to bring them forward.

Ladies in Red
15" × 22" (38cm × 56cm)

The Experimental Method

The experimental method is just what the name suggests—a spontaneous and expressive use of materials used in an unrestricted manner. There are countless ways to put paint to paper. A "color splash" is just one way to try that is fresh and free—the opposite of the traditional method. By using the experimental method, you break loose from preconceived concepts and use your imagination—opening up new areas of thought and crossing boundaries in ways not possible with any other method. Paint with gusto. Only as the painting progresses does the artist slowly build order out of chaos and begin to think about composition. The "color splash" is my preferred method for creating unplanned subject matter. For different textures, try adding salt, tissue paper, Plexiglas or other materials.

MATERIALS LIST

BRUSHES
Nos. 4, 8 and 14 rounds

1-inch (25mm) flat

3-inch (76mm) wash brush

WATERCOLORS
Da Vinci: Hansa Yellow

Grumbacher: Prussian Blue, Thalo Blue, Thalo Green, Thalo Yellow Green, Ultramarine Blue

Holbein: Opera

M. Graham & Co.: Dioxazine Purple

SURFACE
Full sheet (22" × 30" [56cm × 76cm]) 140-lb. (300gsm) Arches cold-pressed paper

ADDITIONAL SUPPLIES
Acetate, black marker, broken pieces of Plexiglas, drafting tape, rocks or books (for weights), table salt, tissue paper

1 Get Started
Tape the edges of the paper so the border remains white. Wet down the entire sheet with water using a large wash brush. With the no. 14 round, use broad sweeping strokes to lay down paint. Start with Thalo Blue, Thalo Green and Thalo Yellow Green, blending with the other colors. The paper is already wet enough for the paint to flow freely, so use very little water in thinning the paint. New colors will emerge. Don't worry about hard edges or runbacks. At this stage there is no preconceived subject matter, so just have fun sloshing on beautiful color.

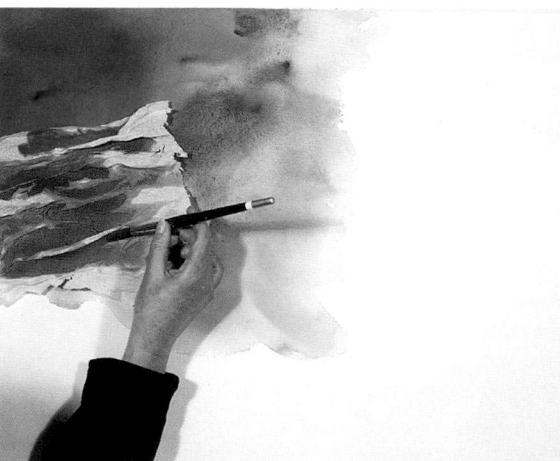

2 Add Texture
Work one quadrant at a time so the paint won't dry out before using the texturing devices. After filling the top left quarter of the paper with color, lightly press crumpled tissue paper into the wet paint. Gently stroke over some of the sections with a wet no. 8 round to press them into the paper while leaving some of the ridges unstuck.

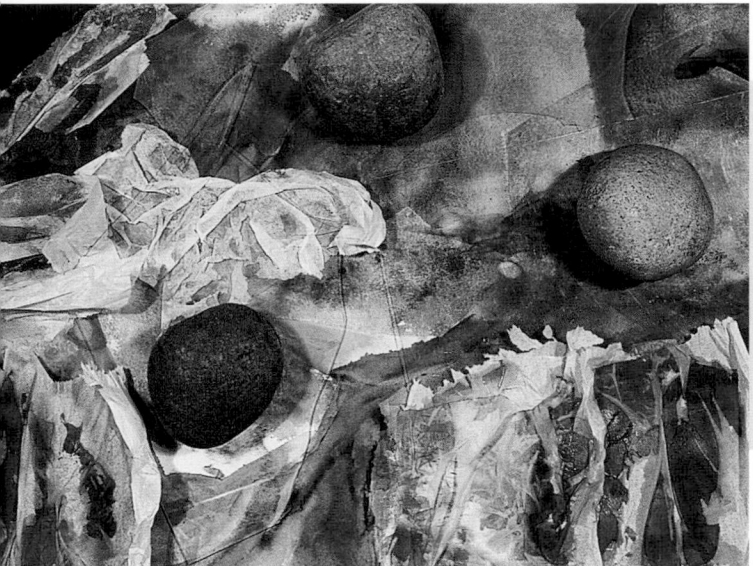

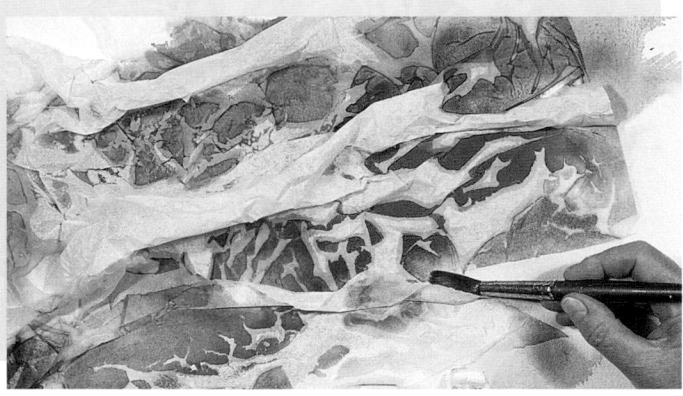

Detail: Using Tissue Paper

Crumple the tissue paper before pressing it into the wet paint so that some parts of the paper stick to the paint while the ridges don't, creating a natural, uneven effect. With the no. 8 round, paint into the valleys of the tissue paper to control the pattern a little. When it is dry, pull off the tissue to reveal a beautiful design.

3 Cover the Entire Painting

Put tissue paper in some areas of the painting and press the Plexiglas pieces into other sections of the wet paint (not overlapping the tissue paper) and weigh them down. Add a little table salt for a different texture.

Move on to the other three quadrants of the paper, repeating the same procedure until the entire page is covered. Let everything dry completely to allow the surface tension of the tissue paper to take full effect and the printing of the Plexiglas to work.

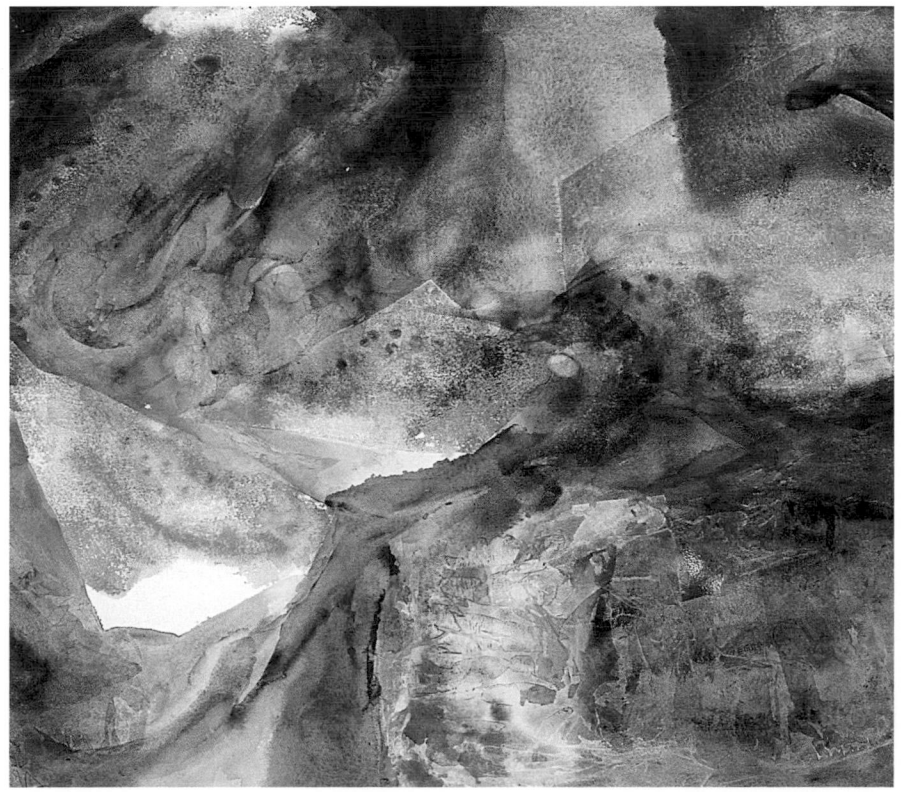

4 The Great Unveiling

When everything is completely dry, take off all the stones, Plexiglas and tissue paper. Brush off all the salt residue to discover what will appear underneath. Usually, it looks like large swirls of nothing decipherable. But, if you stand back and turn the paper in all directions, something starts to reveal itself. The looseness of the paint flow allows colors to merge so that organic and natural forms emerge. Shapes begin to appear, such as fish, flowers, trees or birds.

5 Use Acetate to Define Shapes

After deciding on a subject, lay a sheet of acetate on top of the painting and use a black marker to delineate the outlines of the general forms to help identify the subjects more clearly. In this case, fish seem to present themselves as an idea for the painting's subject. (Note: The white streaks noticeable in some areas of the painting represent the shine of the acetate, not a deliberate highlight.)

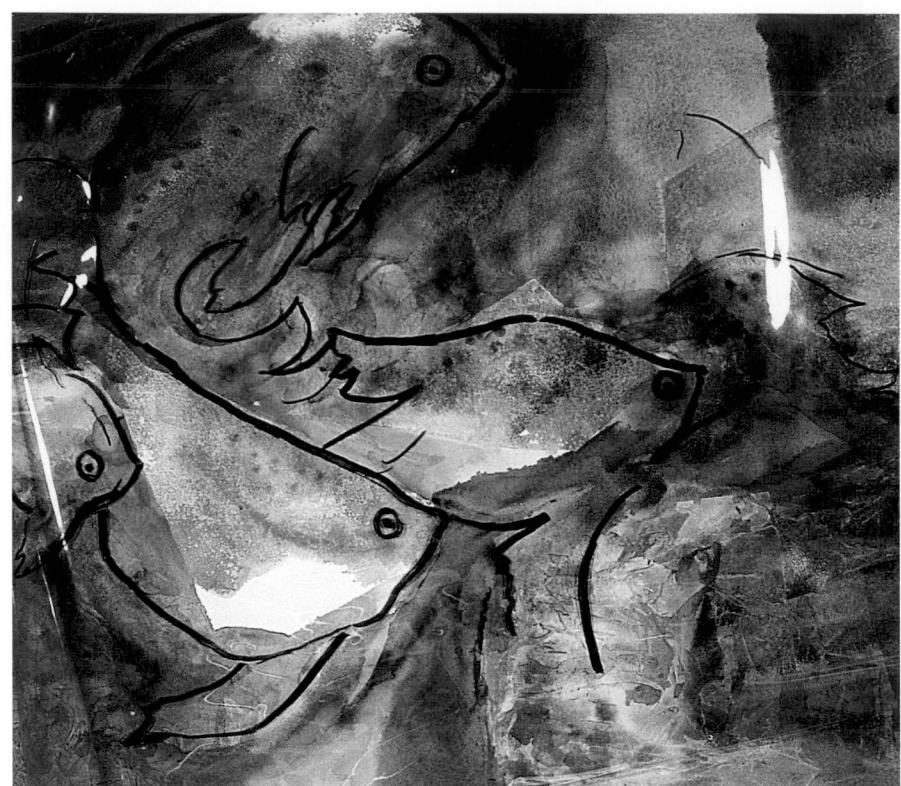

6 Develop the Forms

Use dark colors and medium-sized brushes to paint behind and between the fish shapes to identify them more clearly. Clarify other colors by adding more paint to areas that have become dull when dry. Define the fish more fully by painting directly into them, adding details such as eyes, fins and tails. Make fish scales by pressing your finger into the wet paint of the fish shapes or, after the paint dries, by dipping your finger in paint and then printing scales on the fish. Leave some bits of tissue paper on the painting if you wish. Sometimes the tissue paper makes a beautiful pattern. It can also add another variation in the texture of the painting. If you like the way it looks, leave it.

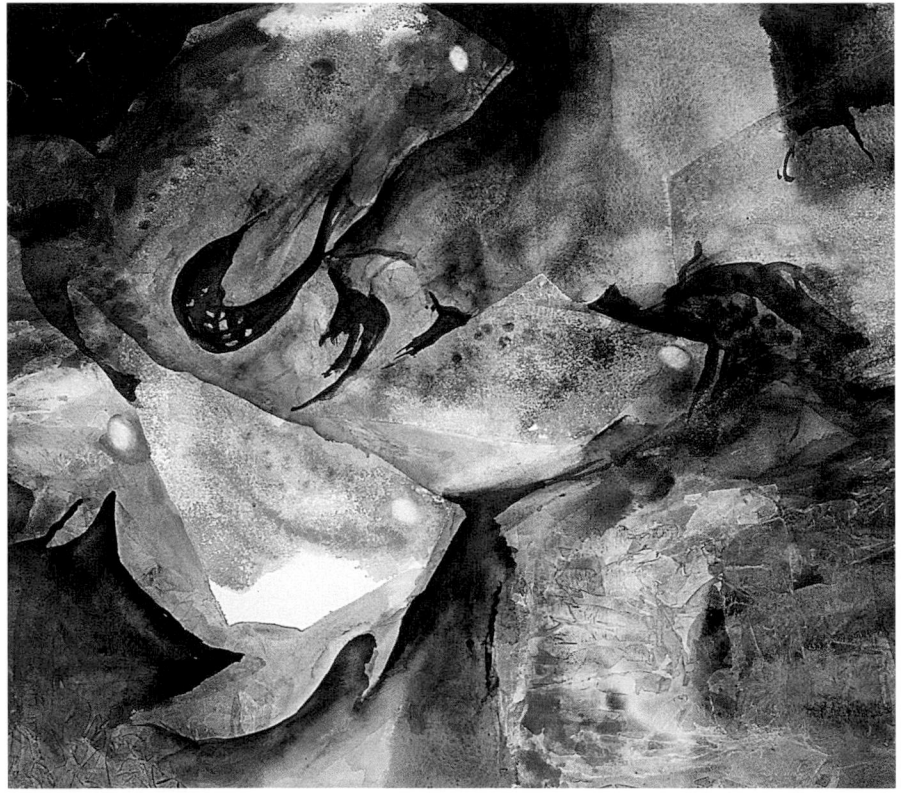

Helpful Hint NUMBER 3

Go beyond what the eye sees and paint what the mind sees. That way, you will get a personal and individual interpretation that represents you.

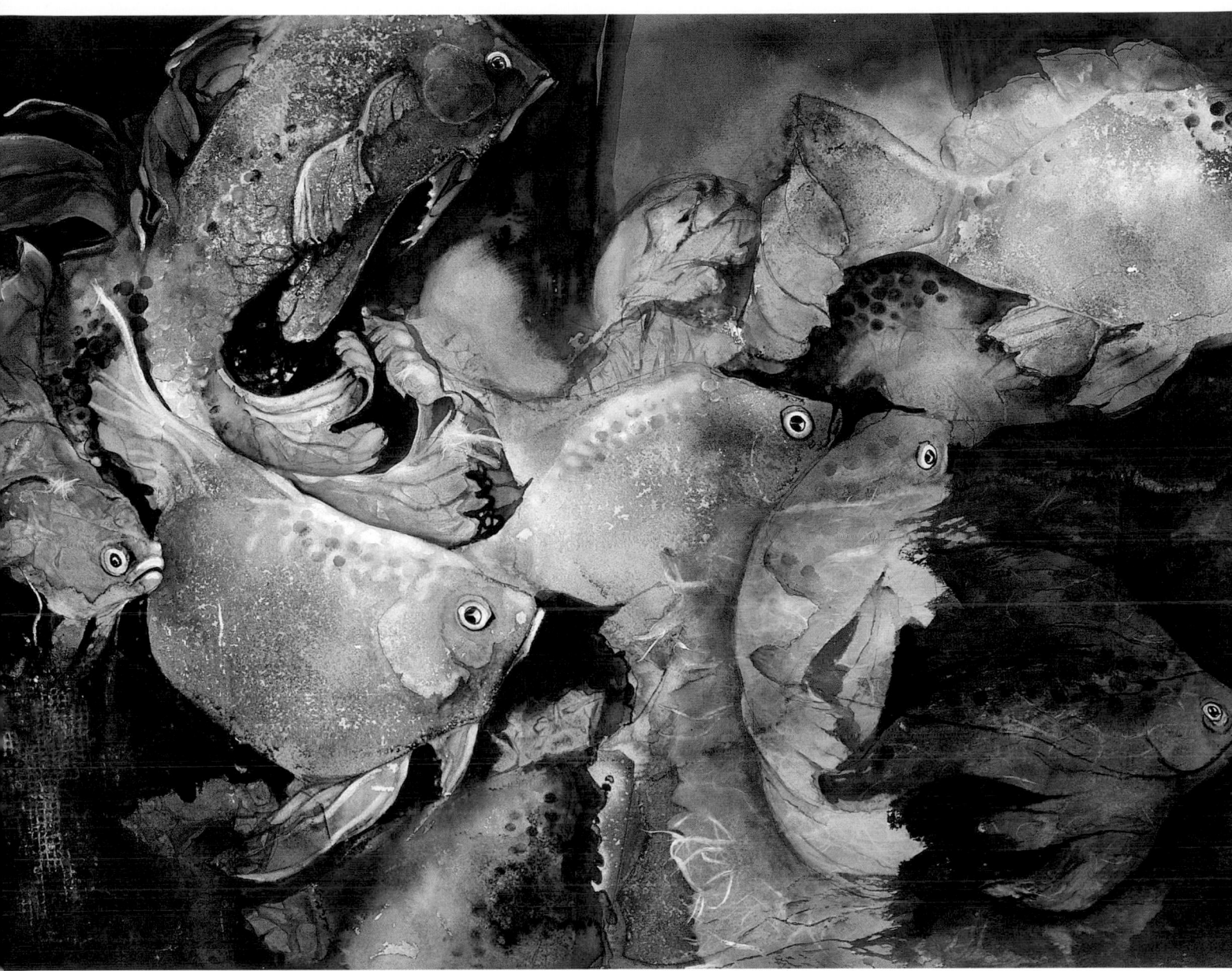

7 Finish the Painting

Step back and review the results. Make final adjustments by adding more fish or altering colors to create an overall balance. The feeling of the painting is loose, somewhat abstract, and not realistic. Put the painting away for a few weeks before giving it a final evaluation.

Fish Fantasy
22" × 30" (56cm × 76cm)

The Combined Method

The *combined method* painting technique offers the best aspects of both the traditional and experimental methods. By pre-planning with thumbnails and line drawings, you will be able to avoid many compositional pitfalls and know exactly how all the elements relate because they act as guidelines. Still, you are able to retain the freshness and looseness of the free-flowing approach that make the experimental method so appealing.

MATERIALS LIST

BRUSHES
Nos. 4, 8 and 14 rounds

3-inch (76mm) wash

WATERCOLORS
Grumbacher: Burnt Sienna, Cadmium Yellow Medium, Davy's Gray, Mauve, Payne's Gray, Sap Green

Holbein: Opera

SURFACE
Half sheet (22" × 15" [56cm × 38cm]) 140-lb. (300gsm) Arches cold-pressed paper

ADDITIONAL SUPPLIES
Drafting tape, pencil, salt, tissue paper

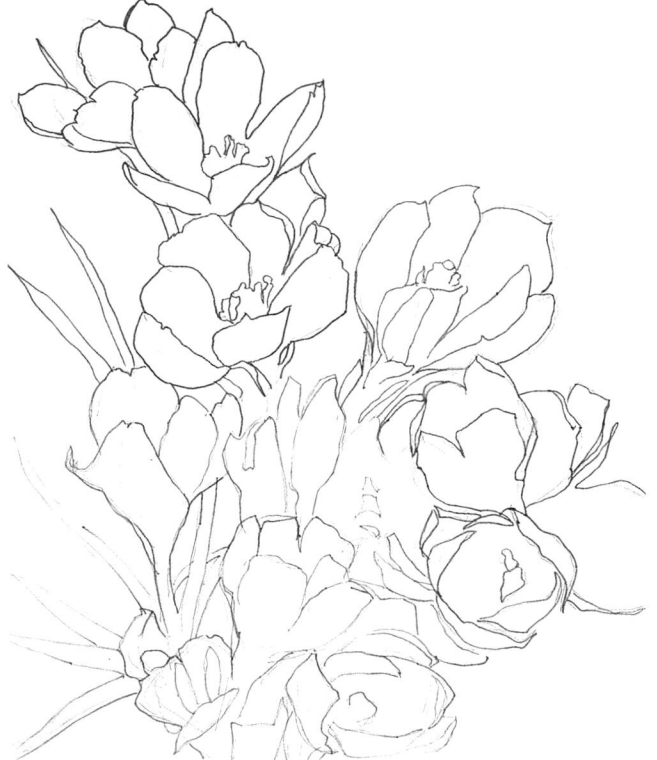

1 Make a Value Statement
Just as in the traditional method (see page 14), start by preparing several thumbnail sketches to help you determine a pleasing pattern of values from the darkest darks to the lightest lights. Then choose the one you like best.

2 Create an Outline Drawing
Use a line drawing to define the exact shapes and their placement. This drawing will be the exact size of the watercolor paper. Transfer the drawing onto the paper using very light pencil lines.

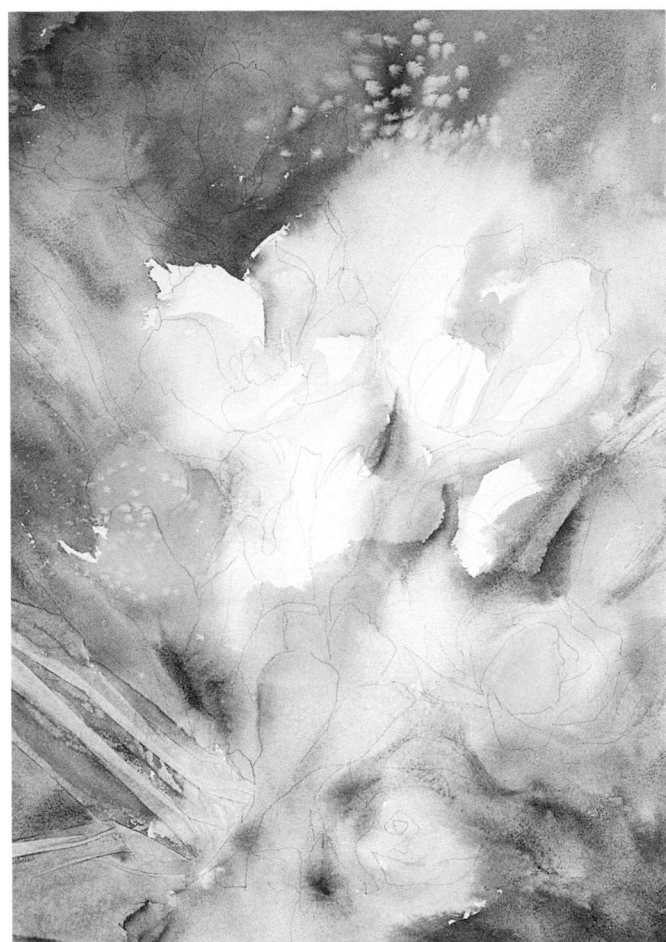

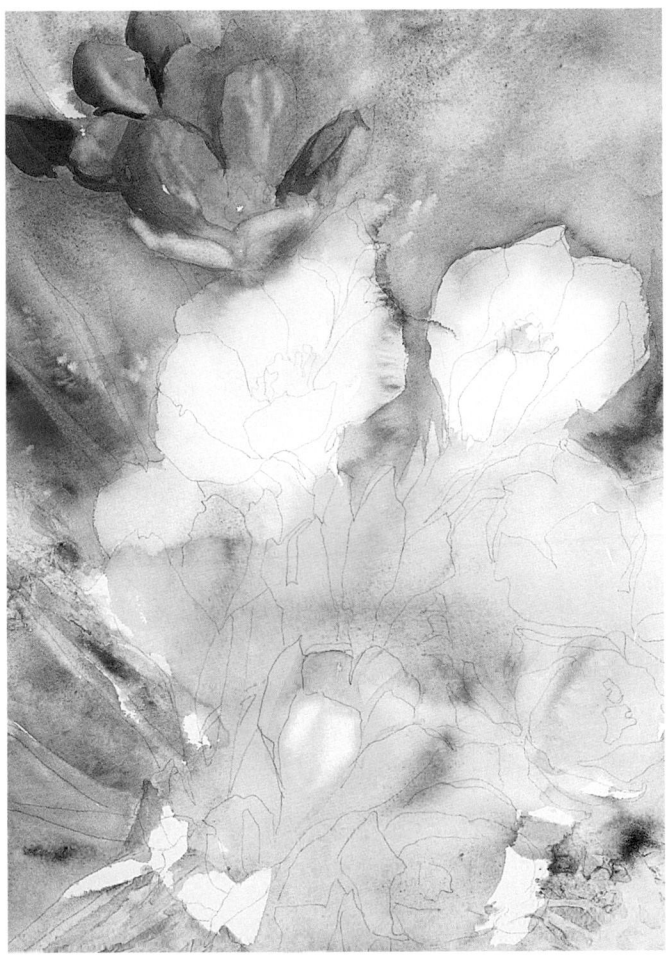

3 Add Color

Tape the edges of the paper to define the format, wet the entire surface, then add colors freely as in the experimental method (see page 18). This time, however, since you have a general idea of the subject (flowers), you won't be splashing colors on quite so randomly. Begin by washing in a soft Payne's Gray background, then use the larger rounds to add touches of Opera. Create the flower colors with Cadmium Yellow Medium, Mauve and Sap Green. Add Davy's Gray for the foliage. Place the colors in the general location of the drawn flowers. Throw salt here and there and lay down tissue paper for added texture.

4 Define the Forms

When everything is dry, remove the tissue paper and brush off the excess salt. Paint behind and around the flower shapes, leaves and stems. Use the same colors to identify the forms that appear in the background. Add Cadmium Yellow Medium to the flower centers and Burnt Sienna to the flowers' shadow areas. Lift paint for highlights. Add color to push some elements into the background and pull other elements into the foreground.

Helpful Hint NUMBER 4

By "pushing" and "pulling" different elements, you add depth and dimension to a painting. Add darker values to the areas that you want to sink into the background (push). Bring other areas into the foreground by lifting paint for lighter values (pull).

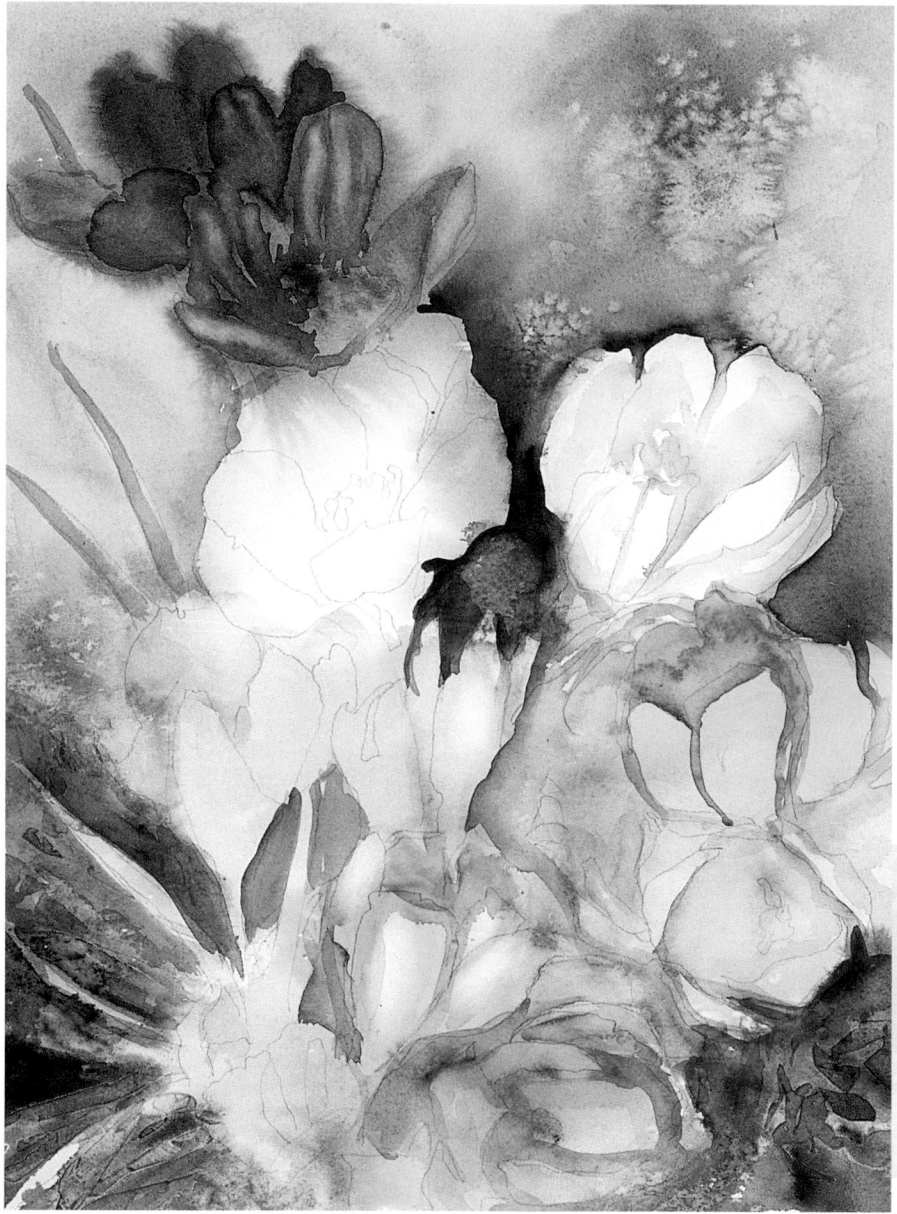

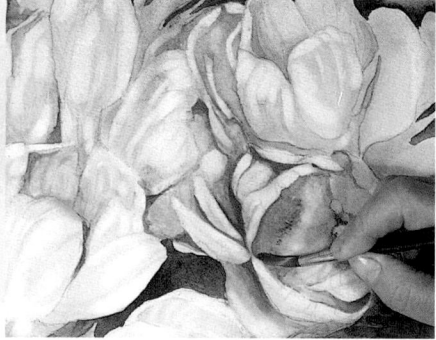

PREFERRED PAINTING METHODS

You've learned about three different painting methods in this chapter, and you might be wondering about my preferred method. The short answer is, it depends. My painting method is determined by whichever one works best to execute the concept of the painting. The nature of the subject matter (loose, flowing fish or a realistic still life) always helps to determine which method to choose.

5 Clarify the Postive Shapes

Paint directly into the flower forms to further identify them. Begin to separate and enhance the different petal shapes.

Detail: Creating Form and Volume

Paint the darks into the yellow flowers in the lower right side of the painting to give them form and volume.

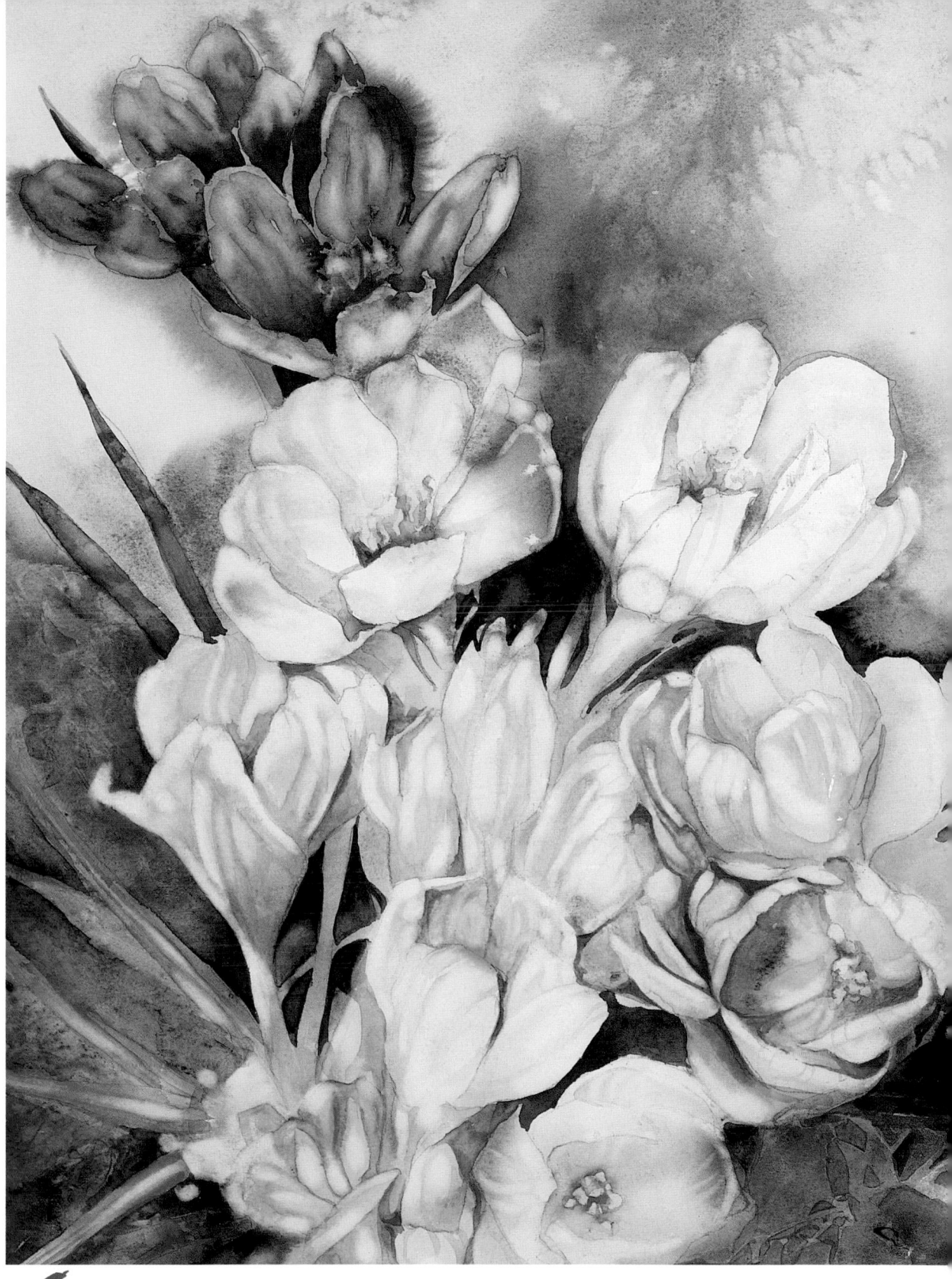

6 Add Details, Finish the Painting

By adding the details of veins, centers and stems, each blossom is brought into full focus and definition within the painting. The final result is a painting that is halfway between the two methods because it has some soft and some hard edges, some pre-drawn petals and leaves, and others "found" along the way. Some areas are quite detailed, while others are deliberately indistinct.

Early Crocus
22" × 15" (56cm × 38cm)

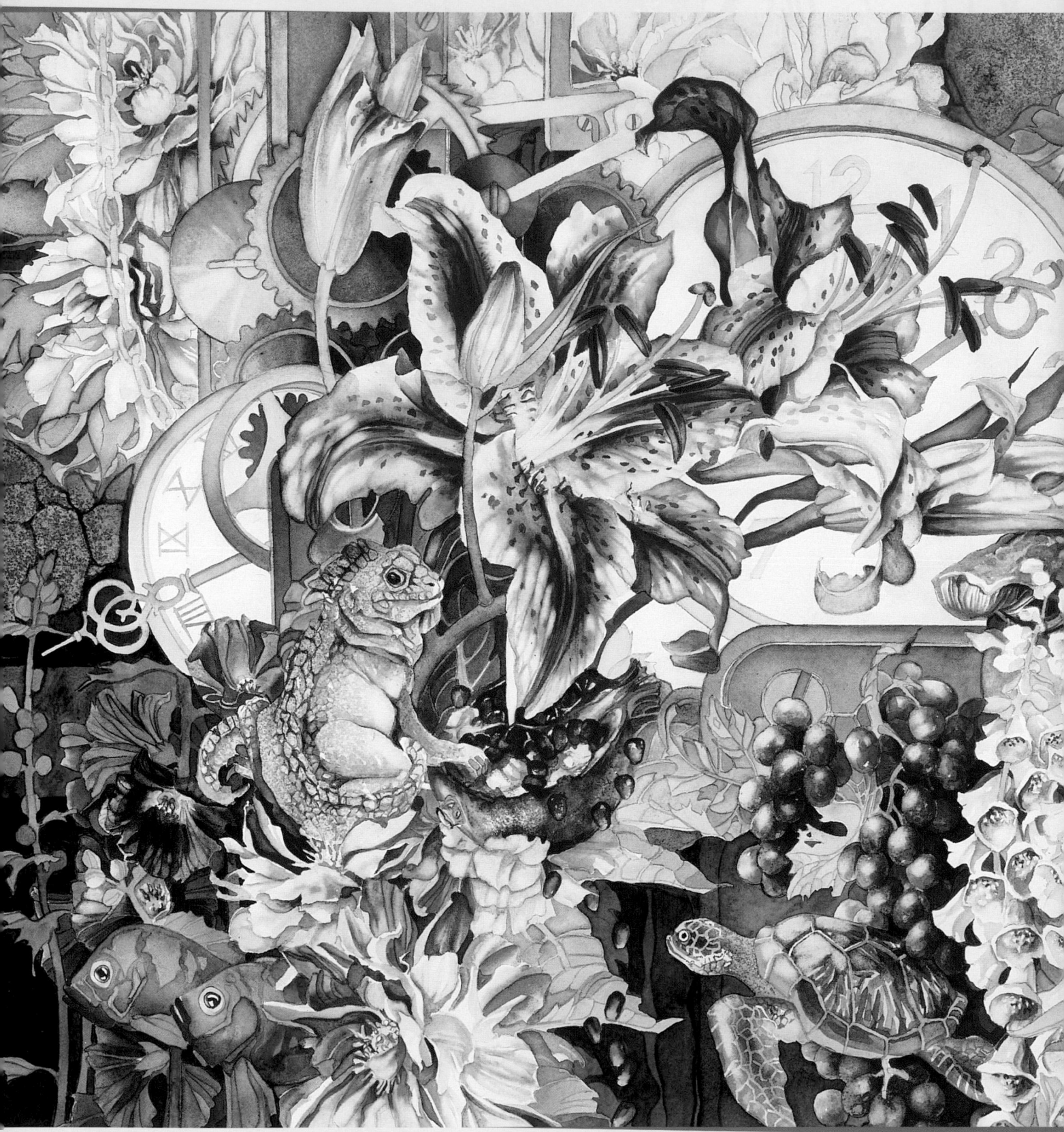

Enigma
22" × 30" (56cm × 76cm)

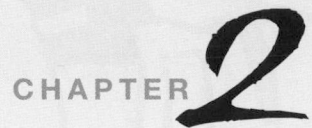
composition

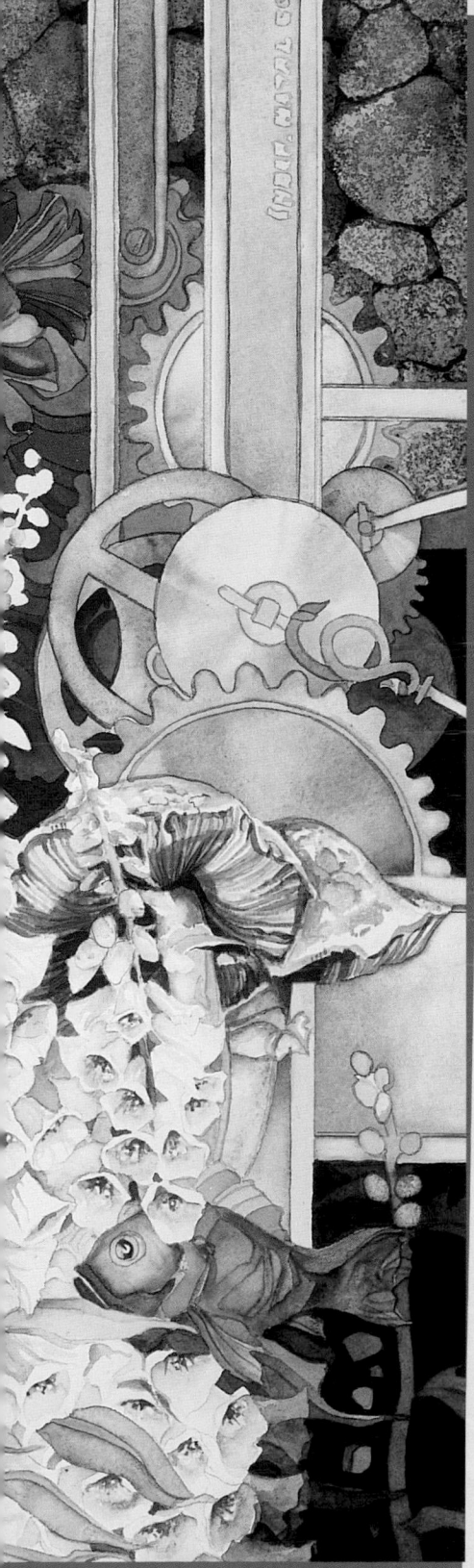

IT'S VERY IMPORTANT TO ESTABLISH A SOLID FOUNDATION early in the planning stages of a painting. Even if you work for hours and hours and your craftsmanship is perfect, the end result will not be successful without a solid structure based on the rules of composition. This is why a painting's composition—the total content, everything about the work of art—is so important, even in the experimental method.

Good composition and design, the arrangement of various elements within a painting, is innate for most of us. Just imagine yourself straightening up a messy coffee table strewn with Sunday's newspaper, several magazines, remote controls, a bowl of popcorn, and a centerpiece pushed to the side. Without too much thought you will stack the magazines, remove the remote controls, recycle the newspaper, throw away the popcorn, and move the centerpiece. When you create a painting, you are essentially doing the same thing. You are arranging the different elements in your painting (line, color, shape, value, texture, space and form) and eliminating unneeded elements to create a balanced and pleasing composition. The principles of design are how an artist uses the various elements within the painting to create balance, harmony, repetition, contrast, rhythm, gradation, unity and dominance. In this chapter you will learn about these principles of design and elements of composition and practice them through various exercises.

Any artist will tell you that there are plenty of things to think about while painting. Total concentration is required from the beginning of the process until the final result. As the artist, you are required to make judgment decisions both large and small during each step of the painting that will dramatically affect the eventual outcome.

Deciding on a composition is one of the most important choices that an artist must make. Composition involves careful positioning of all the elements that constitute the painting as a whole. The artist must direct and control the viewer's eye flow throughout a painting.

Look at the thumbnail illustration on the right. Notice how much of the painting is mapped out before any color is added. In this example, the top of the painting will be different from the sides in both the chosen shape sizes and distribution. Likewise, the bottom of the painting also will differ from the sides.

Remember that your painting should be divided roughly into two-thirds dark values and one-third light values, or vice versa. This "one-third rule" helps create a heightened interest in your painting. In addition to value, an artist can utilize a number of approaches to create an eye-catching painting, including the use of both warm and cool colors, rough and smooth textures, shape sizes large and small, as well as using a mixture of soft and hard edges in your painting. All of these terms will be explained in more detail later in the book.

1 Interlocking positive shapes and negative shapes add interest to a painting (see page 53).
2 A repetition of shapes with variation of forms creates a good composition (see page 36).
3 The top of the painting is different from the sides.
4 Be sure to incorporate small, medium and large shapes within the painting.

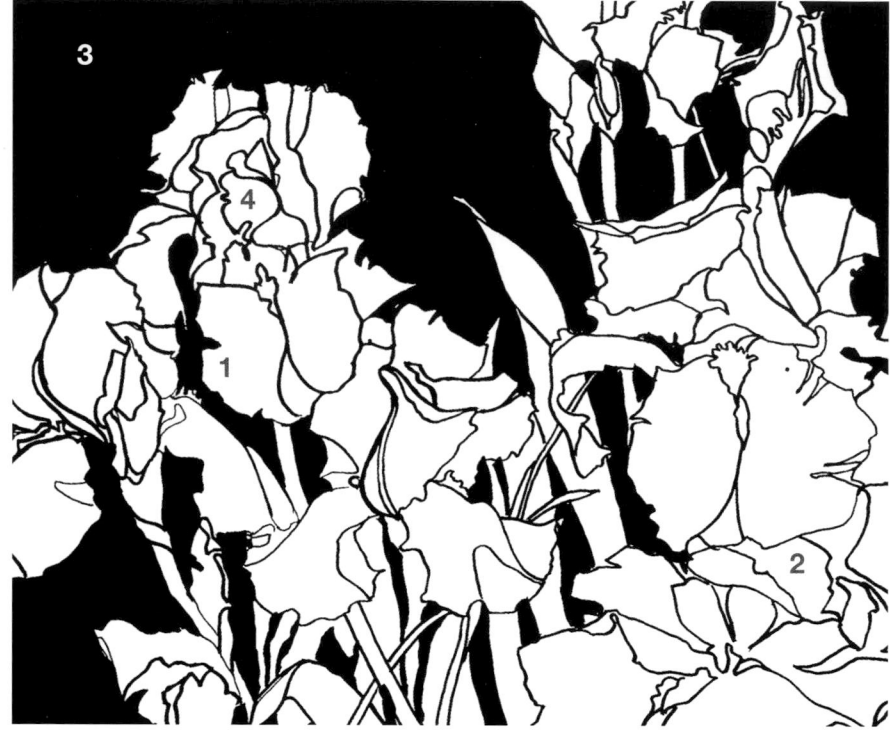

Elements of Composition in Action
This enlarged version of a black-and-white thumbnail illustrates some of the things that you need to think about while working through the steps of a painting. Notice how the thumbnail construction is based on a vertical thrust that provides an anchoring device, holding all the different elements of the painting together. You'll learn more about each of these elements later in the book.

Helpful Hint NUMBER 5

Each edge of the painting should be different from the other. Edges also should be divided by small, medium and large shapes. For instance, in the thumbnail above you can see the top edge is a large area first on the left, medium-sized next, and small on the right. Think about the highest point and lowest point of the painting. Don't put one directly above the other.

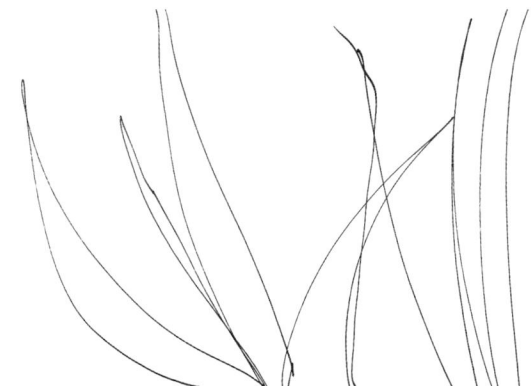

1 The Value Sketch

Make value sketches or thumbnails to assemble a harmonious arrangement of lines, masses and shapes, as well as an abstract value pattern of lights, midtones and darks. Thumbnails help you construct a sound composition from the beginning. This will serve as a roadmap for the entire painting process.

The composition should have dynamic divisions of space in order to be interesting and deliver the most dramatic impact. Notice the strong upward thrust used as an anchoring device to provide structural emphasis and help support other shapes. There is a repetition of shapes, but also variation, including a mixture of large, medium and small shapes, both in the positive and negative areas. There are interesting interlocking shapes like a jigsaw puzzle. Don't forget to add overlapping shapes for interest, depth and dimension.

2 The Gesture Drawing

Next, get into the feeling of the painting by making gesture drawings. On a larger sheet of paper, make long sweeping lines in the general directions that the painting will take. Use your entire arm and draw freely. This is also a great warm-up exercise. In the gesture drawing above, notice the different directional movement and counter-movement. Some flower shapes will lean to the left and some to the right.

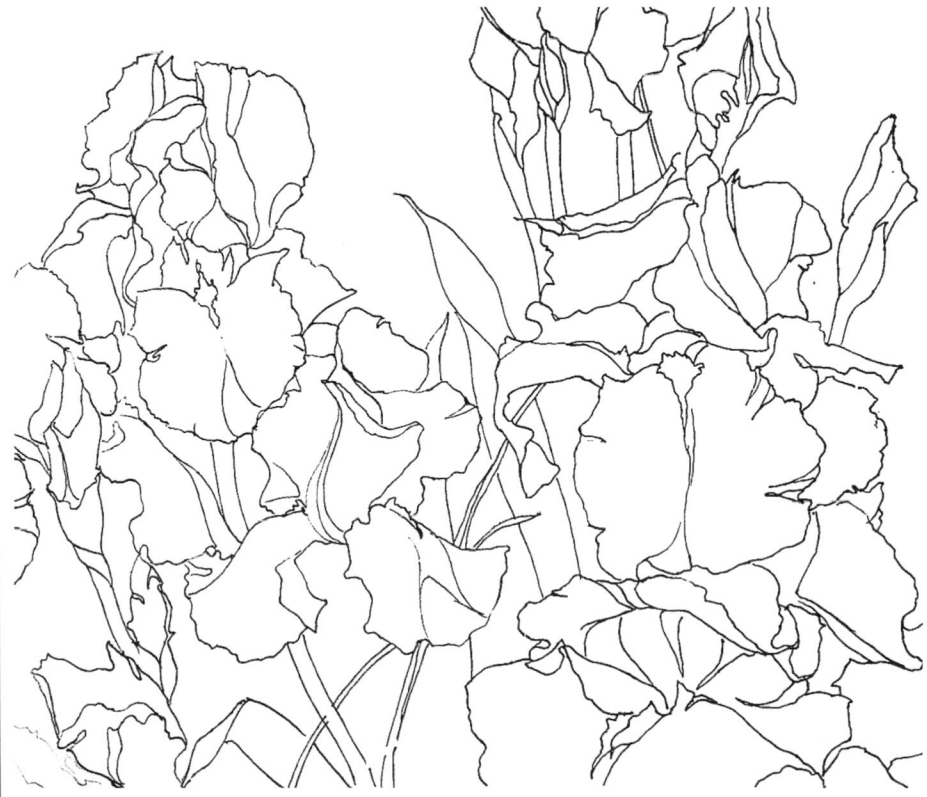

3 The Outline Drawing

Make a detailed outline drawing and trace it onto the watercolor paper. At this stage, begin to paint using the traditional method. Use the "one-third rule" for determining color, value, shape and the edges. One-third of the color should be warm and the other two-thirds should be cool. One-third of the painting should have darker values and two-thirds lighter, or vice versa. Edges also should be divided by thirds relating to softness and hardness.

4 Final Paintings

These two paintings from the same outline drawing show the different mood and feeling that can be created by using a different palette of colors. Sometimes during the painting process, a title for the painting comes to mind. This helps to indicate where the emphasis will be directed.

In *Standing Ovation*, the emphasis is on warm pinks and greens blending into an equally warm background of browns, greens and violets. Indefinite and lost edges give the painting a gentler essence.

Standing Ovation
15" × 22" (38cm × 56cm)

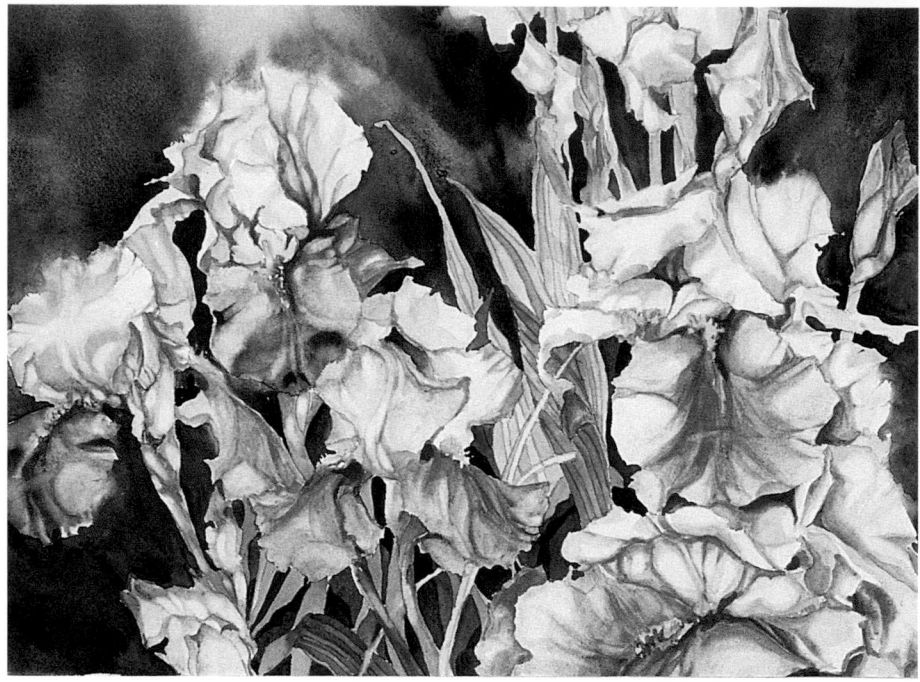

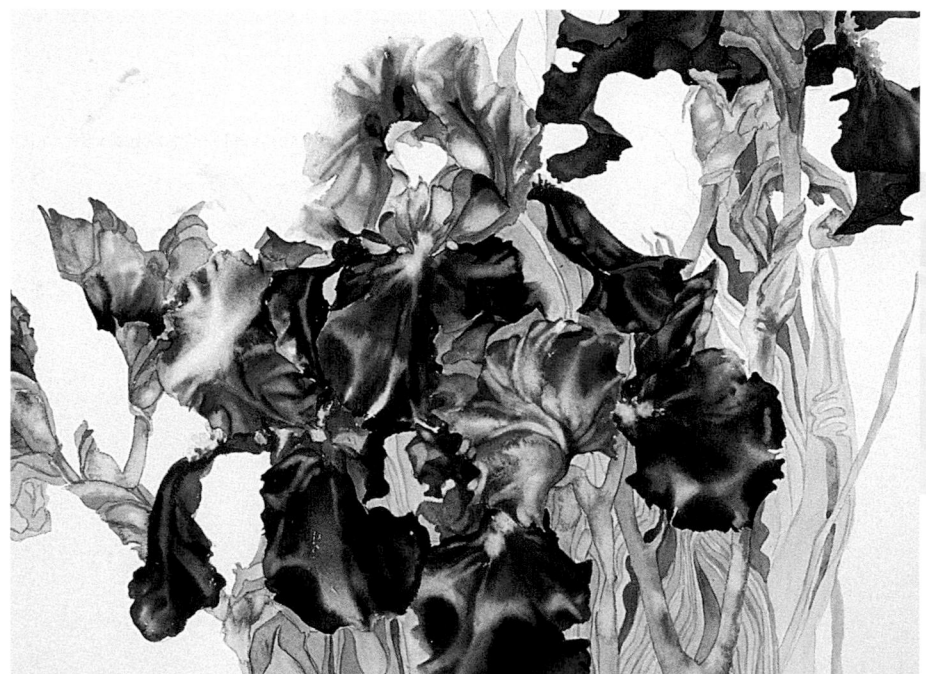

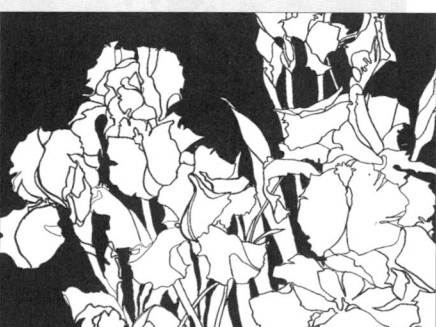

Original thumbnail

In *Twist of Fate*, cool, dark blues and purples are contrasted against a stark white background, giving a greater sense of drama and intensity. The hard edges and sharp focus emphasize a feeling of strength and definition, compared to the gentler *Standing Ovation*. The strong upward thrust of the stems and leaves (apparent in both paintings) creates a scaffolding upon which the other flowers and leaves are hung.

Twist of Fate
15" × 22" (38cm × 56cm)

choosing a format

When planning the contents of a painting, you must decide on a *format*. This refers to the dimensions of the ground upon which you plan the painting. The format can be any shape that best complements the pictoral content, but is oftentimes a square or rectangle.

To check whether your subject works within the format, consider its abstracted shape. Is the shape pleasing? Does it fill the format?

Also, you must decide which subject elements receive the most attention. You can divide the format several different ways, using large, medium and small shapes.

■ Format   ■ Shape   ■ Content

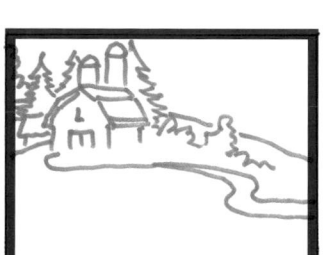

Place Your Subject

First, choose your subject and place it within the format. A pleasing shape will have varied edges and fit comfortably within the format.

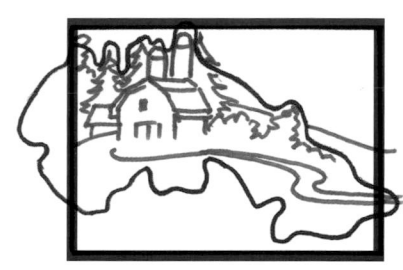

Check the Shape

Next, draw an interesting shape around your subject to confirm that this is the proper placement for the pictorial content.

DIFFERENT FORMATS

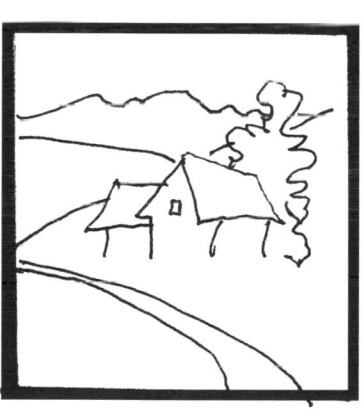

Square

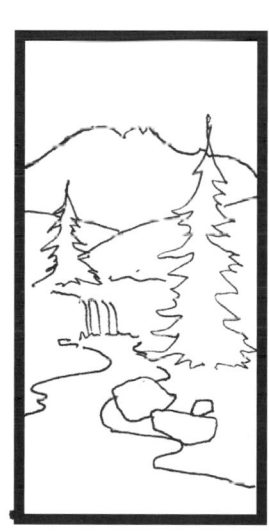

Tall and Vertical

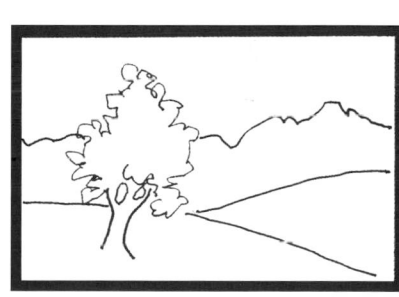

Rectangle

DIVIDING THE FORMAT

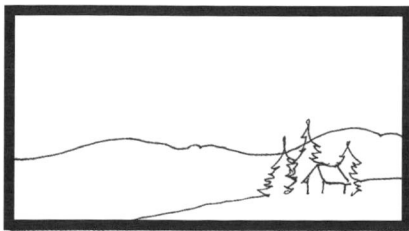

Sky Is Dominant

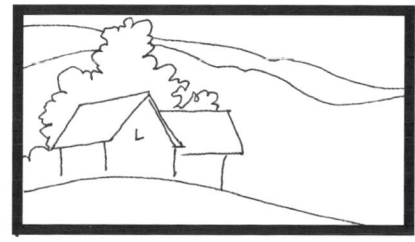

Land Is Dominant

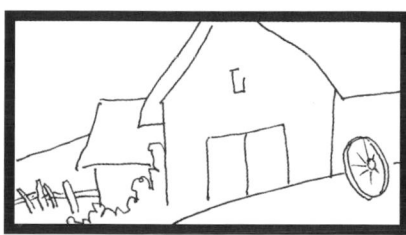

Buildings Are Dominant

working with a format

Even after deciding on a format, you can crop the edges of your painting in order to create the very best result. The most important elements of the painting should be placed in a position to receive the most attention from the viewer.

As a learning exercise, practice cropping your paintings to see how different types and sizes of formats can affect the work as a whole.

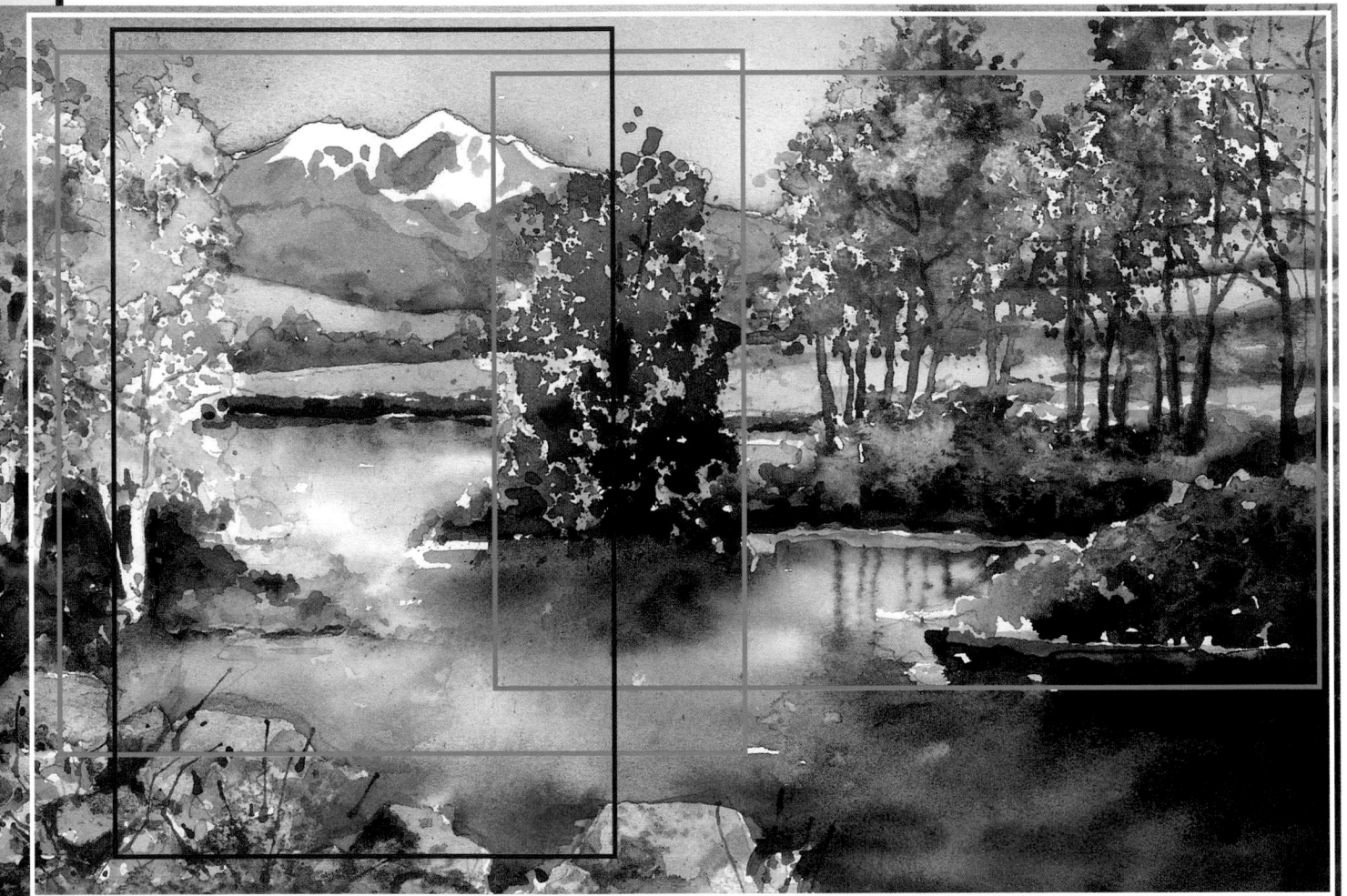

Crop Your Painting

You can crop your painting after it is finished in order to highlight the parts of the painting that you want to emphasize. The result should be a satisfying composition, regardless of what is included or excluded. The first crop (in blue) is a smaller rectangle that emphasizes only the grouping of trees on the right. The second crop (in red) is a vertical format that eliminates many elements of the original painting and focuses solely on the mountains and water with minimal trees. The third crop (in green) encompasses all the components of the painting with the mountain area as the main focal point. The water leads the viewer's eye through the painting. In all three formats the subject matter falls comfortably within the picture plane. While each is a good composition, individually they provide a different emphasis. Which of the three new formats do you like the best?

Helpful Hint NUMBER 6
Don't try to paint everything: focus on what drew you to the subject matter in the first place.

the elements of composition

Once the subject and format are decided, you must use the various elements of composition (including line, color, shape, value, texture, space and form) as tools to develop the painting.

SPACE AND FORM
Space and form give volume to a painting and add mass or density. The form of an object is determined first by its outline and then how it rests within its space, according to the light and shadow that give it dimension and depth.

SHAPE
Shape refers to a defined area within a painting, different from what is around it. Shape has two dimensions, while form has depth. They are interrelated elements—form is the space around the shape. Shapes can be curvilinear or geometric, as determined by the line around them.

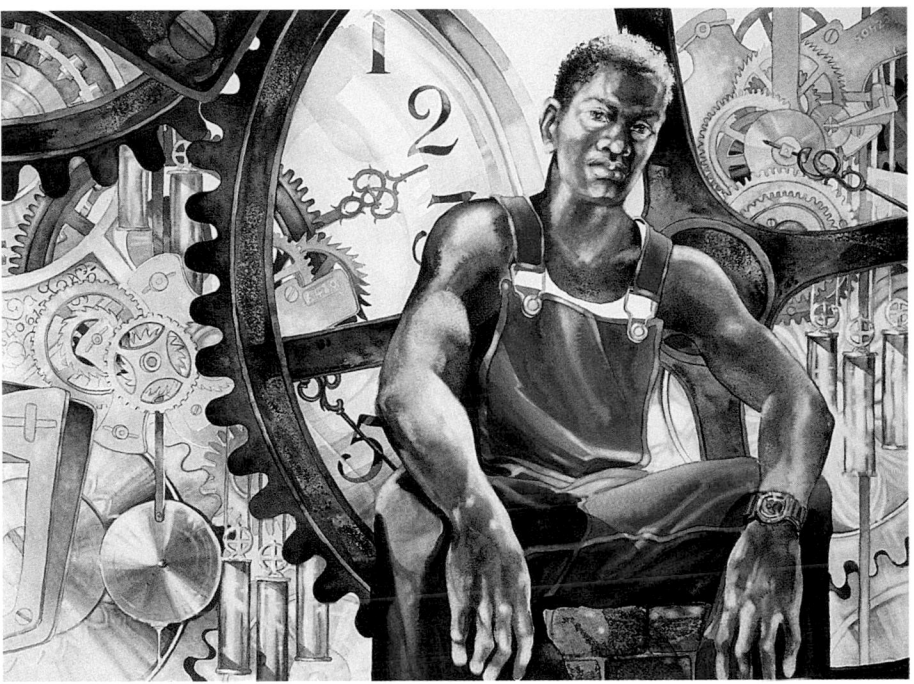

Using Space and Form
The figure in this painting has been molded in a three-dimensional form. This is contrasted with the flat shapes of the background clockworks, which are two-dimensional. On a deeper level, the painting is a contrast between humanity and machine.

Deus ex Machina
22" × 30" (56cm × 76cm)

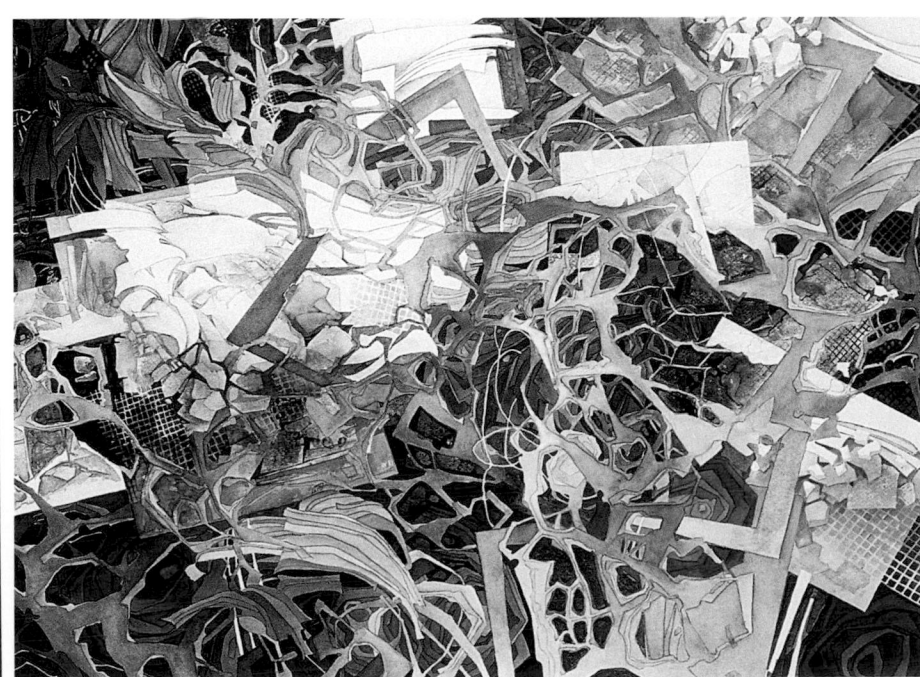

Using Shape
In this painting, every sort of shape is played against each other, from geometric to curvilinear, as well as both large and small. Note the negative shapes created by the positive ones. The square-spotted blue is an endangered species of butterfly found high in the Sierra Nevada mountains. Letters seeking the butterfly's preservation are written to newspapers, but such letters usually get tangled up in political bureaucracy. This painting is about the letters caught in that web.

Square-Spotted Blue
22" × 30" (56cm × 76cm)

LINE

Line is one of the fundamental tools of art. It can suggest mass, texture, light and shadow. It has its own character and can be an erratic squiggle or a smooth curve. It establishes boundaries, denotes direction, defines contours, creates pattern and sets mood. Horizontal lines are peaceful, vertical lines denote strength, diagonal lines suggest movement or energy and curved lines create rhythm.

VALUE

Value refers to the degree of light or dark existing in a painting. Darker colors are said to have low value; lighter colors have high value. Placing strongly contrasting values (such as black and white) next to one another in a painting creates greater visual excitement than two similar values.

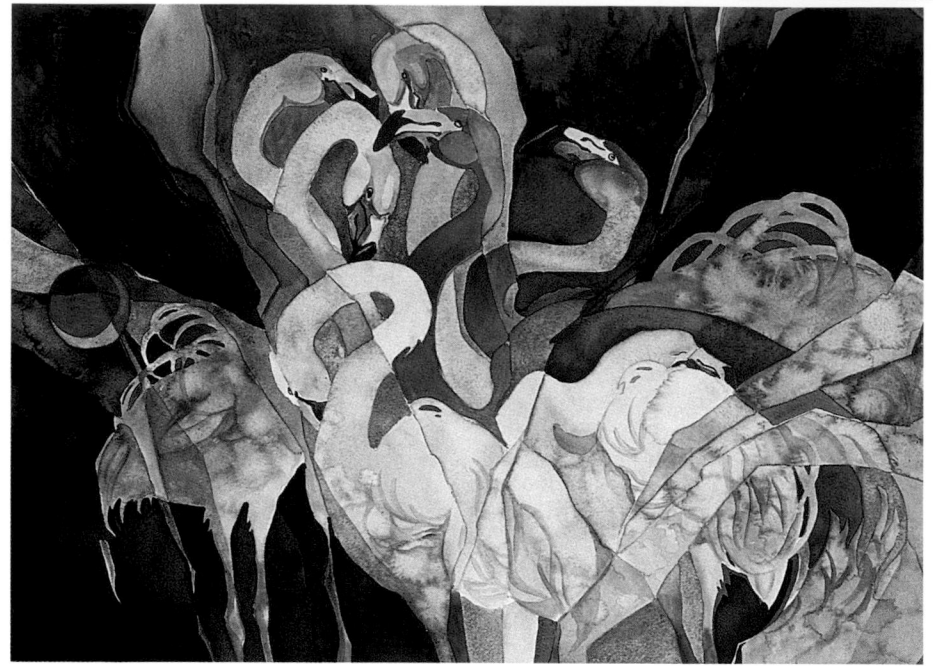

Using Line

Line helps determine how a painting will flow across the format as well as defining the parameters of the shapes themselves. In this painting, the lines have outlined the fluid curves and arches of the sinuous flamingo shapes as well as the upward vertical movement of the background spaces.

Flamingo Flamenco
22" × 30" (56cm × 76cm)

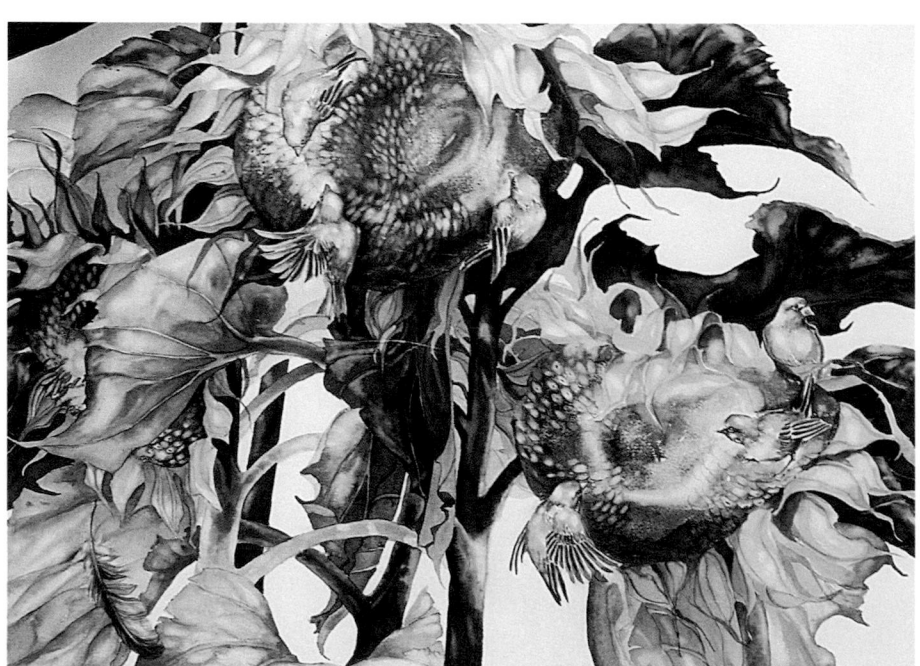

Using Value

Value is one of the most important features in a compelling picture. It is always good to use a full range of values when making a strong statement, but a medium value range can be used if a softer sentiment is desired. *Sunrich Gold* uses a full value range from the lightest light of the white paper for the background to the darkest darks of the contrasting leaves. If you have difficulty determing value, try placing red plastic on top of your painting to subdue all the colors. This will show the value pattern more clearly.

Sunrich Gold
22" × 30" (56cm × 76cm)

COLOR

A painting is a symphony of *color*. A pleasing arrangement of color can create movement, advancement or retreat, as well as mood, harmony or agitation. Color can also balance a painting through visual weight by the use of lights and darks and intensity. Cool colors must have warm colors, darks need lights, luminous colors need opaques, intense color needs some dullness and any color needs a little of its complement.

TEXTURE

Texture refers to the variations in surface quality that can be seen or felt. It gives interest by drawing attention to a specific area in the painting and helps to establish mood.

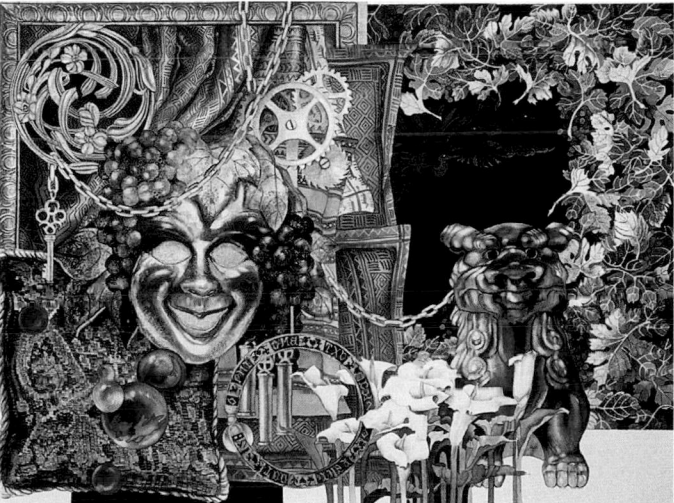

Using Texture

One way to avoid a bland and lifeless painting is to incorporate a variety of different textures within its components. *Bacchanalia* uses a number of textures that define fabrics, metallics and ceramics (man-made) and some flora and fauna (natural). This diversity holds the viewer's attention as the eye travels from one interesting element to another in this rich tapestry of effects.

Bacchanalia
22" × 30" (56cm × 76cm)

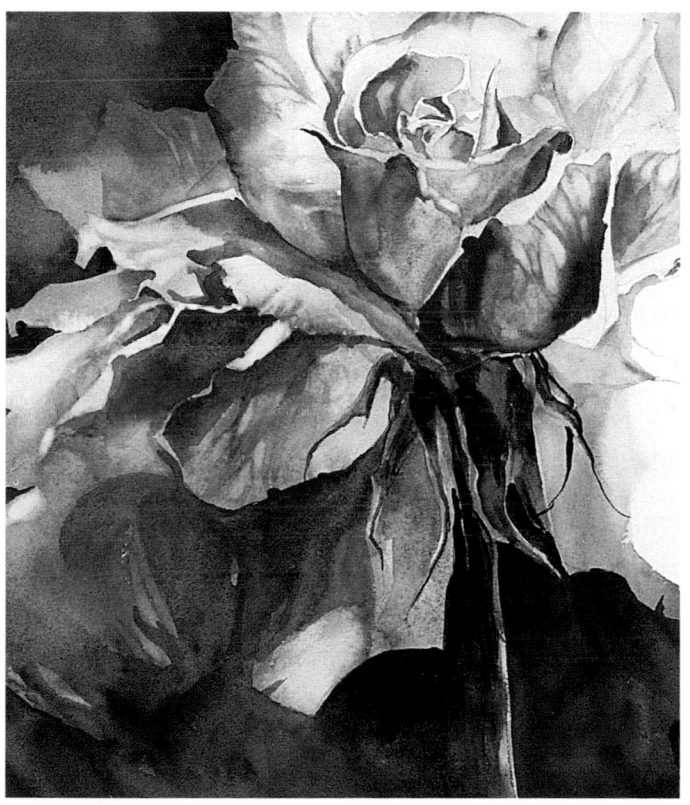

Using Color

What could make your painting more eye-catching than the use of brilliant color? Color can infinitely change the mood of a painting from the most subtle to the most vigorous statement. In *Peace*, the vibrant pinks and reds present the image of the rose in full force, and the contrasting greens add interest.

Peace
14" × 13" (36cm × 33cm)

From the elements of composition we move onto the *principles of design.* These are the objectives that artists have in mind when combining different elements to make an effective composition. They include balance, harmony, repetition, contrast, rhythm, gradation, unity and dominance. A composition is well balanced when all elements sit comfortably on the format.

If these rules of good composition are used, a painting will just "feel" right and have a certain synergy of all its parts. Proper positioning of all parts of a painting creates the perfect relationships between all of the pictorial components.

BALANCE
Balance is an equal distribution of visual weight within a painting. In formal works of art, symmetrical balance (equal weight on opposite sides) is the preferred way. Asymmetrical balance is more common. It can involve informal or dynamic balance, using unequal weight on either side of a painting counterbalanced by color or value, detail, or subject matter.

HARMONY
Harmony is the close association of objects or compositional elements within a painting. Think of it as a comfortable similarity between colors or shapes.

REPETITION
Repetition is the reoccurrence of compositional elements (for example, color, shape or texture) that results in a harmonious effect. A good relationship between patterns and the flow or progression of the elements is artistically appealing.

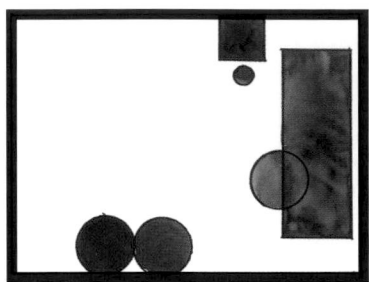 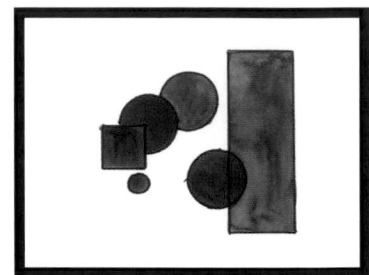

No Balance   Balance

In the example on the left, the viewer's eye jumps from the red shapes to the green shapes and back again. The red circles cause uncomfortable tension because they are on the edge. In the example on the right, the shapes are distributed equally, making the grouping more pleasing to the eye.

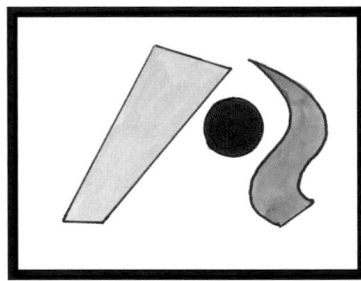 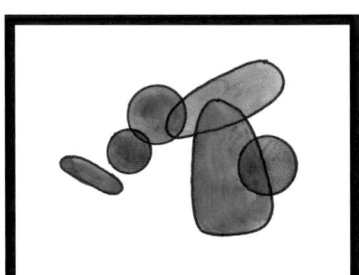

No Harmony   Harmony

In the example on the left, there is nothing that draws these shapes into a happy combination. They are different in their parameters and color. In the example on the right, there is no rivalry because the colors are analogous and the shapes are blended.

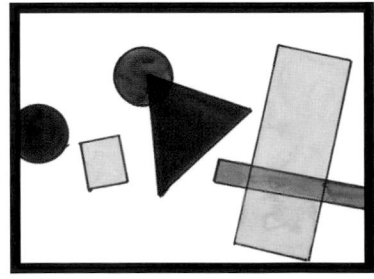 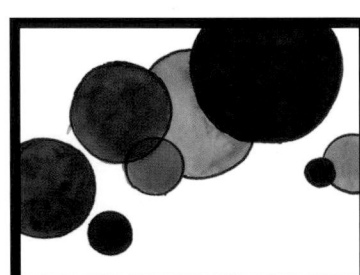

No Repetition   Repetition

In the example on the left, all the shapes are different and each is a different color, which has an uncomfortable, scattered effect. The example on the right shows good repetition because all the shapes are circles. Although different in size, the circles echo each other and their hues vary in shades of the same color.

CONTRAST

Contrast occurs when opposing elements or ideas are introduced into a painting. It can be achieved by color, value, line or form—for example, when adding a round shape to a group of rectangles. Contrast piques the viewer's interest.

RHYTHM

Rhythm is the suggestion of differences between the elements, which causes interest and excitement. It is a sequence of color, texture, or shape differences within a painting.

GRADATION

Gradation is a gradual transition from dark to light, warm to cool, or smooth to rough within a painting.

UNITY

Sometimes confused with harmony, *unity* is a stronger quality in which all elements of a composition are directly linked by one or more attributes. Unity is the order or coherence created in a painting by incorporating similar colors, forms or lines. It is a pleasing relationship between interlocking elements within a painting.

DOMINANCE

Dominance is the supreme importance given to one part or feature of a painting in respect to size, color, shape, volume or placement. For instance, a shape can be made more dominant by making it bigger or brighter, by making it happen more often, or by providing more value contrast around it.

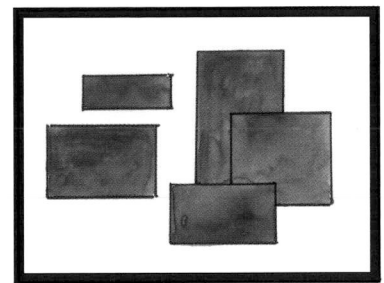
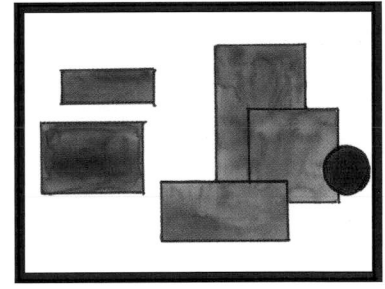

No Contrast   Contrast

In the example on the left, all the colors and shapes are the same except for slight variations, creating a boring design. In the example on the right, the addition of one shape different in form and color instantly creates interest in the entire composition. The eye moves directly to the red circle.

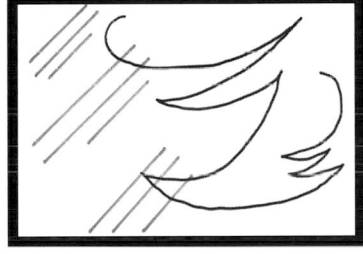
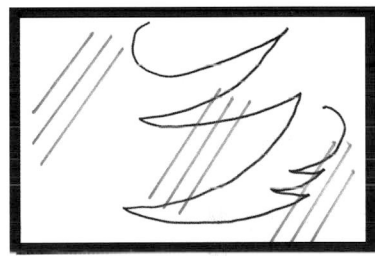

No Rhythm   Rhythm

In the example on the left, there is no blending of tempo or pace in this grouping of straight diagonal lines placed on the left and freeform lines on the right. In the example on the right, a pleasing rhythm occurs where the diagonals are merged with the freeform lines. The colors, no longer divided between left and right, help maintain an even pace within the format.

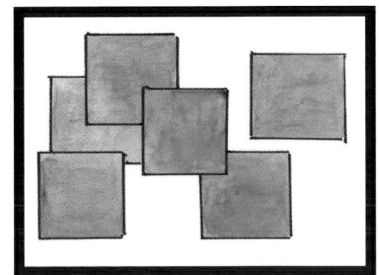
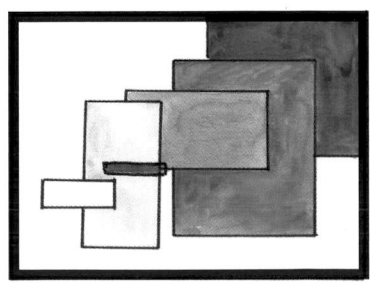

No Gradation   Gradation

In the example on the left, each blue square is the same value as its neighbors and there is no variation within the entire format, creating a flat and uninteresting compositon. In the example on the right, the range of values varies from very pale blue to darkest blue with many shades of blue in the entire range resulting in a much more interesting whole.

The *focal point*, or center of interest, is the one-fourth of a painting that is a "feast for the eye," the part that first attracts the viewer's eye by using compositional elements such as line, color, shape or value. Focal points are frequently established by using dominance and contrast.

The focal point itself should have dominance and act as a force to hold the composition together. It can be very large, very light or very dark. It can be the area of greatest contrast, brightest color, most detail, or where lines intersect. It can also be achieved by subject. If you have an entire painting of flowers and one small human figure in the corner, your eye will be attracted to the figure. In a painting of mainly cool blue, a small shape of orange will draw the eye. Attention is attracted by the most detail, the sharpest edges, the greatest difference between light and dark, and incongruities. If you have a painting of fish and add a clock, the clock will be the focal point. There should also be lesser, secondary focal points that are appealing enough to draw the viewer's attention to other parts of the painting. Hidden elements can make the viewer look a second time.

There are eight ways to establish the primary area of interest in your painting (see illustrations). Try taking a different approach to your artwork by using a focal point technique that you don't usually employ.

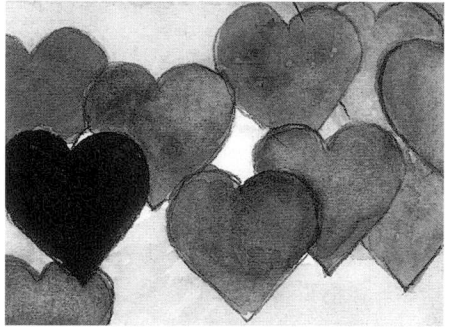

The Brightest Bright

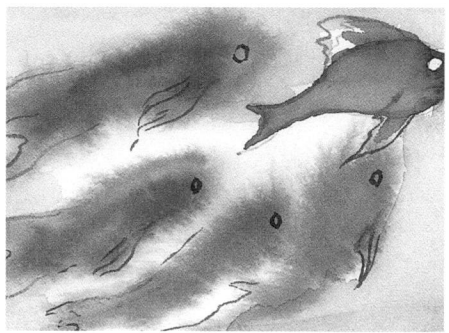

The Sharpest Edges

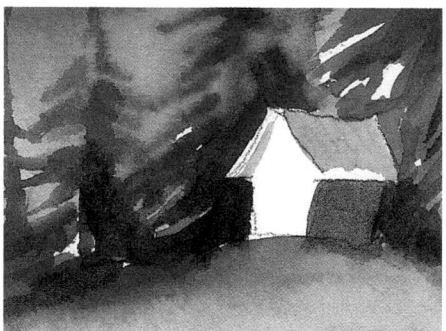

The Lightest Light Against the Darkest Dark

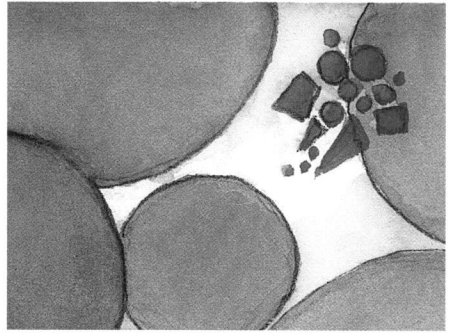

The Most Detail

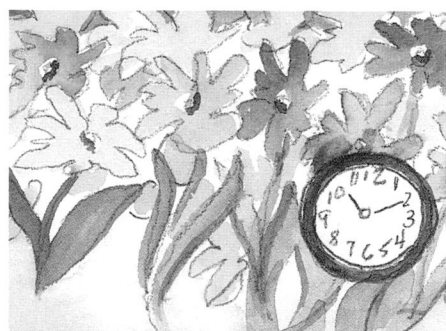

An Odd Object Among Similar Objects

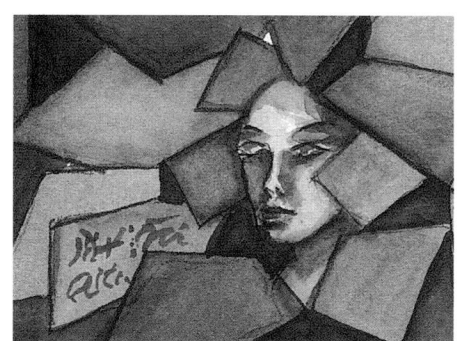

The Human Face or Writing

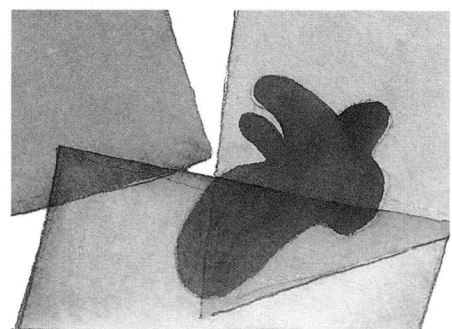

A Curvilinear Form Among Geometrics

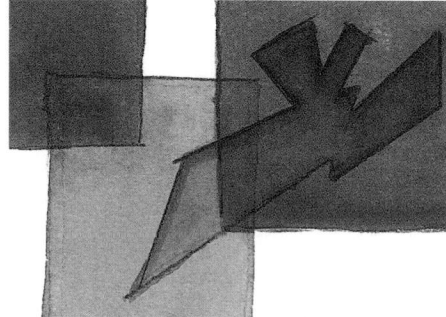

The Most Interesting Shape

placing the focal point

It is important to place the focal point in one of the appropriate areas of the painting to create a pleasing composition or the painting will feel off-balance. Divide your format into balanced sections with a basic "tic-tac-toe" pattern, then arrange the composition by placing the pictorial content along the lines of the divisions. This easy guide assures a comfortable design pattern by imposing order on a painting.

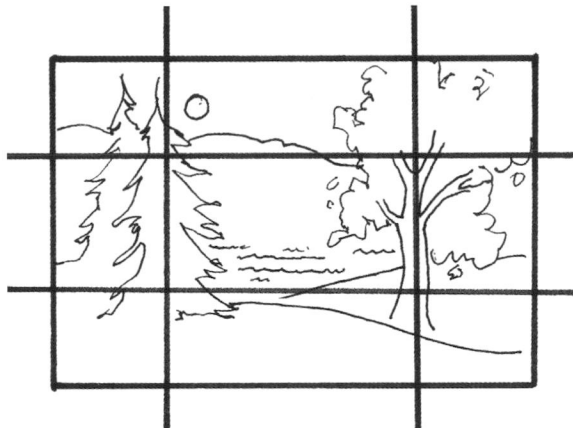

Finding the Focal Point

Although there are many ways to determine a potential focal point, the "tic-tac-toe" pattern is a popular method. Divide the format into thirds, both vertically and horizontally. Where the lines intersect are comfortable places for a focal point.

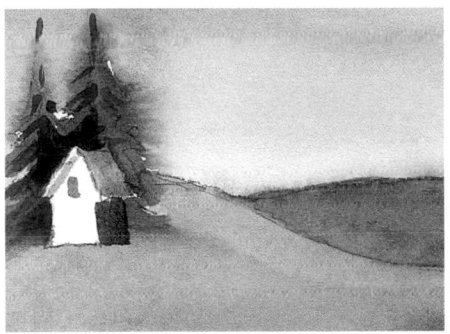

Bad Focal Point
This focal point is too near the left side of the format, causing tension.

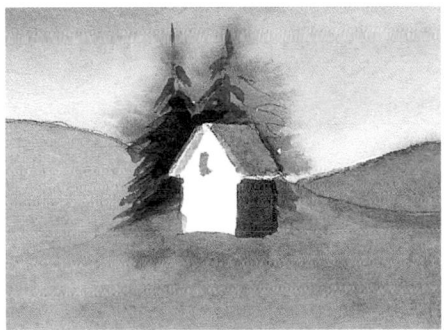

Bad Focal Point
This focal point is dead-on center and feels like a bull's-eye.

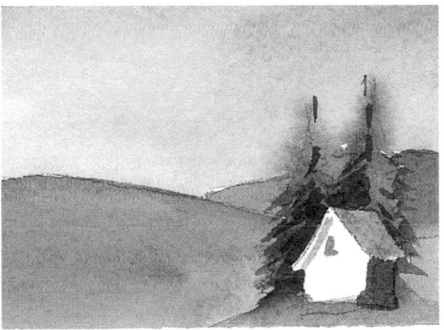

Bad Focal Point
This focal point rests too near the bottom of the format, leaving too much uninteresting space around it.

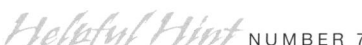

Helpful Hint NUMBER 7

Dramatic contrast draws the viewer's attention into the painting. So does bright color.

Secondary focal point   Primary focal point

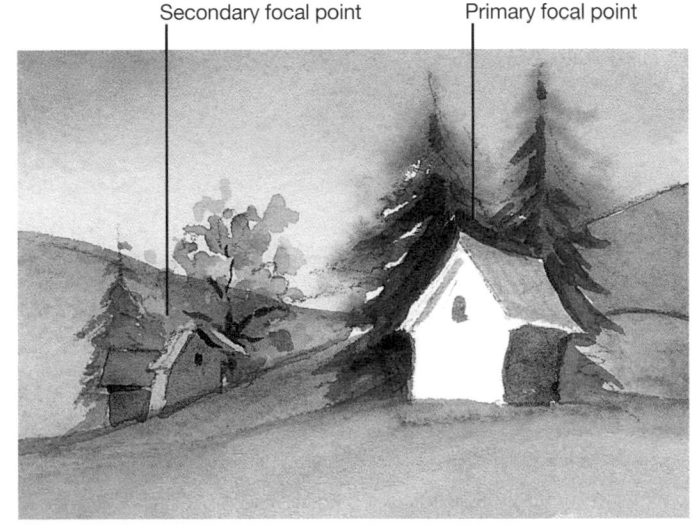

Good Focal Point
This focal point rests in a comfortable space and establishes a pleasing design format.

creating eye flow

Eye flow, or track of vision, is the artist's way to direct the viewer's eye through the arrangement of objects on the canvas. The artist controls how the viewer enters the painting, moves through it finding focal points, and then exits. The artist manipulates the viewer's pathway through the painting by a knowledgeable use of the compositional elements and principles of art.

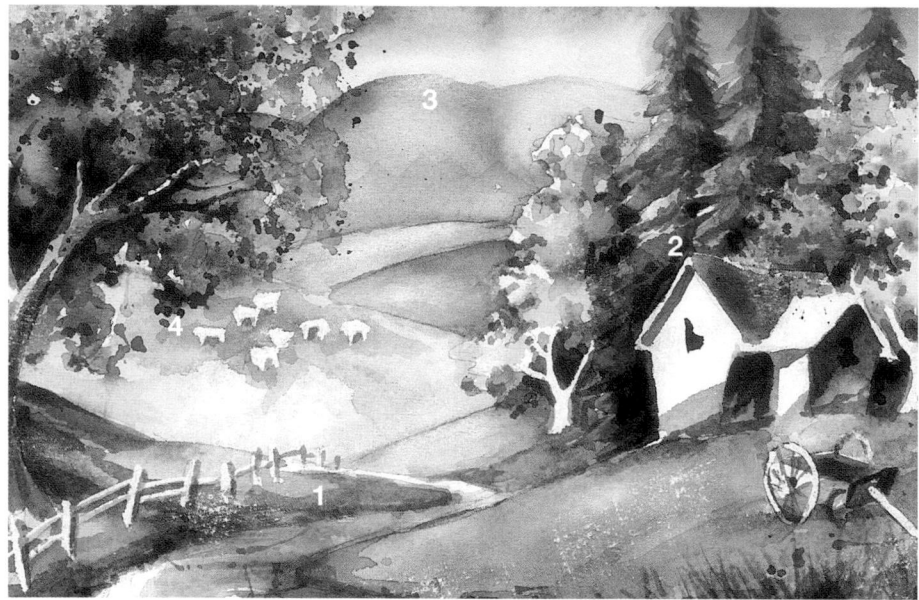

Creating a Visual Pathway

Use directional lines from one focal point to another in order to control a viewer's pathway through the painting. This example shows a counter-clockwise motion through the painting.

1   The road and the fence on the bottom left of the format allow entry into the painting and move directly to the main focal point, the white house.
2   The house's roofline and nearby trees guide the viewer's eye upward.
3   The mountain ridge leads to the other side of the painting to a secondary focal point (grazing cows).
4   The tree branches and trunk move the viewer down the painting and back to the road.

Counter-Movement   Movement

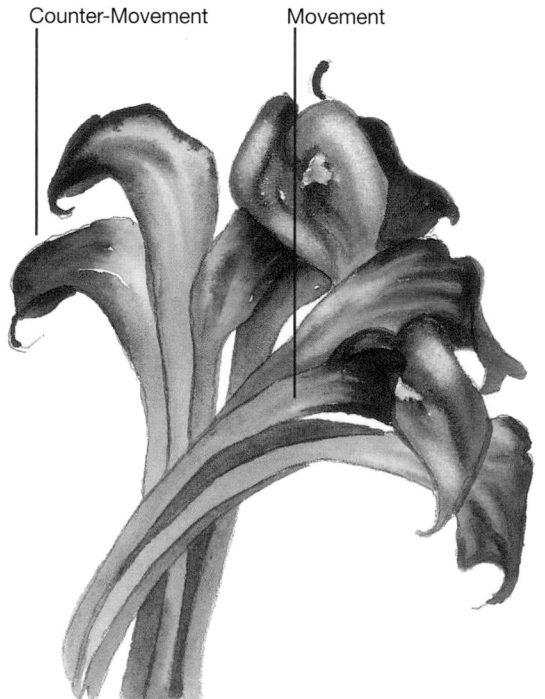

Movement and Counter-Movement

Vitality and flow are evident within a painting when directional lines move the viewer's eye in one direction and other lines move the viewer's eye in the opposite direction.

Helpful Hint NUMBER 8

In addition to areas of interest in your painting, make sure you include "rest areas" to avoid overwhelming the viewer.

These easy-to-follow exercises should stimulate your sensitivity to spatial relationships and are good practice for using the elements of composition and principles of design.

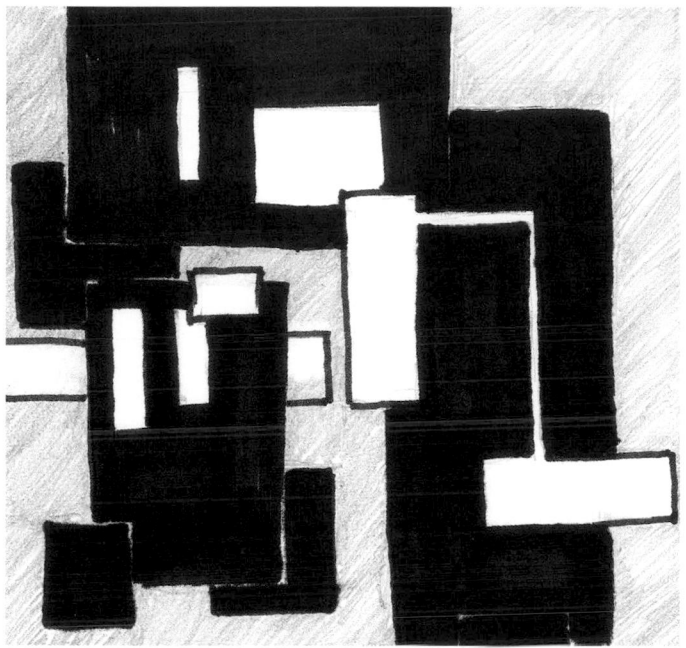

Comparison: Make a Design Pattern
Cut out some black paper squares, rectangles, circles, triangles and lines. Make a design pattern of black and white shapes on a piece of paper.

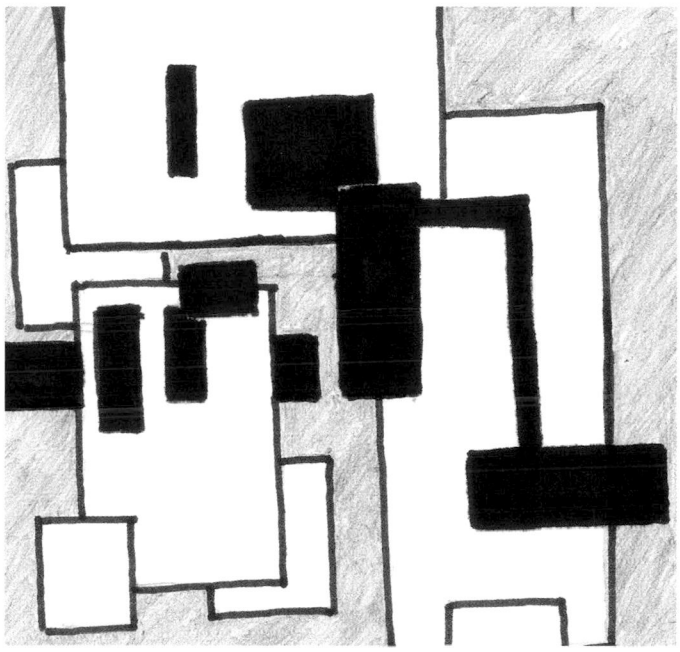

Comparison: Make a Reverse Design Pattern
Do another image of the same design, except reverse the black and white shapes. Note the different mood effects between the two. Which is more expressive?

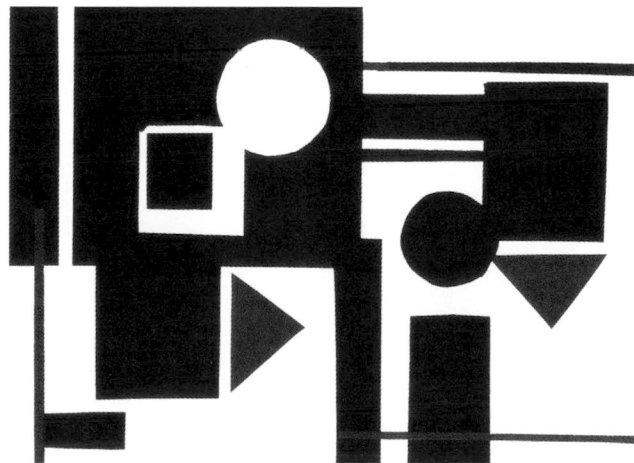

Comparison: Geometric Design
Cut out some black paper squares, rectangles, circles, triangles and lines. Arrange the shapes into a pleasing pattern on white paper. Turn it in all directions to see if it is well-balanced.

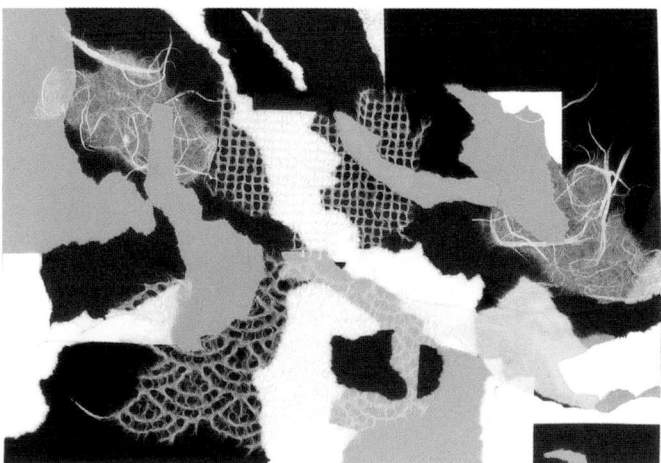

Comparison: Freeform Design
Cut out shapes and tear apart scraps of paper in various sizes, forms, colors and textures. Arrange and rearrange the pieces on white paper, overlapping and placing some on top of others until you have a pleasing freeform design. The finished piece should look balanced if you turn it in all directions and look at it in the mirror.

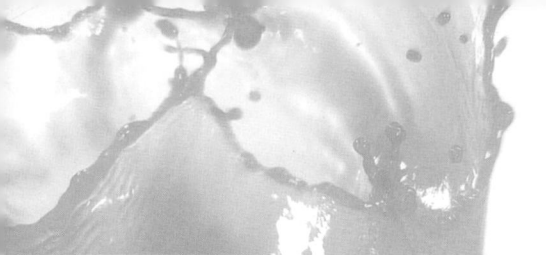

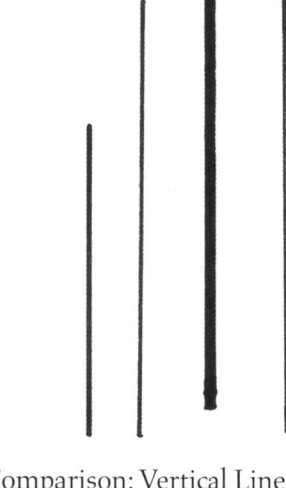

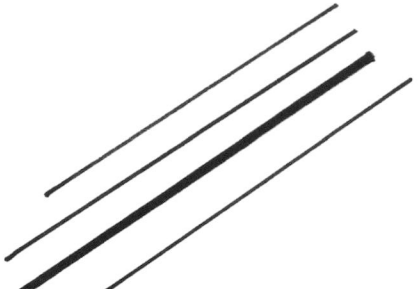

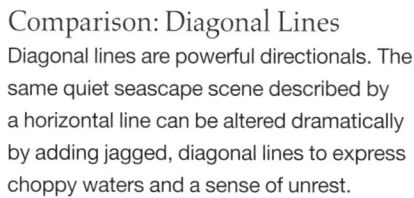

Comparison: Horizontal Lines
Horizontal lines create calmness and serenity. In nature, a quiet seascape with barely a ripple in the water can be expressed with a simple horizontal line.

Comparison: Diagonal Lines
Diagonal lines are powerful directionals. The same quiet seascape scene described by a horizontal line can be altered dramatically by adding jagged, diagonal lines to express choppy waters and a sense of unrest.

Comparison: Vertical Lines
Lines help to establish mood, rhythm and direction in your painting. By understanding what lines can do, you can manipulate your paintings to create many diverse moods. Vertical lines denote strength and solidity.

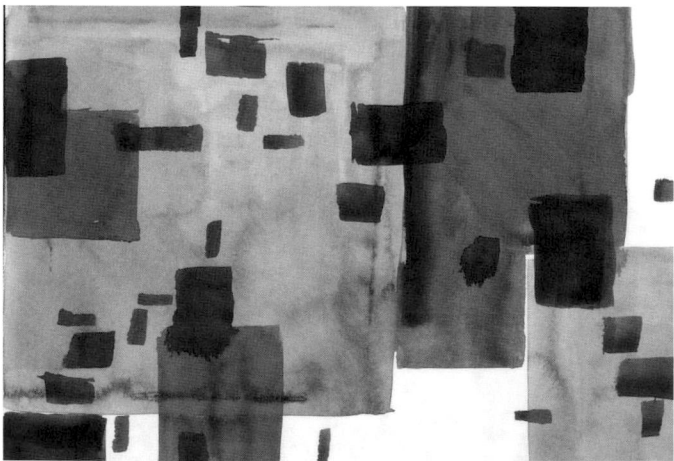

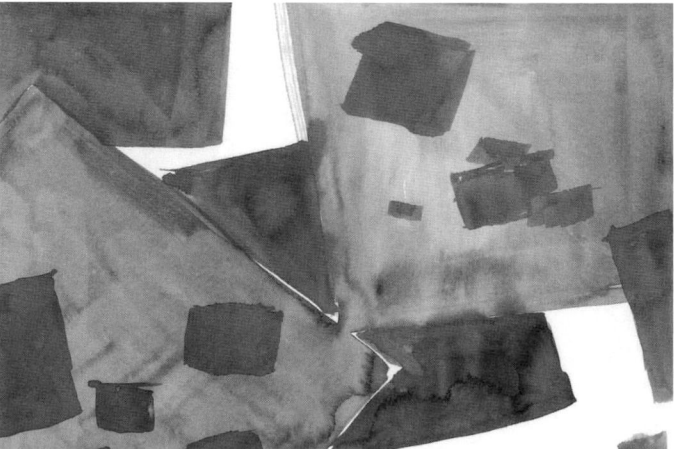

Comparison: Creating Stability
Paint a series of small, medium and large squares in light, medium and dark values. Make them vertical and horizontal to create a stable effect. These exercises will help you learn to focus on design principles such as shape and line and their relationships to one another rather than the subject matter.

Comparison: Creating Energy
Paint small, medium and large shapes and overlap them to create depth. Place them at diagonal angles to create an active effect. By understanding the fundamentals of design principles, you will be able to manipulate the different compositional elements to express your specific concept to the viewer.

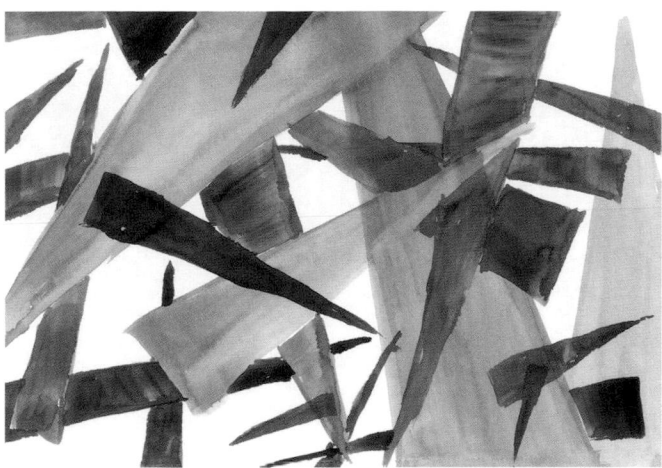

Comparison: Triangles

Practice with shapes by making triangles on the diagonal that show speed, scale and space. They are fast and sharp. There is unity in the repetition of the shapes and variety in size. The triangles, although different in size and direction, are all the same shape and variations of the same color. By repeating the shapes you create a pattern of like comparisons.

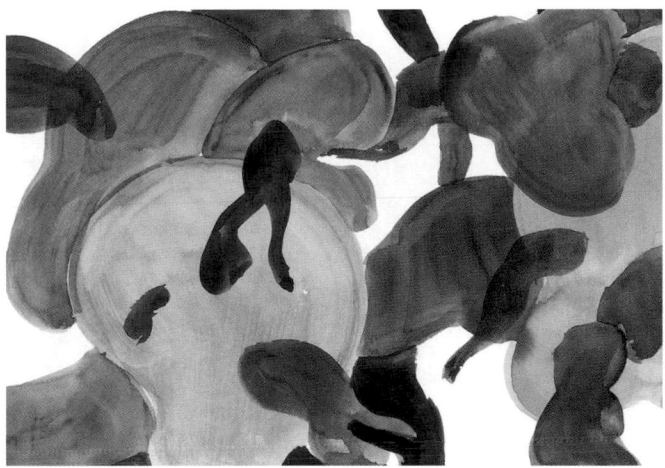

Comparison: Curving Shapes

Now make curving shapes that show unity by repetition and color and variety by size. They show a slower speed and tempo, implying a feeling of calmness. Curving, freeform shapes are more closely related to nature than the sharpness of the triangles.

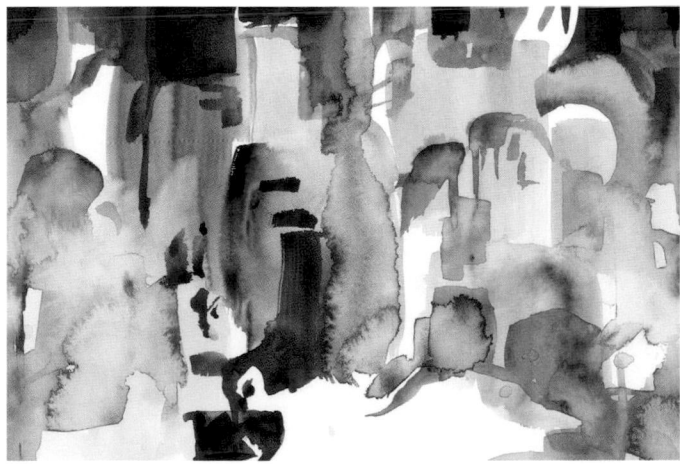

Comparison: Showing Order

Make a small study of shapes with a distribution of mostly rectangles and squares. These shapes suggest order and organization, much like the boxes we use to create order out of disorder in our daily lives. This illustration emphasizes orderliness and a calm tempo. A row of circles drawn in a neat row will accomplish the same goal.

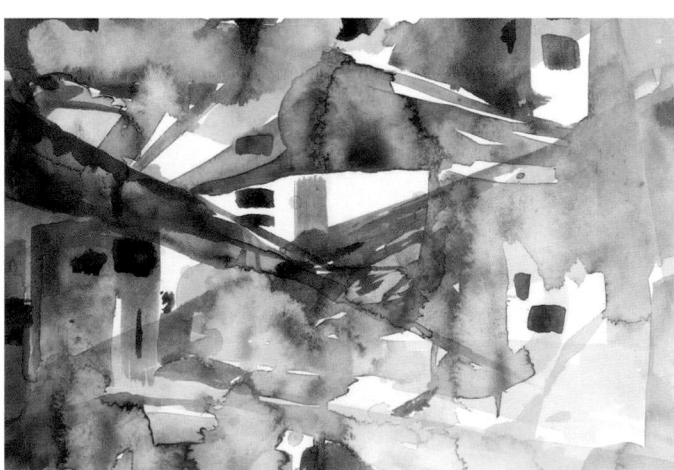

Comparison: Showing Activity

Make another sample that is a distribution of diagonals. The diagonals indicate movement and movement indicates activity. With the diagonals thrust in all directions, the illustration creates energy and the feeling of a fast pace.

testing object placement

Select three objects that are different from each other in size and shape.

Arrange the objects in all different ways and make small sketches of them. Out of all your arrangements, choose the grouping that is the most effective. Ask yourself the following questions:

- Is it well-balanced?
- Does each object relate well to the whole?
- Is it unified?

In this case, the last example seems to be the best arrangement of the objects because it best adheres to the principles of design—particularly balance, harmony and unity.

Helpful Hint NUMBER 9
Don't be afraid to change the viewpoint of your subject matter. Put it on the floor for an aerial perspective, turn it around or zoom in close to show details.

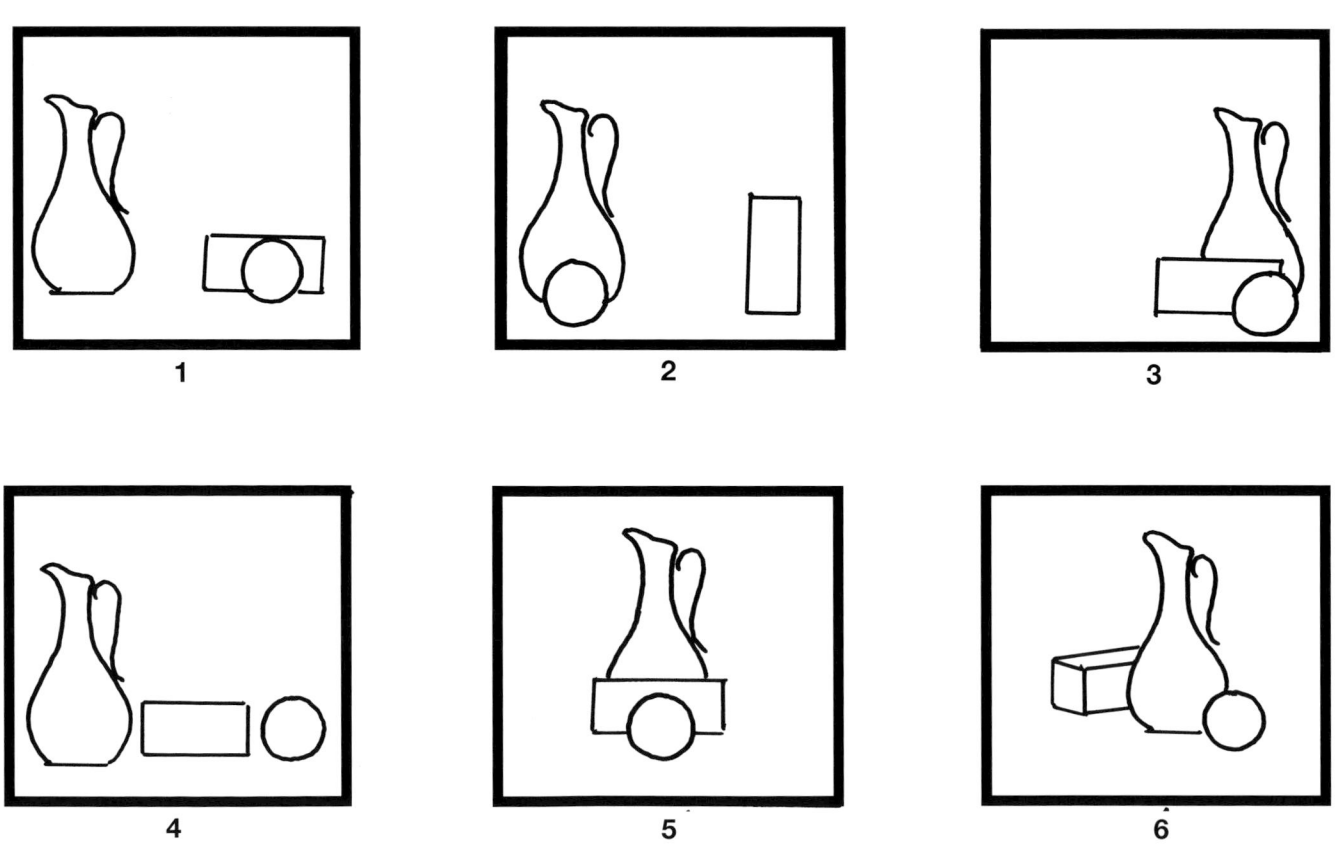

studying value relationships

Next, practice different value relationships by painting your chosen arrangement in values of light, medium and dark.

For each sketch, change the values of the background, foreground and subject. Notice how different the feeling and emphasis is in each different statement.

Value is one way to create an effective mood. In each of these examples, the mood is different, ranging from quiet and somber in the darker illustrations to starkness in the illustrations with the most contrast.

There is a comfortable balance between lights and darks in the third example.

Helpful Hint NUMBER 10

Arrange the white areas of your painting to help lead the viewer's eye through the composition.

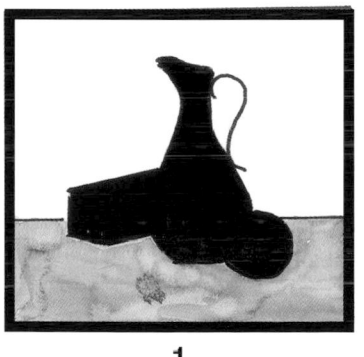

1

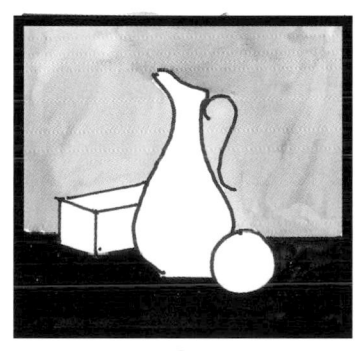

2

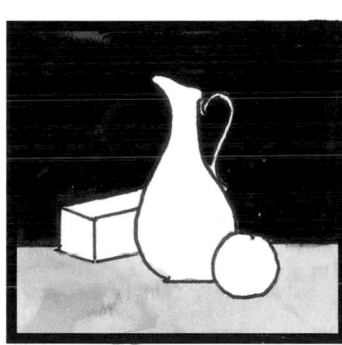

3

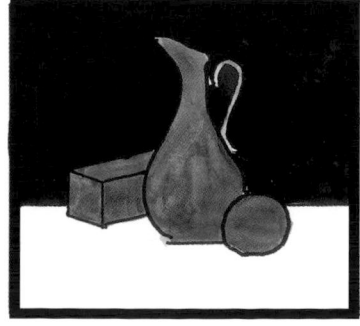

4

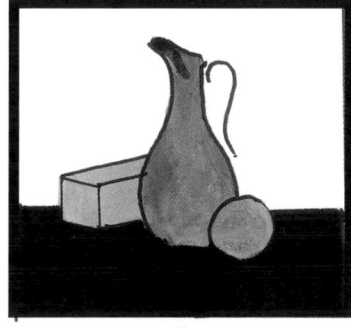

5

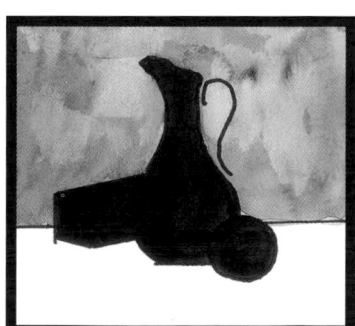

6

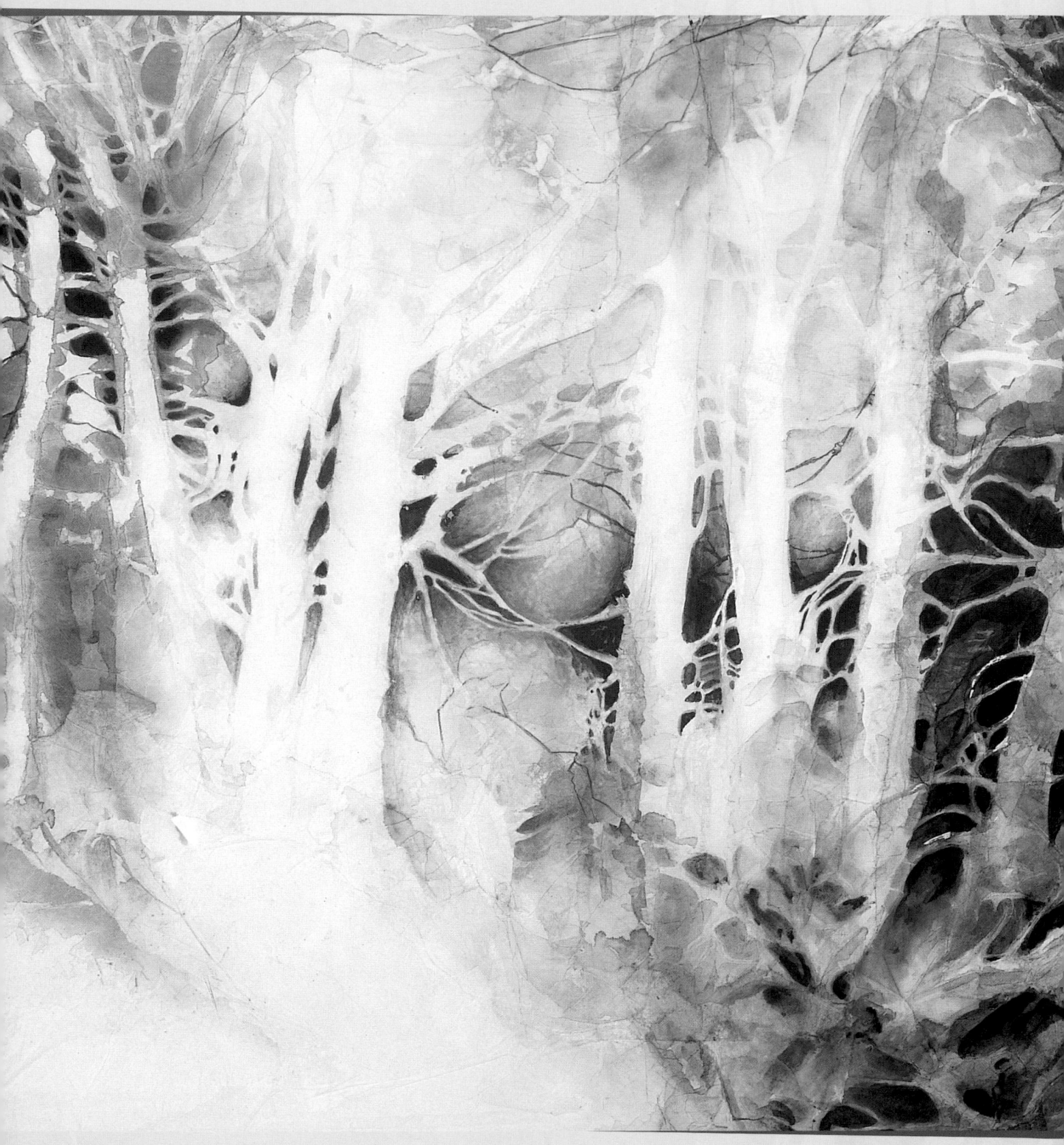

Tissue Trees
22" × 30" (56cm × 76cm)

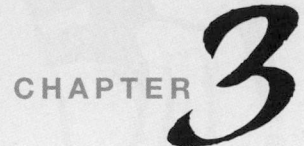

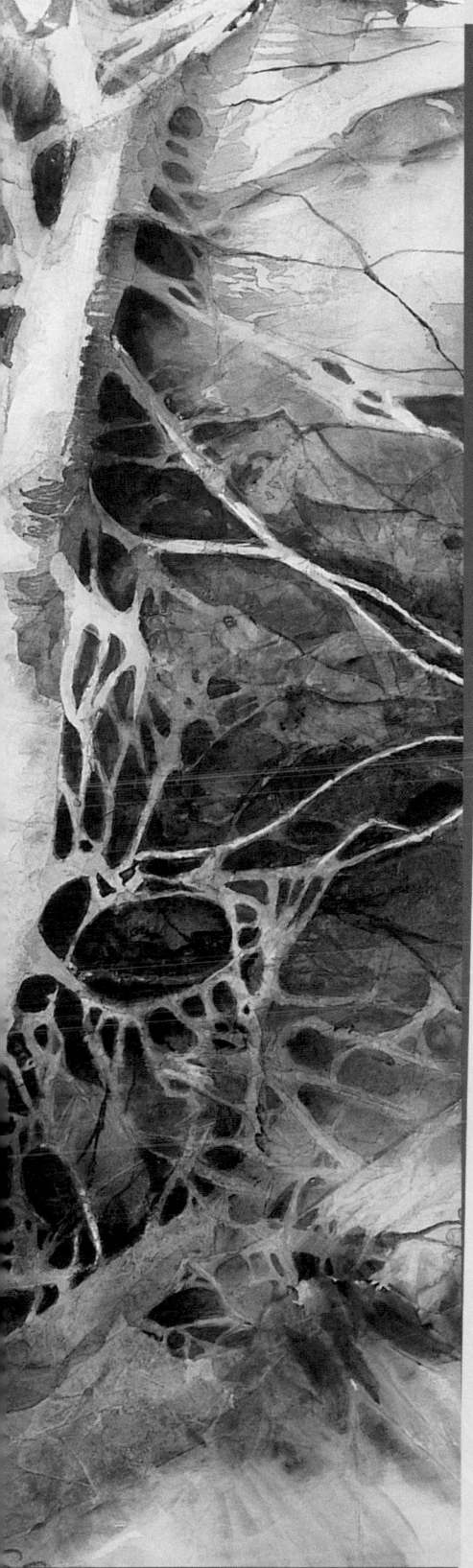

techniques

THE WATERCOLOR MEDIUM IS SO EXCITING BECAUSE OF THE infinite variety of ways to fashion a tapestry rich with expressive imagery. Think of yourself as a magician, as well as an artist. You are devising an illusion to fool the viewer's eye by creating a three-dimensional image with brush and paint on a two-dimensional sheet of paper. To do so, it is important to understand the nearly unlimited ways a 3-D effect can be created by using various techniques or approaches to apply paint to paper. Splashy watercolor with lost edges has a different feel and look than drybrush with hard edges, for instance.

In the spirit of learning, we must constantly strive to develop a style of painting we can call our own by first practicing as many techniques as possible, and then by exploring different painting methods.

This chapter will provide instructions on how to apply paint to paper, which brushes to use, and what quality of wetness or dryness is required for a specific result. You will learn wash techniques and their purposes, and practice layering, glazing, dropping color into wet paint, overlapping, drybrushing, wet-into-wet and lifting. You can even combine different techniques to create new effects to expand your creativity. By practicing these methods you will have a head start in being able to achieve the exact results you're looking for in your paintings.

Before you can create any "technique," first you must be comfortable with some of the many different brushes at your disposal. Don't be afraid to venture outside your artistic comfort zone. Try using several kinds of brushes to see what effects they can make. Every artist has a unique approach, so practice holding the brushes in various ways and at different angles. Don't be afraid to experiment. Alter the amount of pressure you apply and use the tip of the brush as well as the full body. Practice on different weights of paper. Watercolor paper surfaces can vary between *hot press* (a smooth, shiny surface), *cold press* (slightly textured) and *rough* (heavy texture). The majority of paintings in this book, including the examples on this page, were done on cold-pressed paper.

Compare the differences between the brush mark examples for flat, round, wash and rigger brushes shown on this page.

A *flat brush* has a flat, rectangular head with relatively long filaments.

A *round brush* has a round, pointed head. It is used in all mediums.

A *wash brush* is wide and flat, ideal for fluid wash finishes over large areas.

A *rigger brush* (or line brush) has a long, narrow head relative to its diameter. Some are pointed and some are blunt. It is used to paint long lines and fine details.

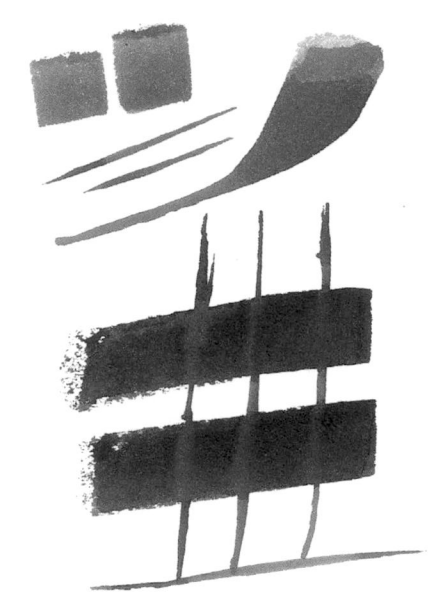

Flat Brush

A flat brush is ideal for creating geometric forms such as barns or fences and is perfect for laying on flat washes or covering large areas evenly.

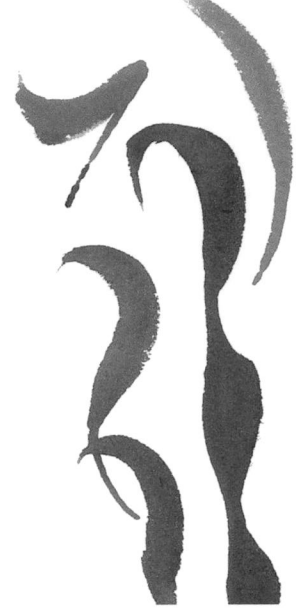

Round Brush

A round brush is very versatile in manipulating the paint onto intricate and irregular shapes and freeform sections of your painting.

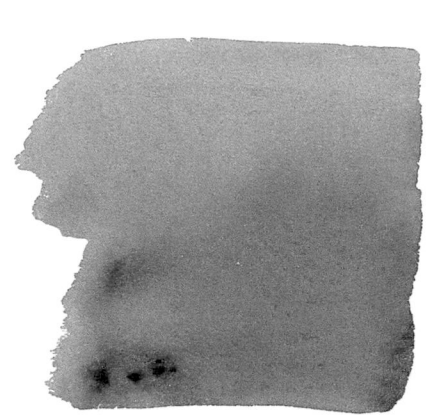

Wash Brush

Wash brushes come in different shapes but are usually flat and large. They are useful for laying in large areas of water or color, for wetting the surface and for absorbing excess media.

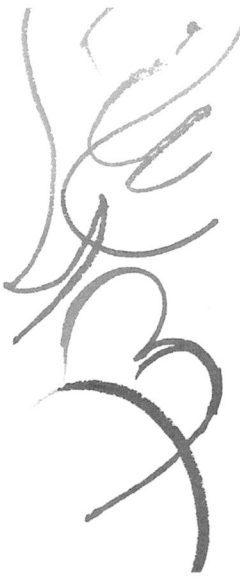

Rigger Brush

A rigger brush is used to paint long lines and fine details. Its long, slender shape allows you to paint delicate twigs, branches or petal details without having to reload too frequently, creating an uninterrupted flowing line.

The foundation of your painting is oftentimes the *wash,* a thin, fluid relatively transparent coat of paint usually applied over a large area. The rest of the painting can be built upon the first wash to create any number of results. Whether you choose a flat, graded or variegated wash depends on the pictorial content and what you wish to convey to the viewer. Use a flat wash for large areas of even color. A graded wash is ideal for variations of color. Use a variegated wash to merge different colors.

Variegated Wash

There are two ways to create a variegated wash, which blends two or more colors.

(1) Using two colors, mix a wash on your palette that begins with one pure color (blue) gradually blending with another pure color (yellow) to create several shades of green in between. Wet the paper and lay down a stripe of blue at the top of the page. The next stripe should be blue-green, the next green, the next yellow-green and the last pure yellow. Tilt the paper to let one stripe bleed into another.

(2) Using the same colors (blue and yellow), lay on a wash of blue stripes until you reach the center of the paper. Turn the paper upside down and paint a wash of pure yellow starting from the top and moving to the center of the paper where the blue wash ends. Tilt the paper to allow the blue and yellow washes to blend into green.

Flat Wash

Wet your paper with a large brush. Load the brush with a thick mixture of paint and water. (Start with a flat, but experiment with other types.) Add water for a paler wash. Tilt the paper at an angle and paint a horizontal stripe across the top of the page. Add a little more paint and water to the brush, then paint another stripe below and slightly overlapping the bottom edge of the first. Continue to the bottom of the page. Tilt the paper back and forth so the stripes blend together.

Graded Wash

Using the same technique as in the flat wash, paint a dark stripe across the pre-wet paper. This time, instead of reloading your brush with paint, dip it in water and then make the second stripe. Add more water to each successive stripe until the page is covered with paint that gradually moves from very dark to very light.

Using Combined Washes

Now that you have learned to create different types of washes, use the flat, graded and variegated washes together in one composition. In this short demonstration, practice putting washes to use for a small landscape and then add detail for further interest.

1 Paint the Sky

Use masking fluid to draw tree trunks and branches wherever you choose your focal point. Let dry. For the sky, use the wash brush to lay a variegated wash on the center of the page with a peach color (Opera mixed with Cadmium Yellow Pale) blending into pure yellow.

MATERIALS LIST

BRUSHES
Nos. 8 and 14 rounds

3-inch (76mm) wash

Rigger

WATERCOLORS
Grumbacher: Cadmium Red Light, Cadmium Yellow Pale, Cerulean Blue, Sap Green, Thalo Blue

Holbein: Opera

SURFACE
¼ sheet (11" × 15" [28cm × 38cm])140-lb. (300gsm) Arches cold-pressed paper

ADDITIONAL SUPPLIES
Masking fluid

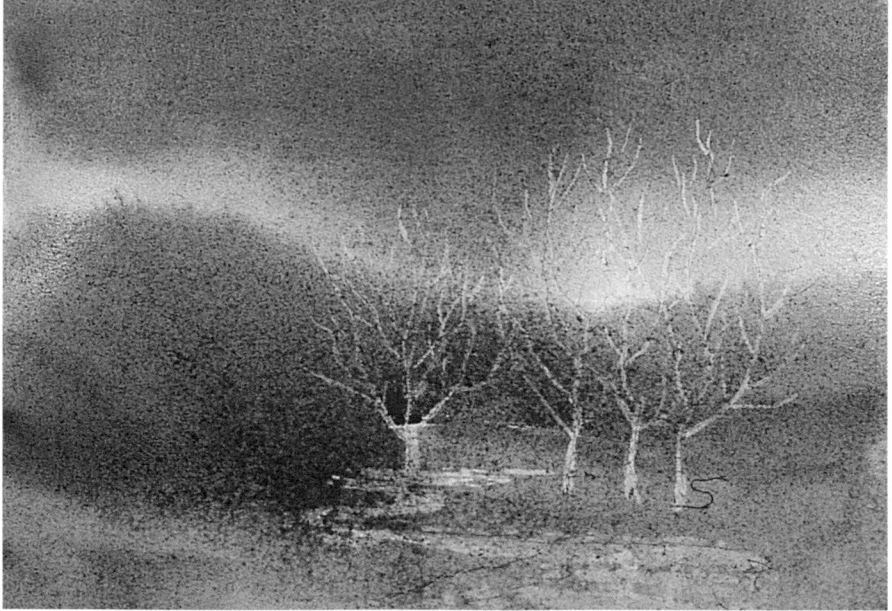

2 Add Hill Shapes and Another Wash

While the paper is still wet, add some hill shapes with a soft gray made by mixing Cerulean Blue and Cadmium Red Light. Start at the bottom of the yellow wash, overlapping in some places and carrying the gray wash to the bottom of the page. You are still using the wash brush to create a graded wash that becomes lighter towards the bottom of the page. The very bottom of the page becomes a flat wash. Note: The original sky wash was gone over a second time to enrich the colors, darkening the painting.

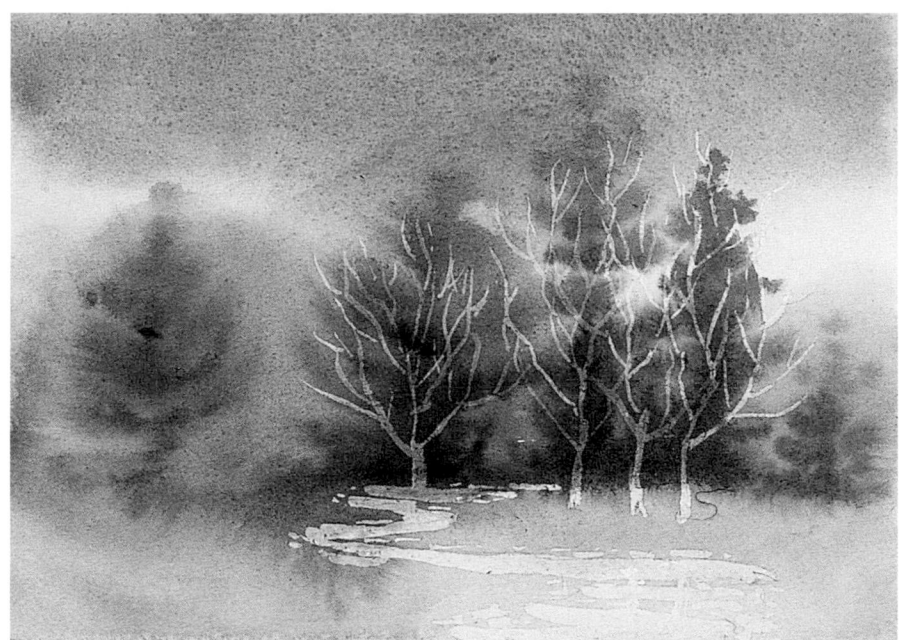

3 Put in More Tree Shapes

While the paper is wet, add tree shapes with the no. 14 round using a mixture of Sap Green and Thalo Blue. Let everything dry.

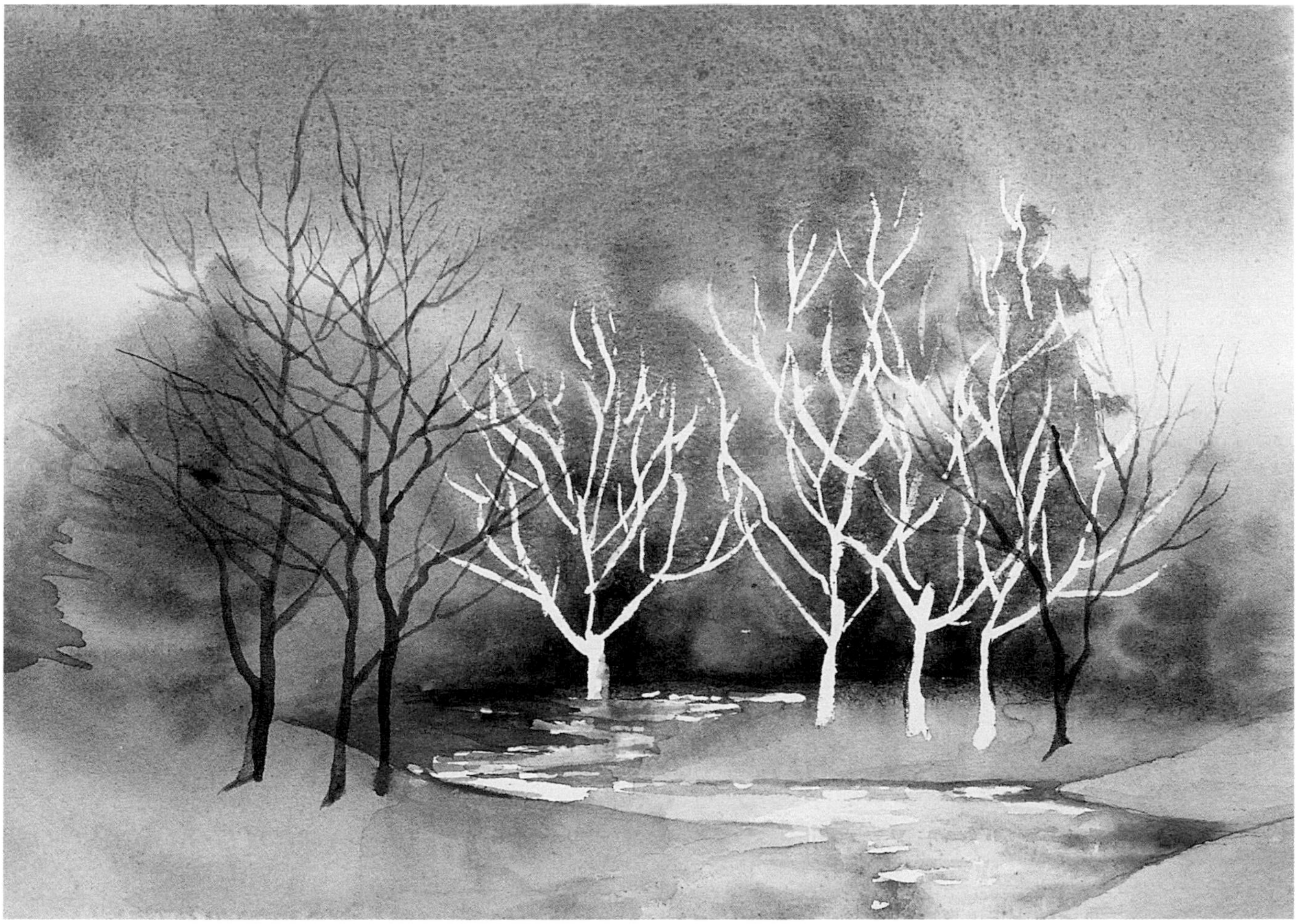

4 Finish the Painting

With a dark green mixture, darken the focal point so the white trees stand out. Use the rigger to add some trees and branches in the foreground for more detail. Remove the masking fluid and add the final details, such as the dark trees in the foreground on the left.

Helpful Hint NUMBER 11

To redo an area of wash that has dried unevenly or with brush-strokes showing, rewet the area with clear water. Let sit for a few seconds, then gently brush over the area to loosen the paint. Tilt the paper in every direction until the area is smooth.

Winter Sunset
7½" × 11"(19cm × 28cm)

layering basics

By using the *layering* technique, you take advantage of the wonderful luminosity and transparency characteristic of the watercolor medium. In layering, you are painting one coat of paint over another, building a series of washes on top of each other to create depth and richness of color. If the coat is transparent, it is called a *glaze*.

This is the first of several exercises designed to help you practice various application techniques. By learning a variety of skills, you will become more versatile in your paintings.

EXERCISE

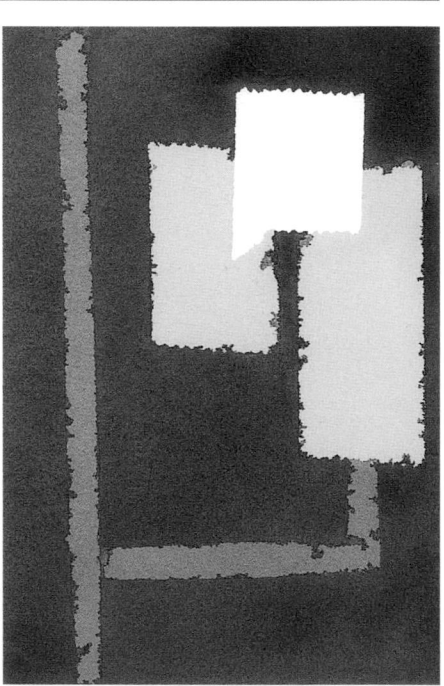

1 Apply the Yellow Wash
Place a square of masking tape on the upper right corner of the format to preserve this square shape throughout the various steps. Lay on a yellow wash.

2 Add a Green Wash
When dry, add two more squares of masking tape to preserve the yellow layer. Lay on a green wash on top of the yellow.

3 Add a Blue Wash
When dry, add more masking tape strips to preserve the green layer. Lay on a blue wash. When everything is dry, remove the tape to reveal all four layers, starting with the white of the paper.

layering with negative and positive shapes

Now that we've learned that layering can create depth and dimension, it's time to move on to negative and positive painting—other forms of layering.

Negative painting means identifying the subject by painting the background in between and around it. *Positive painting* means painting the subject itself. In this example, you will be adding one layer of leaves behind another layer, going further into the background behind the primary foreground leaves.

NEGATIVE PAINTING

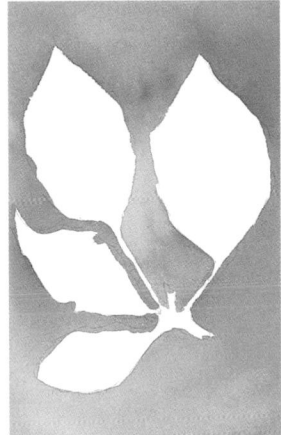

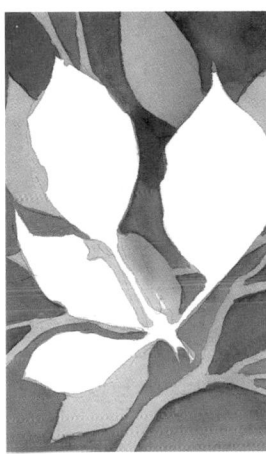

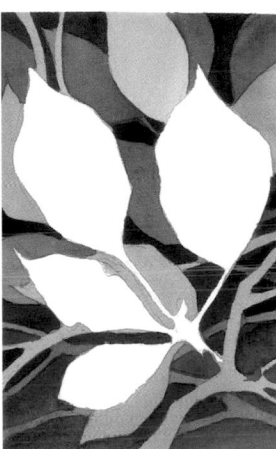

1 Paint the Negative Space
Create depth by painting the negative spaces. Paint around, between and behind the leaf subject.

2 Add Another Layer
Add another layer behind the first one by adding more negative leaves and branches.

3 Darken With More Layers
Repeat this procedure with more layers. The painting will become darker with each subsequent layer.

POSITIVE PAINTING

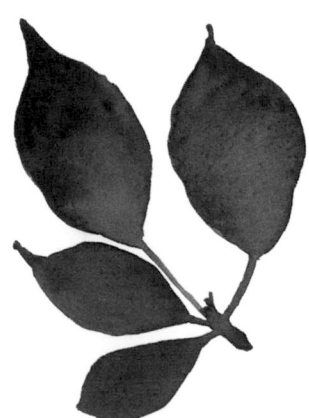

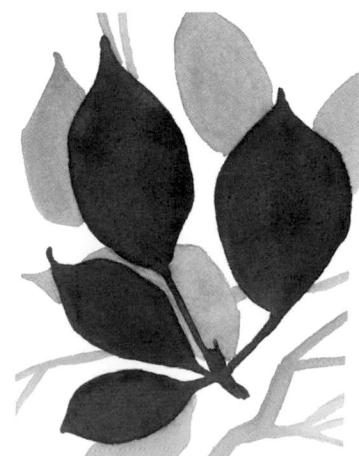

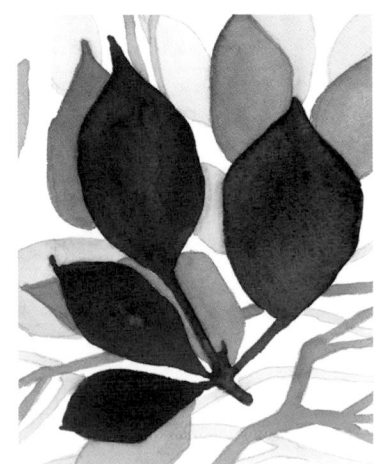

1 Paint the Positive Shape
Add depth by painting positive layers, one behind another. You can add as many layers as you like.

2 Add Another Layer
Paint a second layer of pale blue leaves behind the first layer.

3 Finish
Paint a third layer of paler leaves behind the second layer to add even more depth.

Simply put, *glazing* involves painting a thin, transparent layer of color over an existing layer of paint. Adding one color over another (dry) layer can create a range of effects, including sinking an area into the background, changing a section's temperature (the warmth or coolness of a color), or taming an area that is too prominent. The best glazing results occur when using the brightest, most transparent colors so that the other colors can shine through and glow. Sometimes opaque colors can result in *mud*—color that has lost its vibrancy and become dull, usually caused by overmixing.

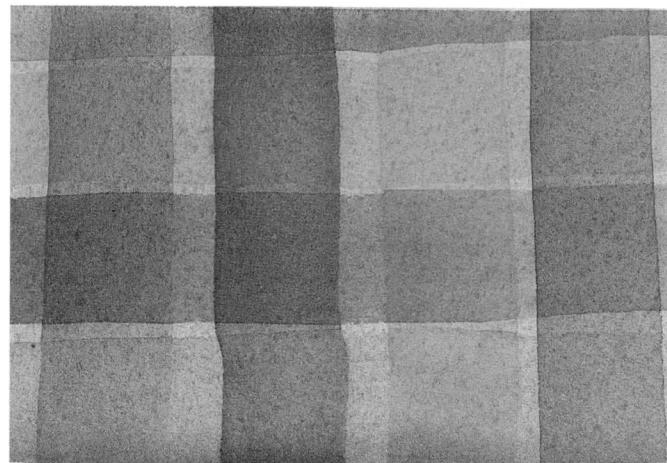

Glazing Basics

Paint a neutral colored square on your watercolor paper. (The neutral color used here is a mixture of all the colors on a dirty palette.) When it is dry, paint stripes of different transparent colors across the square. Then paint stripes in the other direction, overlapping the first set of stripes. Where they intersect you will have three layers of color. Too many layers will often result in mud.

Helpful Hint NUMBER 12

It's a good idea to practice with many combinations of color layers and glazes to discover which ones will work best for your painting subjects.

EXERCISE

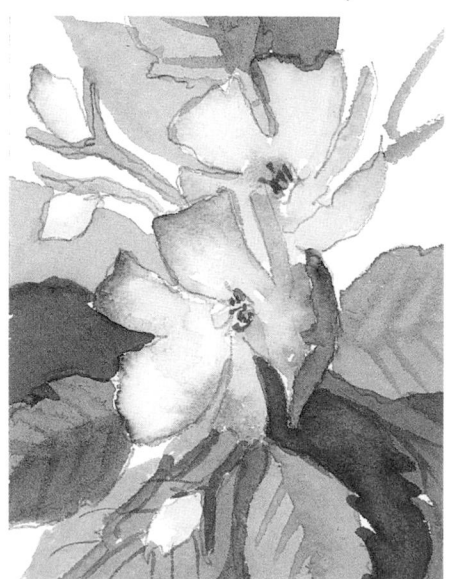

1 Paint Your Subject
Paint basic flowers using the colors pink, yellow and green.

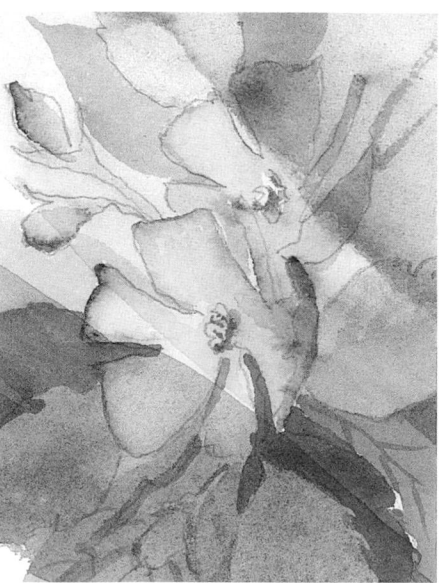

2 Glaze Over Areas
Glaze over different areas with pink (top right corner), yellow (through the center) and blue (lower left corner).

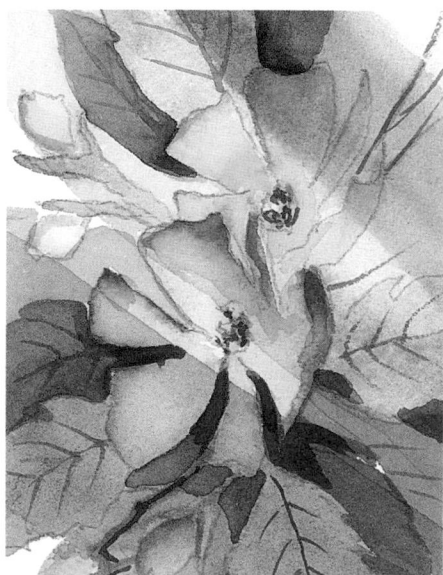

3 Add Finishing Touches
Sometimes, glazing will lift some of the colors from the first layer. Go back into the areas with darker shades of the same color to clarify edges and develop contrast.

blending colors and avoiding mud

Now that you have an understanding of the basics of layering and glazing, it's time to add *blending* to the repertoire. In blending, one color merges with another to create a third color—similiar to a variegated wash.

To achieve a clear, beautiful and transparent blend of colors, practice beforehand. Decide the order of colors that you are using and determine which ones make the best blends as they flow into each other.

Sometimes, the wrong way of blending one color into another creates a muddy effect. The most common mistakes are blending too many colors on the paper, overmixing on the palette or mixing complements together. The good news is that mud can be fixed. Below you will find three different ways to fix a muddy area in your painting.

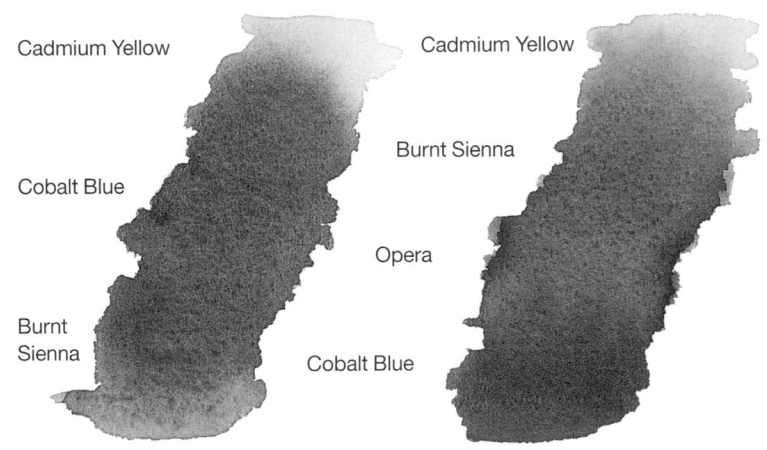

Practice Blending Colors

Wrong way: You will notice that when Cadmium Yellow, Cobalt Blue and Burnt Sienna are blended together in this order, ugly mud is the result.

Correct way: If the order is changed (Cadmium Yellow, Burnt Sienna, Opera and Cobalt Blue), the resulting blends are bright and beautiful.

FIXING MUD

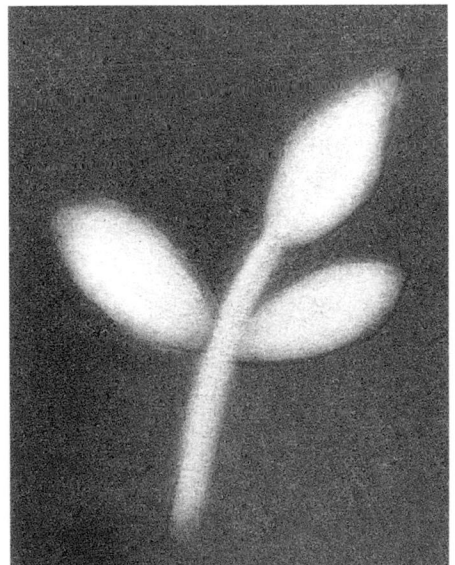

1 **Scrub**
Create a square of mud. Next, scrub out a shape to regain the white of the paper.

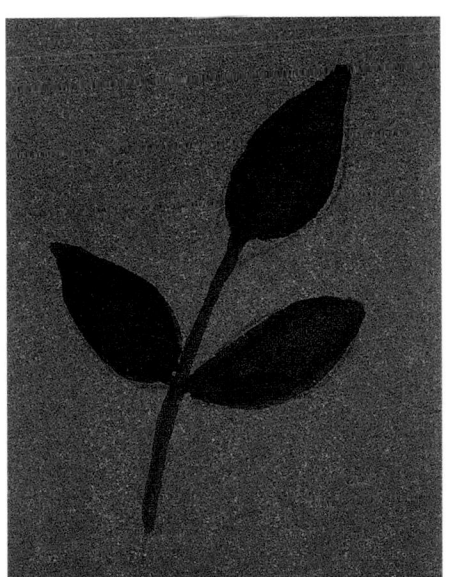

2 **Add a Dark Shape**
Another way to fix mud is to add a dark shape with hard edges.

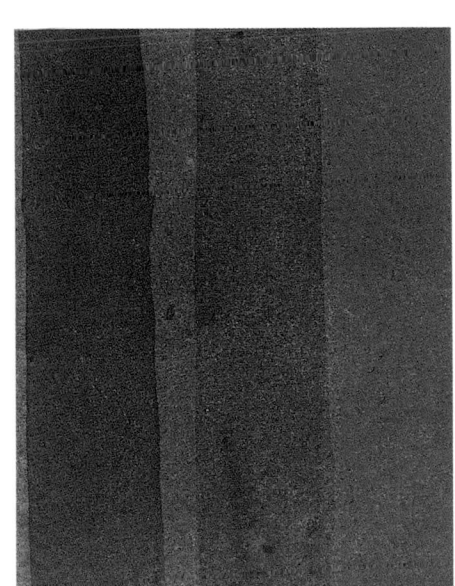

3 **Glaze**
Fix mud by glazing over the area with another color.

dropping in colors

Similiar to blending, *dropping in* colors is an easy technique for adding color variations in an area of wet paint. By creating a shape of a single color and then dropping in other colors, you can control exactly where these variations will appear after the shape is dry.

EXERCISE

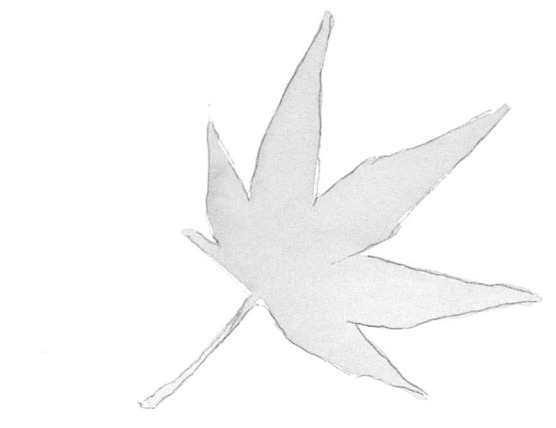

1 Paint a Leaf Shape
Paint a leaf shape with one color (Cadmium Yellow Medium), adding a brush-load of water.

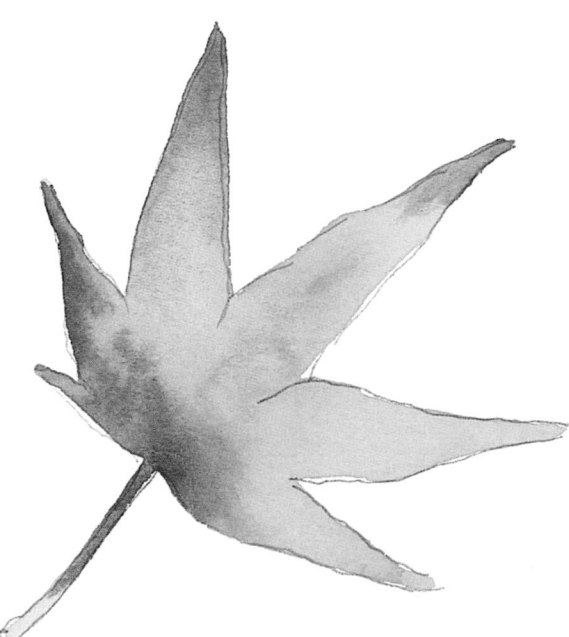

2 Add Another Color
Dip the tip of a no. 8 round into a second color (Burnt Sienna) and dot it lightly into the wet paint in several places, letting it flow into the first color.

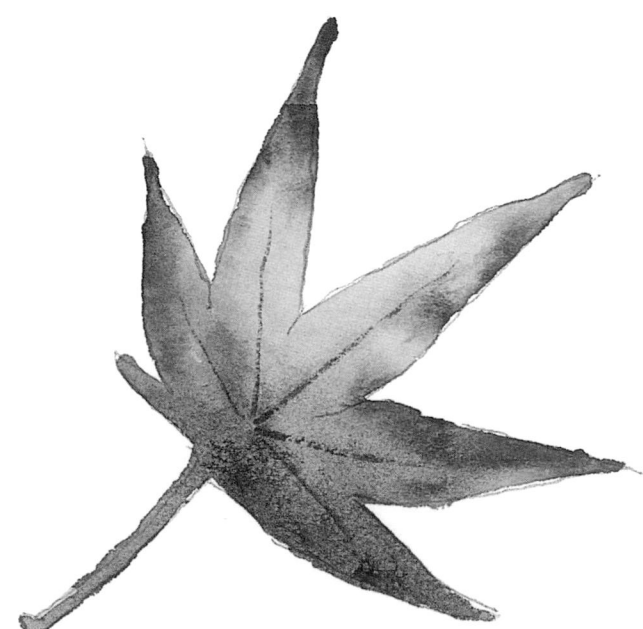

3 Repeat with more Colors
Repeat with several other colors in different parts of the leaf shape. Use these colors in the following order: Burnt Sienna, Sap Green and Permanent Rose.

overlapping objects

Overlapping objects is a good technique to use when suggesting depth and, in particular, showing the delicacy of a flower petal. It involves painting shapes that overlap existing shapes, which have already dried on the paper, to produce an interesting glazing technique that results in a stylized effect. This is one way of adding layers of depth and brilliance to a specific shape or to an entire area of a painting. The overlapping process provides a feeling of translucency because the viewer can see all the way through the layers to the original white of the paper.

Helpful Hint NUMBER 14

Collect paint chip samples from your local paint store. Hold them up to your painting when you are unsure about a particular color.

EXERCISE

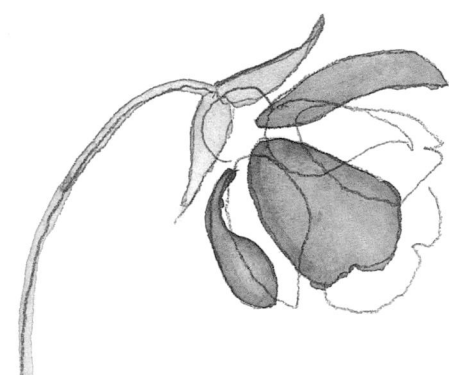

1 Paint the First Set of Petals

After drawing the flower, paint alternating petals that do not touch each other. Add droplets of extra water to push the paint to the far edges of the shape to create hard edges as the area dries.

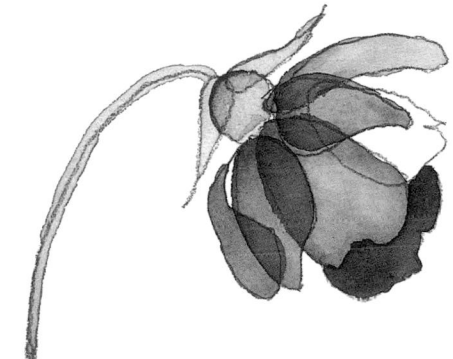

2 Overlap the Petals

When the first set of petals is dry, paint the next set of alternating petals so that the edges overlap the first set. Drop in other colors to add variety if you wish. Let everything dry.

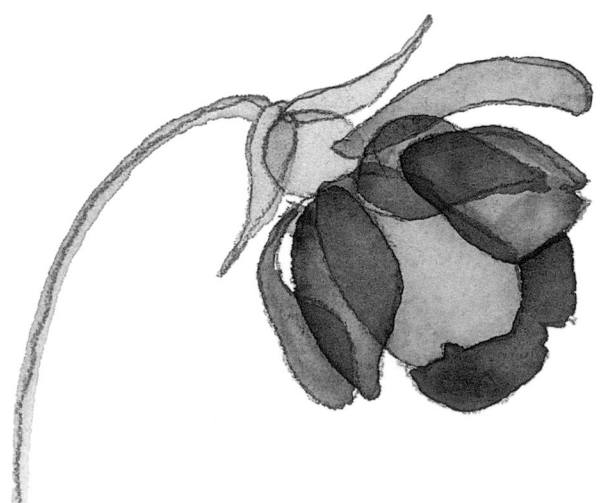

3 Complete the Flower

Keep painting layers of overlapping petals until the flower looks full and complete.

Using the Dry-Brush Method

Drybrushing is a method of laying paint on paper that creates a different effect than normal watercolor. This technique requires less water and less splashy, wet paint. For the drybrush method, use an almost dry brush on dry paper to create controlled lines and shapes. This is excellent for textural effects and it can be used in an entire painting, in small sections or in combination with other methods.

In this demonstration, you will paint a small landscape. Practice on small pieces of paper by first dipping your brush into water, and then squeezing out excess water so the brush is barely damp. Load the brush with fairly thick paint and use only a little water for mixing. Slowly drag your brush across the dry paper to create defined and controlled marks.

MATERIALS LIST

BRUSHES
No. 2 round detail

½-inch (12mm), 1-inch (25mm) flats

WATERCOLORS
Grumbacher: Burnt Sienna, Burnt Umber, Cobalt Blue, Sap Green, Thalo Blue, Thalo Yellow Green.

Holbein: Opera

SURFACE
¼ sheet (11" × 15" [28cm × 38cm]) 140 lb (300gsm) Arches cold-pressed paper

1 Lay in the Background Colors
Using the 1-inch (25mm) flat, apply a variegated wash for the sky with Cobalt Blue, blending into Opera near the horizon. With the ½-inch (13mm) flat, lay on the first layer of the foreground and midground. When it is dry, scumble a mix of Thalo Blue, Sap Green and a little Burnt Sienna over the background so that the first layer shows through.

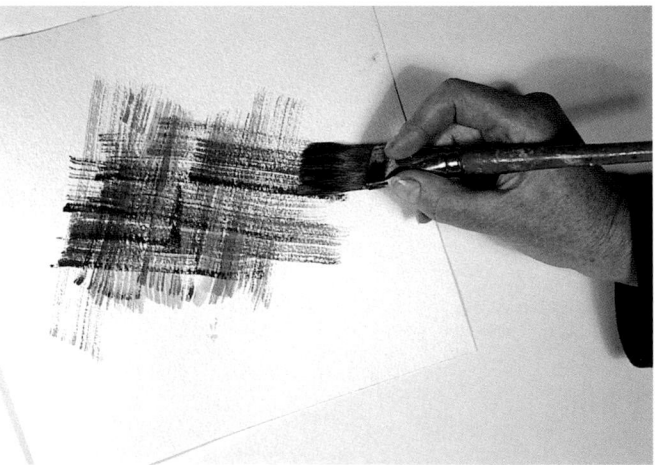

Detail: Scumbling in Action
Scumbling is the dry-brush method used with a lighter touch. Drag the loaded brush across the surface of dry paper so that the paint only touches the tops of the texturing on the paper, leaving valleys of white untouched by paint. This will give an interrupted, dotted appearance, useful if you want the white of the paper to show through. This method is ideal for many textures, including tree bark, barn wood, dirt roads and water sparkles.

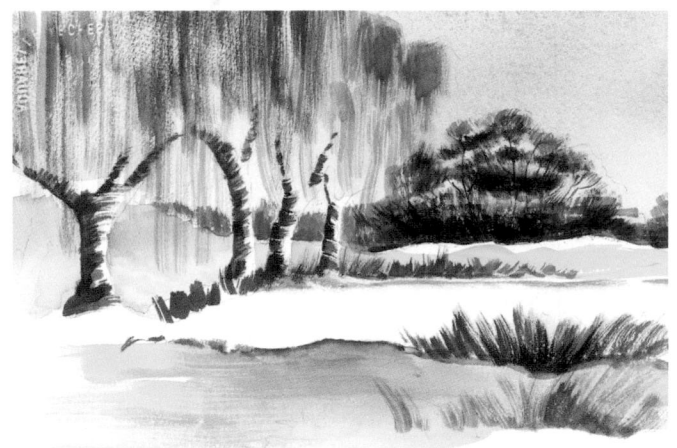

2 Drybrush the Vegetation

Rinse the ½-inch (13mm) flat in water and squeeze out excess water. Begin to dab in the background trees with short, quick strokes using mixtures of Thalo Blue, Sap Green and Burnt Umber, varying the colors with each mix. For the grasses in the foreground, use quick, upward strokes of Burnt Umber. For the willow leaves, use long, downward strokes with green mixes. For the tree trunks, use horizontal strokes with Burnt Umber.

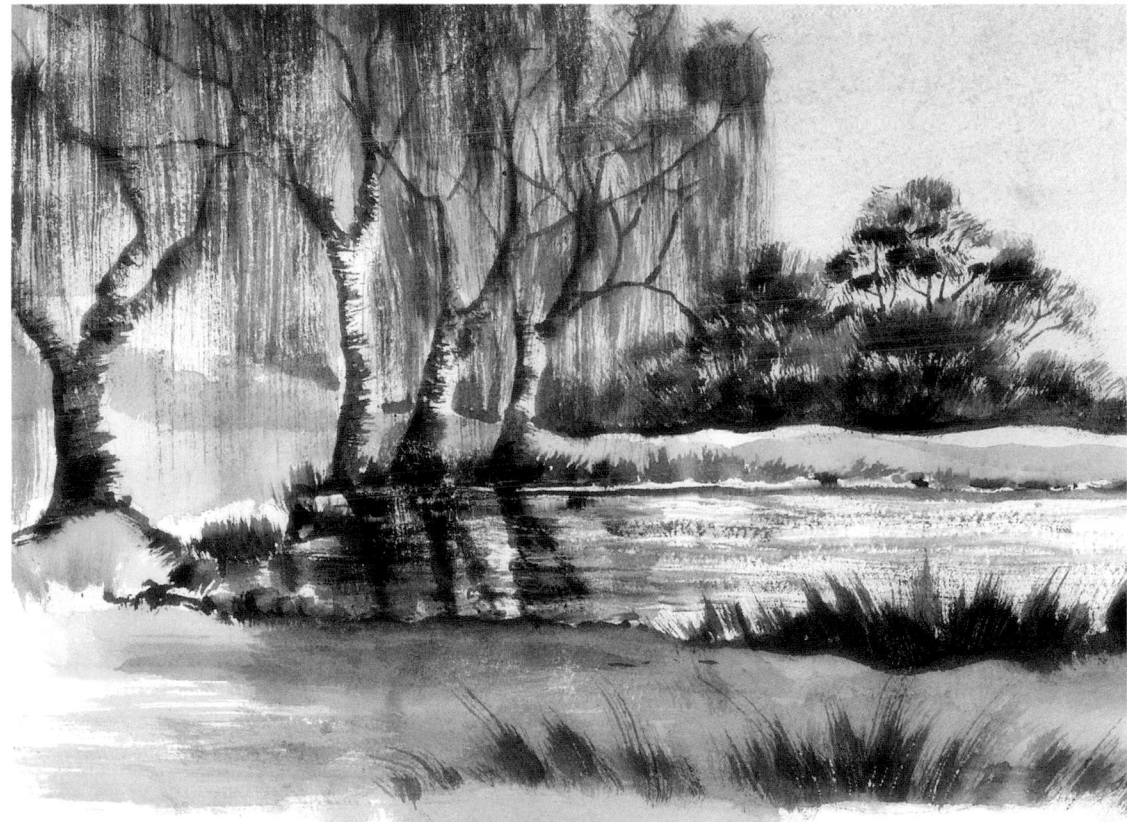

3 Final Version

Continue to refine the trees and leaves by adding more layers of color. Add branches and twigs with the no. 2 round detail. Create the water with horizontal, scumbled bands of all the colors. Notice how many different ways the dry-brush method was employed in this demonstration. The wispy willow leaves differ from the background tree leaves, the water sparkle stands out from the more blended grassy areas, and the foreground grasses contrast against the smooth grass area.

High Gate Pond
7½" × 11½" (19cm × 29cm)

wet-into-wet

Wet-into-wet is a painting technique in which paint is applied to an already wet surface. It is one way to make use of the most exciting and beautiful aspect of the watercolor medium: accidents! Sometimes, wonderful things happen that we cannot control—one color blending with another color to make a pretty, new color or when an area dries with an irregular line, making a new possibility for the edge of an unplanned petal or leaf.

EXERCISE

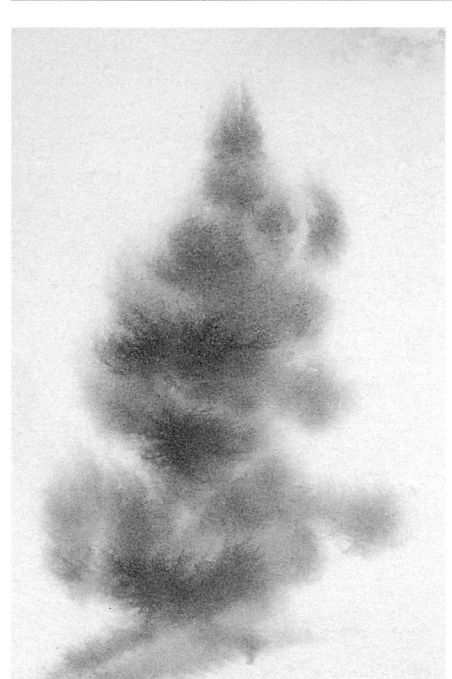 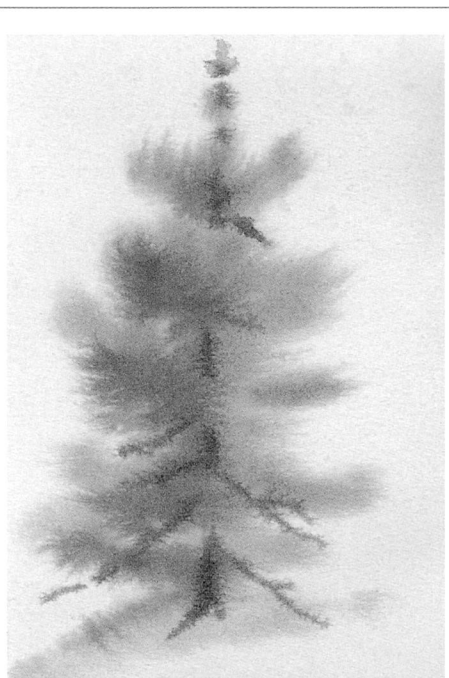 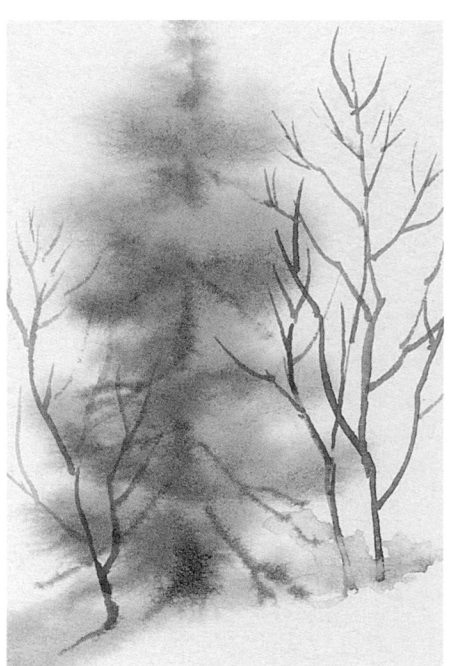

1 Paint the Format

Paint the format with a yellow wash. While the paint is very wet, put in a green tree shape.

2 Add Trunk and Branches

When the paint is semidry, add trunk shapes and some branches with a detail brush.

3 Finish the Scene

When the paint is almost dry, add more trees with a detail brush using the dry-brush technique. By laying on paint when the paper is at different stages of dryness, you can control the shape edges as the paper dries, resulting in nice variations within the painting. Note the difference between the branches of the green tree and the bare trees in the foreground.

Now try painting a small landscape using both the dry-brush and the wet-into-wet techniques. The final result will feature a loose feeling, with plenty of details to draw the viewer's eye.

EXERCISE

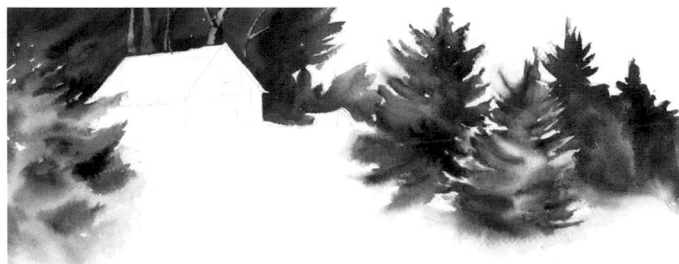

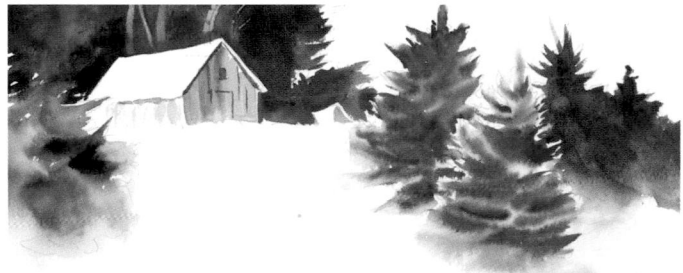

1 Working Wet-Into-Wet

Draw light guidelines in pencil for the general placement of the subject matter. With clear water, wet the area of the trees and maintain a sharp edge near the roof of the building. Using the no. 8 round, add in the blue and green colors (Indigo, Thalo Blue, Sap Green, Cobalt Blue) with quick strokes, letting one color blend into another. Drop in a little Burnt Umber and Burnt Sienna here and there to vary the greens.

2 Working with Dry Brush

Mix Opera and Cobalt Blue to create some purples. On dry paper, using a damp brush, paint vertical lines using the scumbling method to resemble barn wood. Add a few strokes of Burnt Sienna and Opera. Lay in some of the purple mixture (wet-into-wet) for snow effects near the bottom of the painting and to the right.

3 The Final Version: Add Details

Using the no. 2 round, draw in the front bush, the tree in the middle and add detail to the barn with Burnt Sienna. For added interest, place some small, red birds. For the sky, apply a loose wash with the no. 8 round and plenty of water with the purples you mixed, a little yellow, Opera, and a touch of Burnt Sienna.

Winter Gathering
9" × 16" (23cm × 41cm)

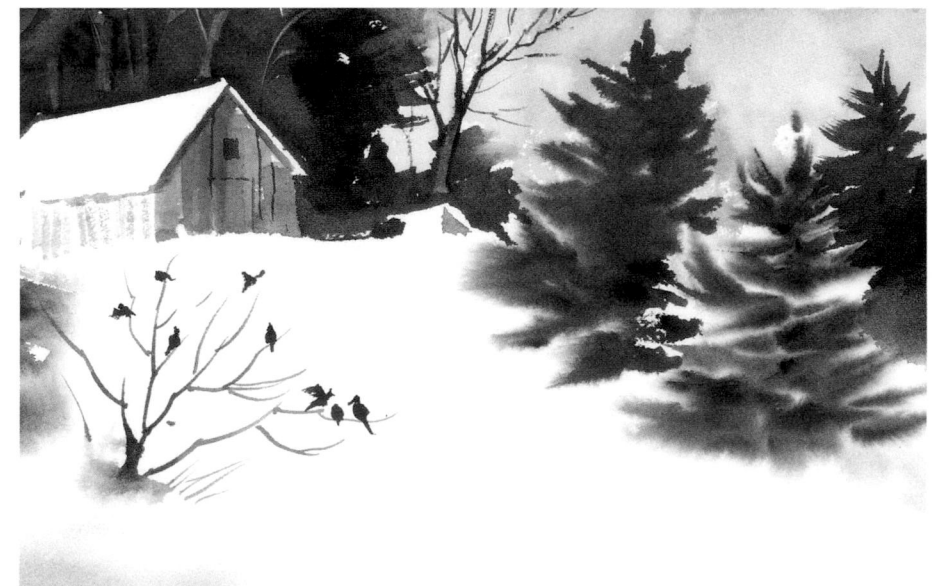

mastering edge control

Once you learn how to purposefully define the edges of your shapes, you will be in complete control of what you wish to express in your painting and how you wish to express it. You can decide beforehand exactly where you want distinct definition in your composition and where softer, more delicate images are preferred. Sometimes it is exciting to let the paint flow and dry at random.

To begin, wet your paper only in some places and then lay down several colors. Where the paper is wet, the colors will blend and create *soft edges*. Where it is dry, *hard edges* (or sharp edges) will form. Also, lost and found edges will appear. Hard edges tend to come forward, so place them near the focal point. Soft edges recede and are ideal for other, less important, areas of the painting.

It is always a good idea to practice on small pieces of paper—watching how the paint dries—before attempting a large painting.

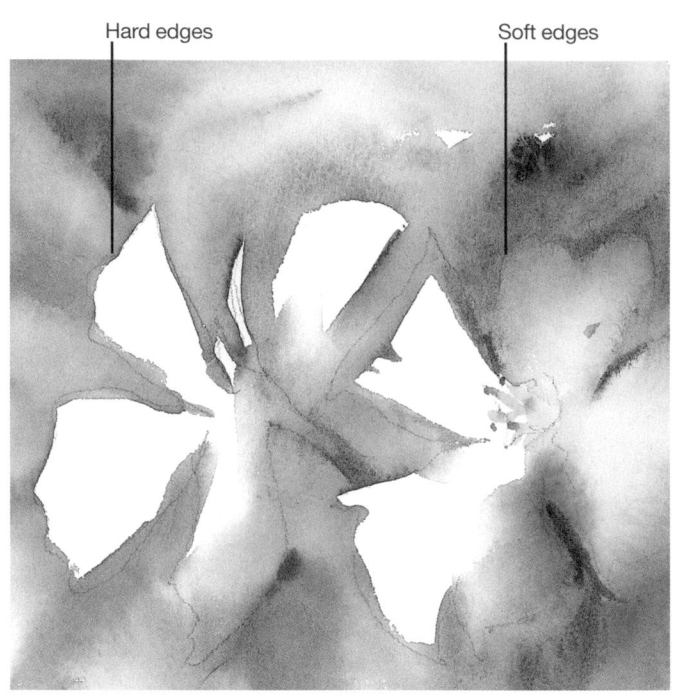

Hard edges   **Soft edges**

Hard Edges, Soft Edges
Hard edges are sharp and crisp and clearly define the perimeter of the shape, distinguishing it from the background.

Soft edges gently blend one shape into another or into the background.

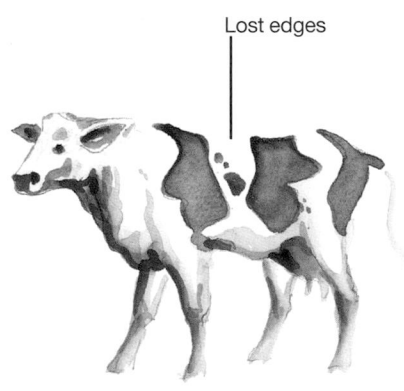

Lost edges

Lost Edges
Lost edges are suggested within a painting, but they are not actually apparent. The viewer's eye assumes the edges are there, making them implied.

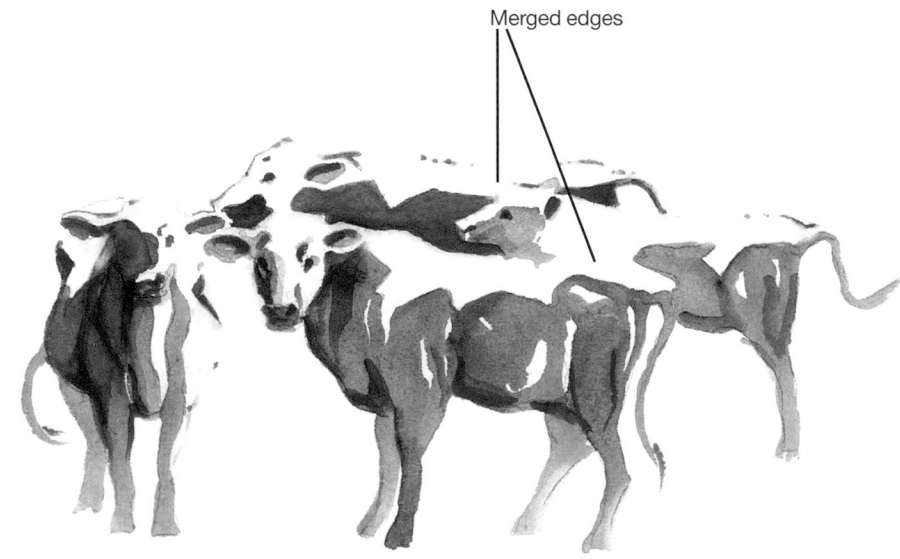

Merged edges

Merged Edges
Merged edges, or found edges, create new shapes as lights blend into lights and darks blend into darks. They create new shapes and new parameters. Lost and found edges appear where the edges of the same shape are sharply defined then disappear into soft indistinctness before being identified once again.

lifting colors

Lifting involves removing paint (or any other drawing or painting material) from a picture's surface. Watercolor may be lifted with a stiff, damp brush. Lifting paint is ideal for creating surface highlights or even veins and other flower details. Practice lifting colors by using the three different techniques listed below.

Helpful Hint NUMBER 16

Don't wait for inspiration. Ideas come while you are painting.

EXERCISE

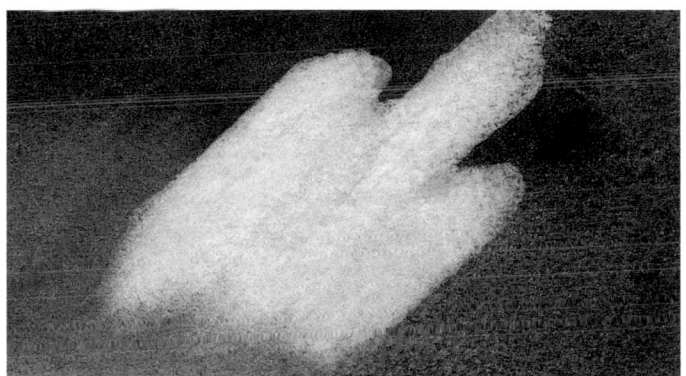

1 Scrubbing
When the paint is dry, scrub the surface with a damp bristle brush and then blot with a paper towel or an old washcloth.

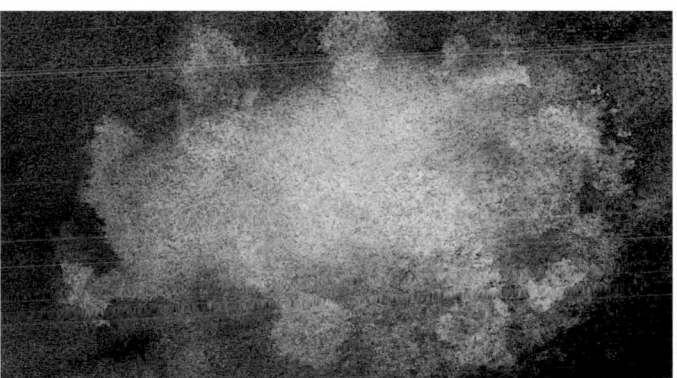

2 Erasing
When the paint is dry, erase the colors with an eraser to create a softer effect.

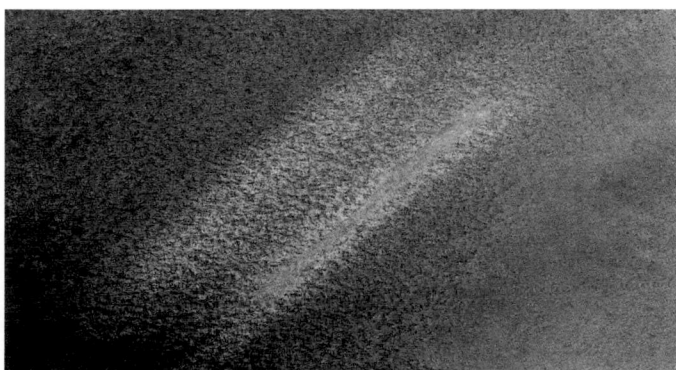

3 Blotting
While the paint is still wet, blot the colors with a paper towel or tissue paper to create irregular edges.

Applying a Combination of Techniques

In this demonstration, you will combine many of the techniques you learned about in the previous pages, such as wet-into-wet, negative and positive painting, glazing and lifting. Also, you will merge colors to create new color blends, plus interesting new shape possibilities or "found" imagery. By starting with wet-into-wet washes, you will achieve that free flowing excitement that is characteristic of the watercolor medium. With your new skills you can control the washes and adapt them toward the statement of your painting.

MATERIALS LIST

BRUSHES
Nos. 4, 6, 8 and 14 rounds

3-inch (76mm) wash

1-inch (25mm) flat

WATERCOLORS
Daniel Smith: Quinacridone Gold, Quinacridone Sienna

Da Vinci: Hansa Yellow

Grumbacher: Alizarin Crimson, Cadmium Yellow Medium, Sap Green, Thalo Yellow Green

Holbein: Opera

M Graham & Co.: Dioxazine purple, Phthalo Green, Quinacridone Red, Quinacridone Violet

SURFACE
15" × 22" (38cm × 56cm) sheet 140 lb. (300gsm) Arches cold-pressed paper

ADDITIONAL SUPPLIES
Drafting tape, pencil, scrubber brush

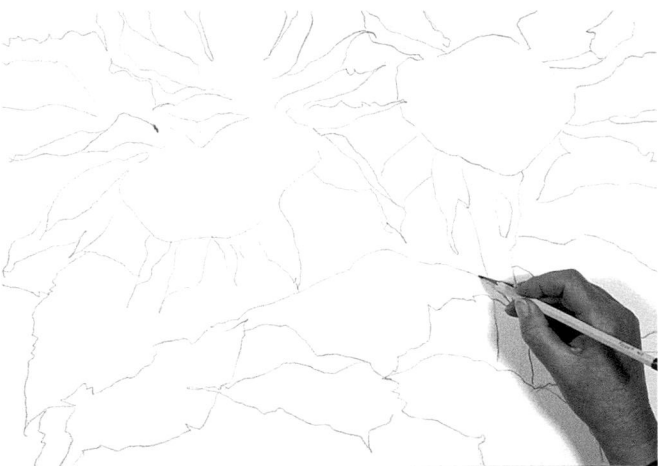

1 Getting Started
Tape the edges of the paper with drafting tape to help define the format. Press down the edges so that paint won't bleed underneath. Then, pencil sketch some general leaf and petal shapes as guidelines. Do not be too precise because the shapes will change during the painting process.

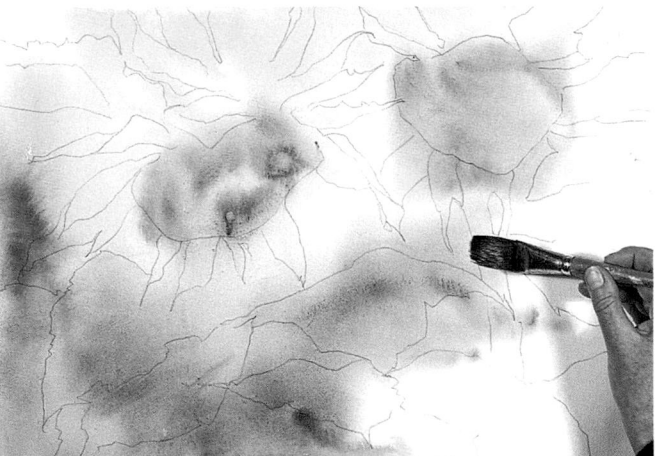

2 Lay on Color
Wet the entire paper with water using your wash brush. With the 1-inch (25mm) flat, charge in Cadmium Yellow Medium, Quinacridone Red, Quinacridone Gold, Quinacridone Sienna, Dioxazine Purple, Sap Green, Quinacridone Violet, Phthalo Green and Thalo Yellow Green. Allow the colors to flow into each other. Don't worry about runbacks or brush marks. Apply big strokes and use several round brushes at once to avoid constant rinsing.

3 Glaze to Enhance the Colors

When everything is completely dry, glaze over the dull areas. Use the same colors for some parts of the painting and different colors in other areas to heighten the values and to harmonize all areas of the painting. Use Hansa Yellow, Alizarin Crimson and Opera in addition to the original washes. Try to keep soft edges as long as possible by washing them out with water and blotting on the edges. Change your water often so you won't muddy the washes. If everything gets too wet to work, stop and let the painting dry completely. For vibrancy, retain some pieces of white.

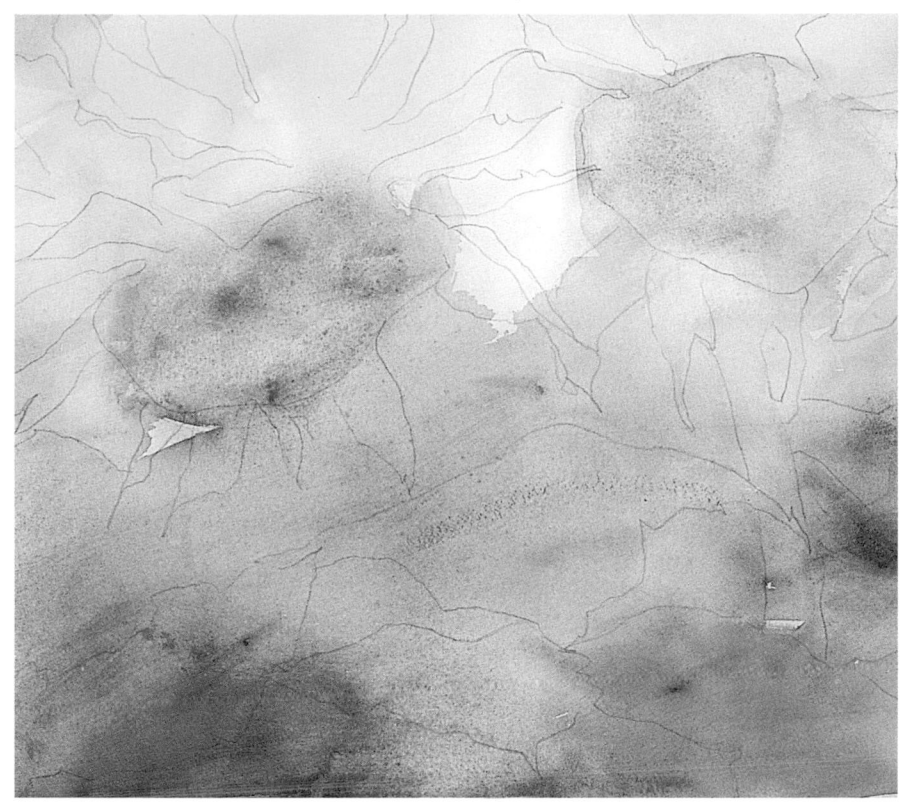

4 Identify Flower and Leaf Shapes

Begin painting negative spaces between and behind petals and leaves. Make hard edges, but leave some soft edges too. Blend out the far edge with water. The shapes of the flowers and leaves will gradually appear as positive forms when the areas behind them become darker and richer.

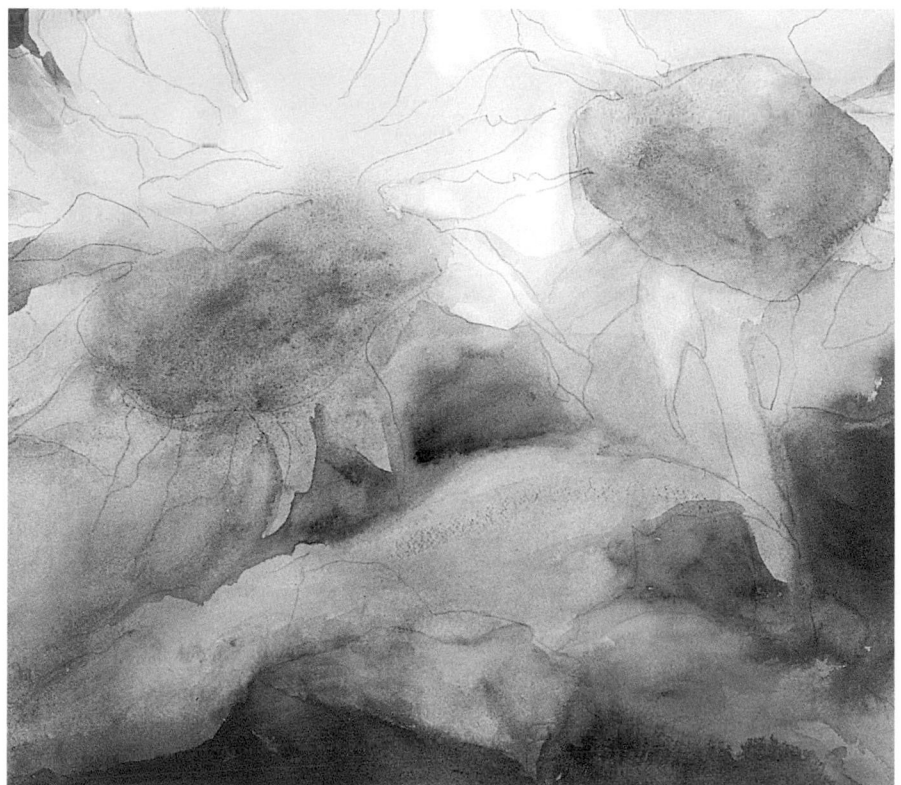

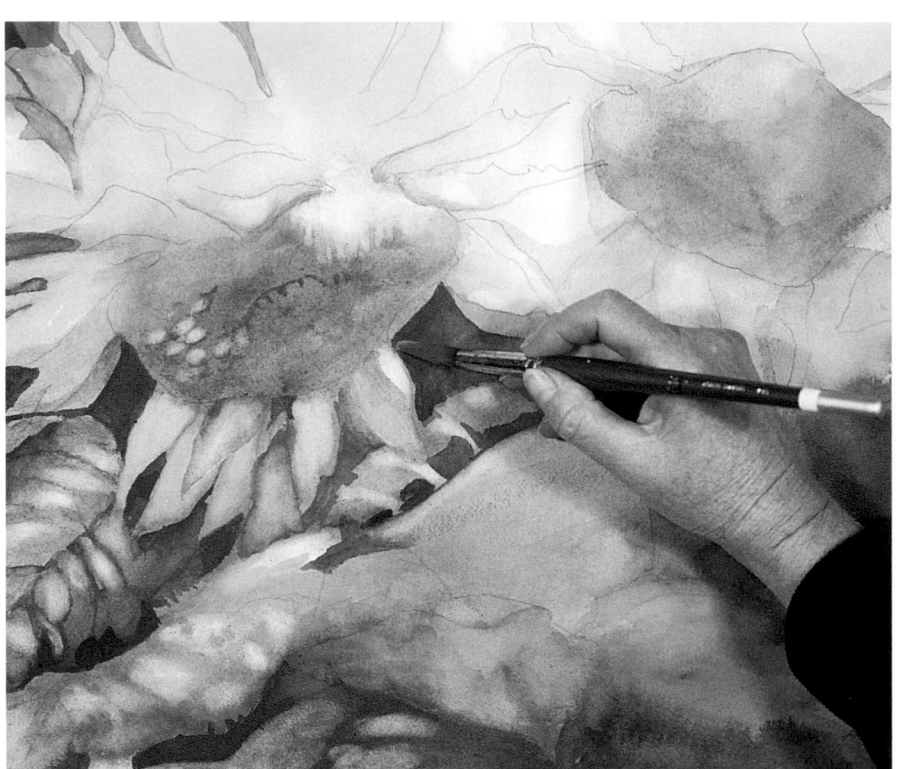

5 Create More Form With Highlights

To create highlights and light veins on the leaves, lift the paint by dampening the paper and letting it sit for a moment to loosen the paint. Then, gently rub the surface with a scrubber brush (be sure not to disturb the paper's surface) and then blot. In some cases, glaze over with a different color once the area is dry. Decide if you want more soft edges or hard edges—one or the other should dominate. In this case, soft sunlit shapes will be the dominant element.

6 Add Details and Make Adjustments

Tidy up edges and further define the stems and veins with your smallest brushes. Adjust colors by lightening and darkening. Lift paint from the leaves if more veins are needed. Glaze until everything looks well balanced. Sometimes, when painting wet-into-wet with a lot of water, the paper buckles. When the painting is finished and dry, gently spray the backside with water and iron.

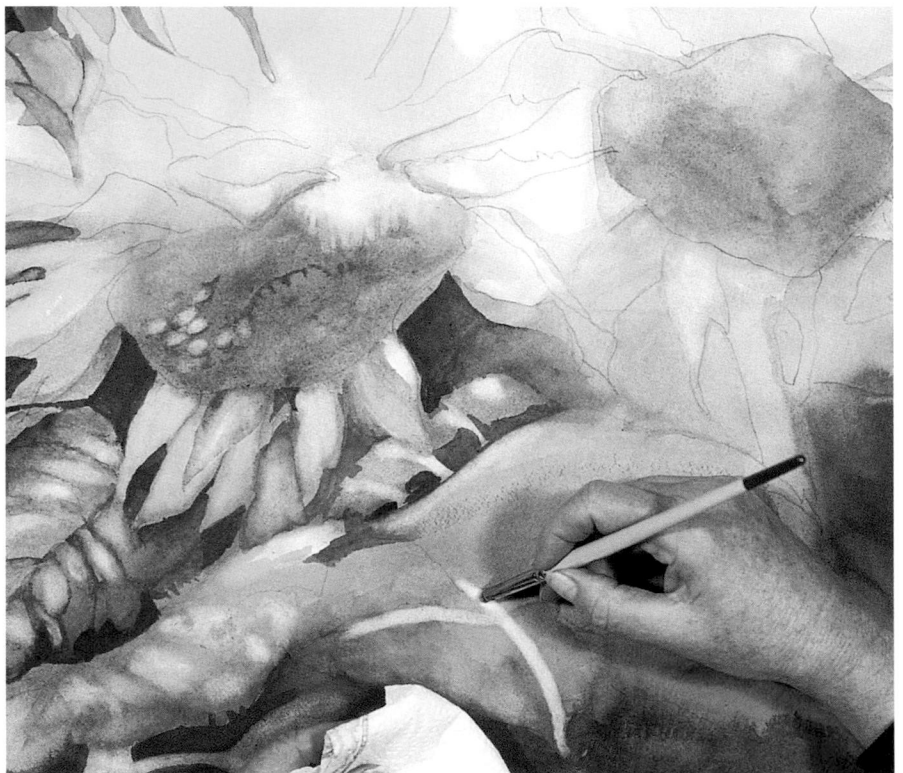

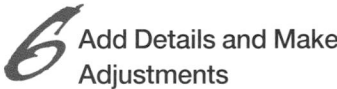 *Helpful Hint* NUMBER 17

When lifting paint, it is important to dry or blot out the paint from the brush so that you will have a clean brush for the next lift. Make sure you have a paper towel or old washcloth within reach.

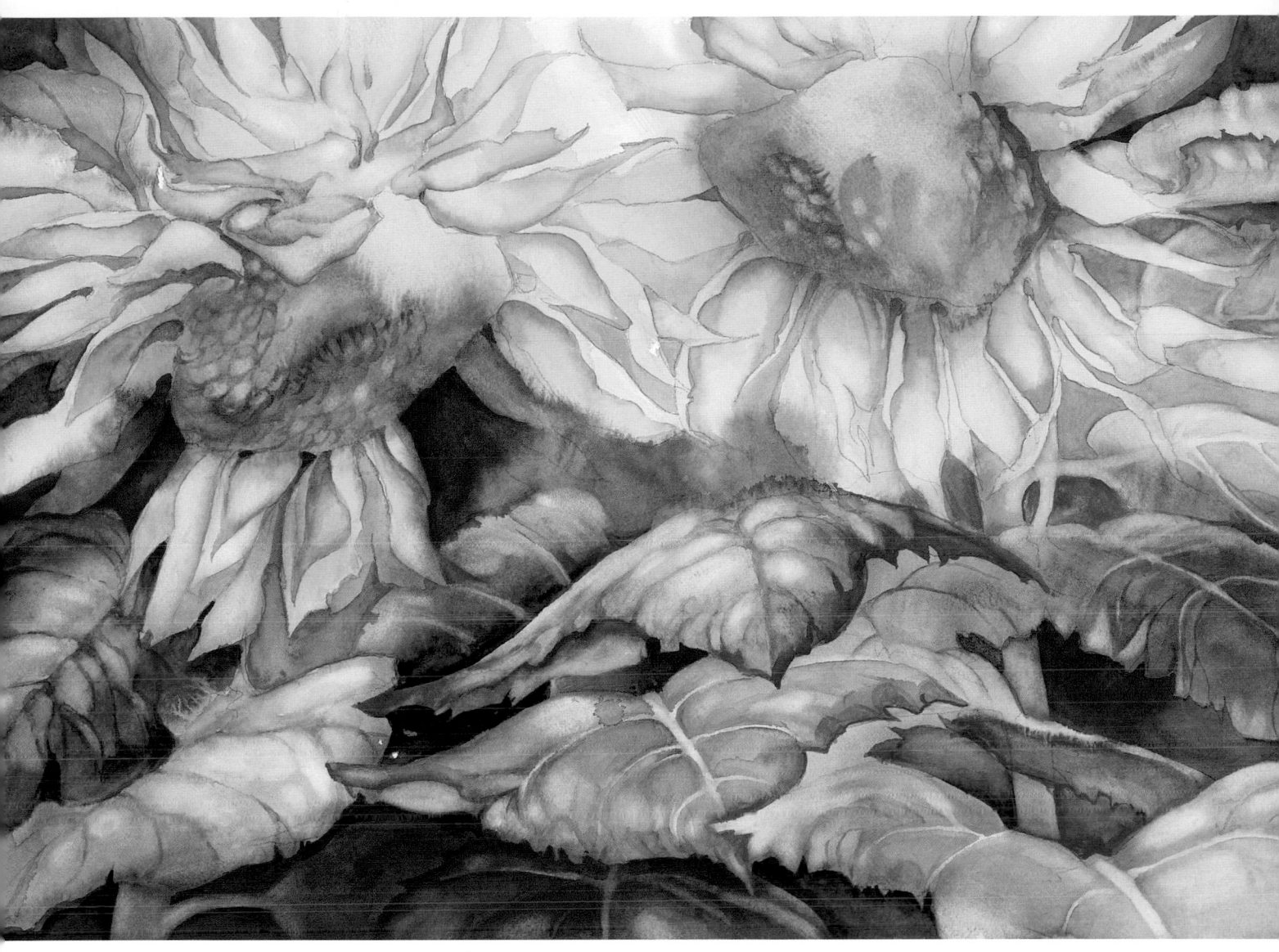

7 Finish the Painting

Continue adding more glazes to certain areas to enrich and enliven the colors so that they glow. Paint negatively to darken behind areas that you want to pop into the foreground in the main focal areas and to sharpen some of the petal edges. Then add the final details such as a few vines and veins here and there.

Sunkissed Sunflowers
15" × 22" (38cm × 56cm)

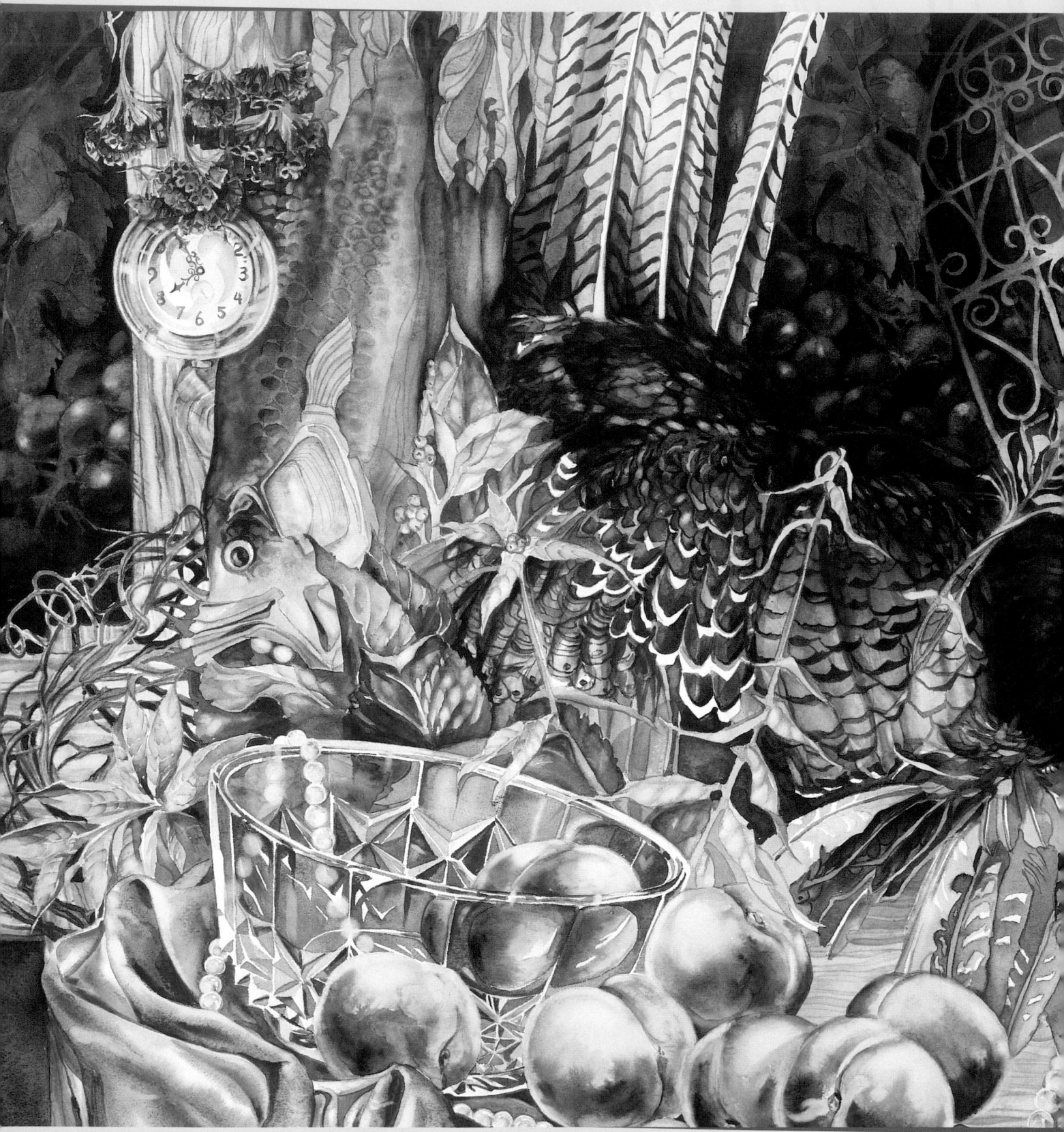

Allegory
21½" × 26" (55cm × 66cm)

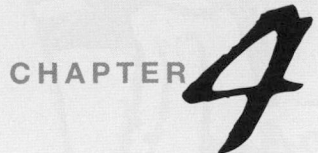
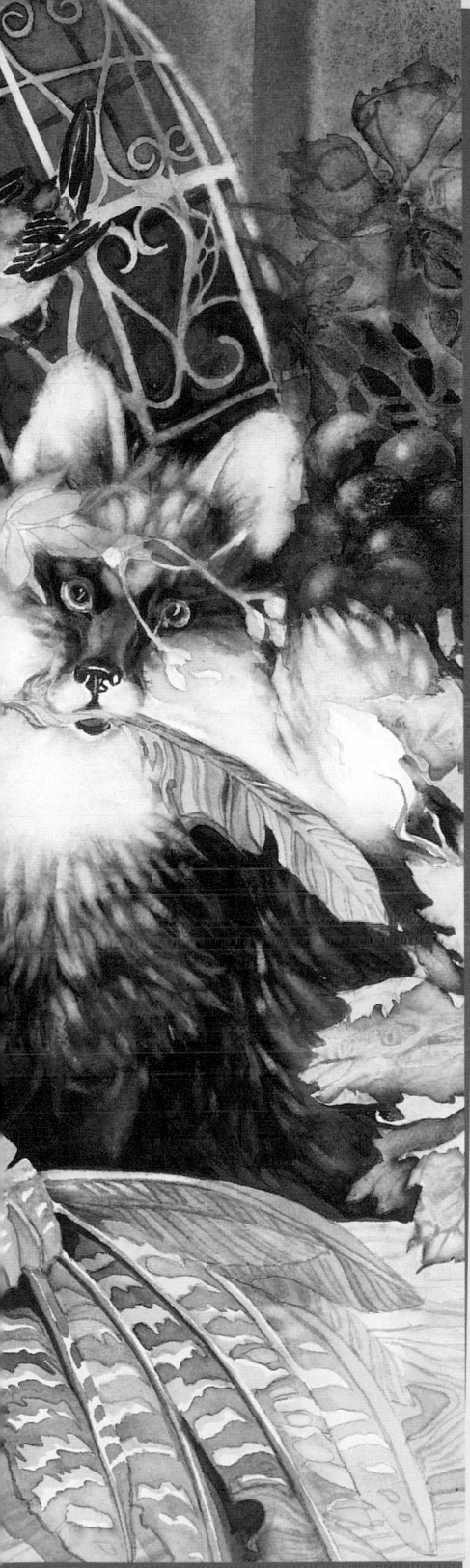

textures

TEXTURE WORKS HAND IN HAND WITH TECHNIQUE TO establish surface interest and to convey a feel of the imagery you're creating. The goal is to make the flat surface of the paper take on the vitality of the images you portray to the viewer. Remember, you are a conjuror of visual effects, a magician of sorts. With a knowledge of textural techniques, you can convey the roughness of barn wood, the delicacy of rose petals, the sharp edges of glass, the fuzziness of peaches or the soft folds in drapery.

Imagine the depiction of a landscape without texture. It would be flat, lifeless and uninteresting—not a memorable painting statement. If you add leaves washed in light, rough bark, rugged stone and sparkling water, the painting gains character and definition, and sings with life.

This chapter combines numerous textural examples using printing methods, resists, sprinkling, spattering, stencils, paper torture and many other approaches. There is only one step-by-step demonstration in this chapter, but plenty of easy examples that you can re-create. Remember, there is an unlimited variety of ways to create texture. Half the fun is to experiment with things from around the house, just to see what they can do in combination with paint on paper. Use your imagination. Anything goes. This chapter will arm you with a number of tools to use towards more vibrant paintings.

Mother Nature describes herself to us in a plethora of forms, patterns and shapes. By mastering these texturing exercises, you will be able to simulate the surface character that defines these natural shapes as well as the characteristics of man-made objects.

Any number of objects can be used to make a pattern when pressed into wet paint. For variety, try using a sponge, corrugated cardboard, burlap, needlepoint canvas, string netting or a rubber stamp. To help the paint adhere to the stamping material, add a little soap to your brush before loading it with paint. Also, try stamping opaque colors over a dark ground.

Through your own experimentation and by combining texturing devices, you can create a wide variety of effects. By using your imagination, you will discover new ways of making texture. Enjoy the creative adventure.

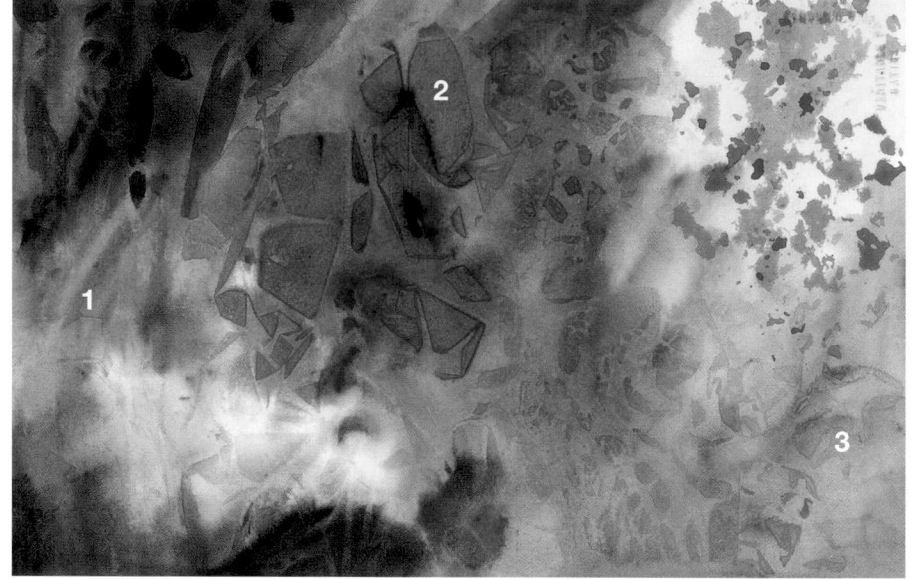

Wax Paper, Plastic Wrap and Aluminum Foil

For a range of interesting patterns and shapes, try crumpling and pressing wax paper or plastic wrap into wet paint. Let dry and remove. Do you see the different effects? Also, crumple up a piece of aluminum foil, paint the ridges and print onto either wet or dry paper. Try tissue paper as well.

All these techniques are excellent for portraying the texture of trees, branches and other vegetation.

1. Wax paper
2. Plastic wrap
3. Aluminum foil

Facial Tissue

Dabbing and blotting wet paint with facial tissue can create subtle changes. Crumple a tissue, blot the wet paint, and then let the pattern dry. By blotting, you are lifting paint and lightening the surface. This is useful for creating cloud effects, sunlit sections in grassy areas or lightening certain parts of your painting.

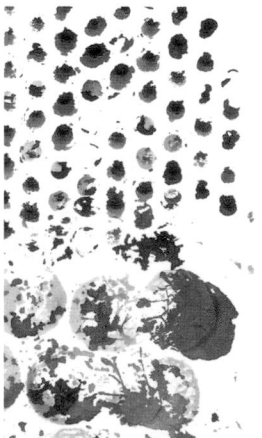
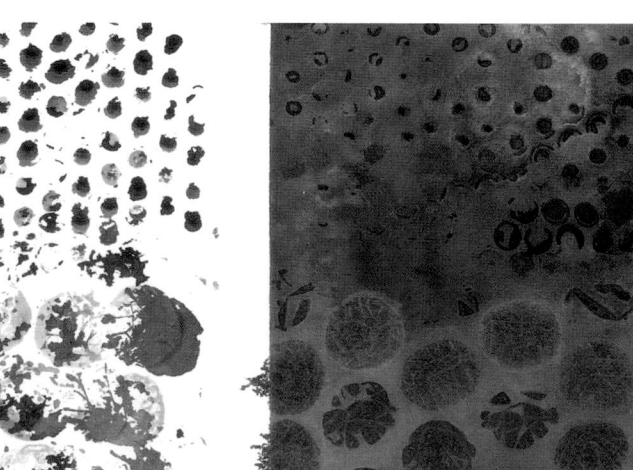

Bubble Wrap

Paint the bubble wrap and press it onto dry paper (left), or for a different effect, press bubble wrap directly onto wet paint (right). When bubble wrap is printed on dry paper, the edges remain crisp. When it is pressed into a wet surface, the edges become softened.

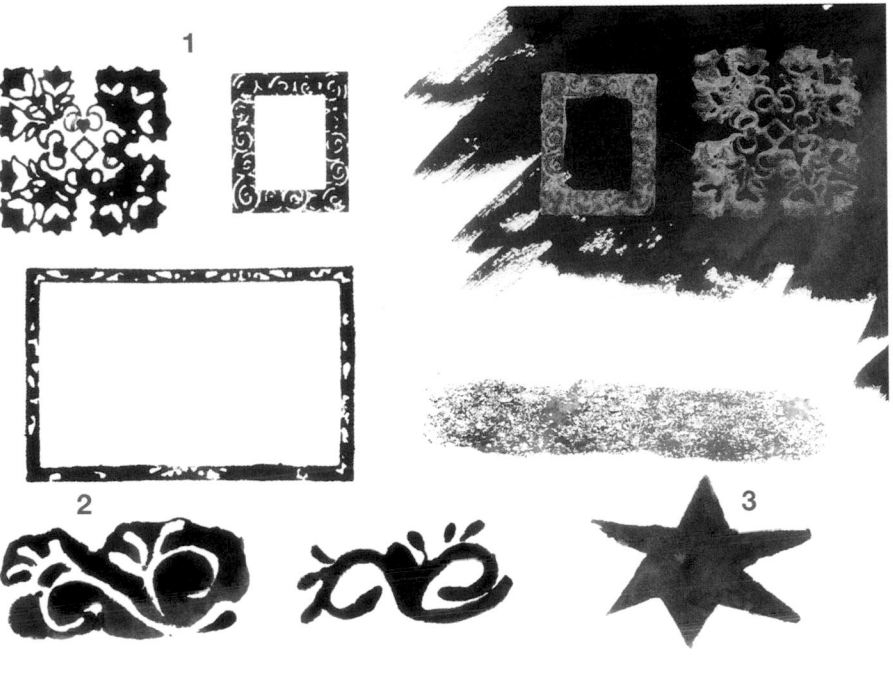

Rubber Stamps, Textured Sponge, Carved Modeling Clay, and Potato

Rubber stamps can be bought in a wide variety of interesting patterns. Have fun printing your paper directly or pressing the stamps into wet paint and then lifting.

With a craft knife, carve a design onto a piece of modeling clay. Paint it with a color and gently press it onto watercolor paper or press it directly into wet paint. Try building up a design with clay and stamping for a postive image.

Cut a potato in half with a paring knife. Remove the sections of the potato that form the background of the shape you wish to print as a positive image. Apply paint to the raised shape and press onto wet or dry paper.

1. Rubber stamp
2. Modeling clay
3. Potato

1. On dry paper
2. On very wet paper
3. On semiwet paper

1. Kitchen utility sponge (2 different sizes)
2. Synthetic sponge
3. Cosmetic sponge
4. industrial sponge
5. Natural sea sponge

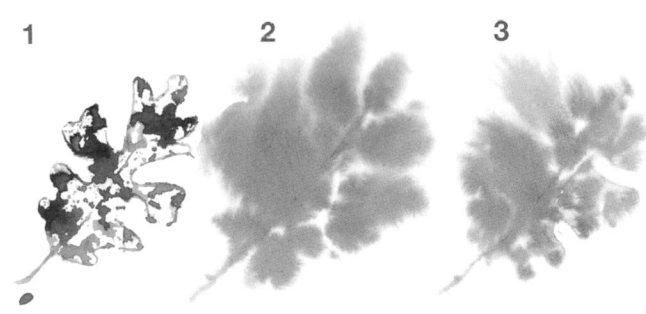

Printing With a Leaf

Use natural materials in your printing, such as leaves, twigs, and feathers. Paint them on one side and press onto either dry, very wet or semiwet paper. Which effect do you like the most?

Sponge Printing

There are many kinds of sponges that are natural or man-made. They have many patterns that can be printed onto your paper for innumerable textural effects. Experiment and see what effects you prefer. Try printing one sponge type on top of another, using different colors. Use this technique for rock textures, ground surfaces, masonry or abstract designs.

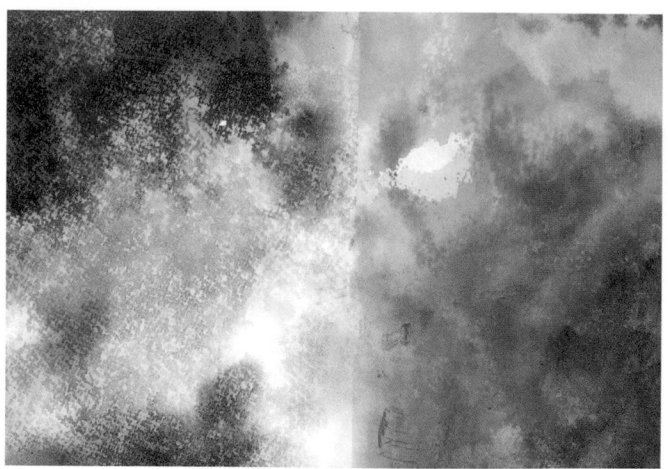

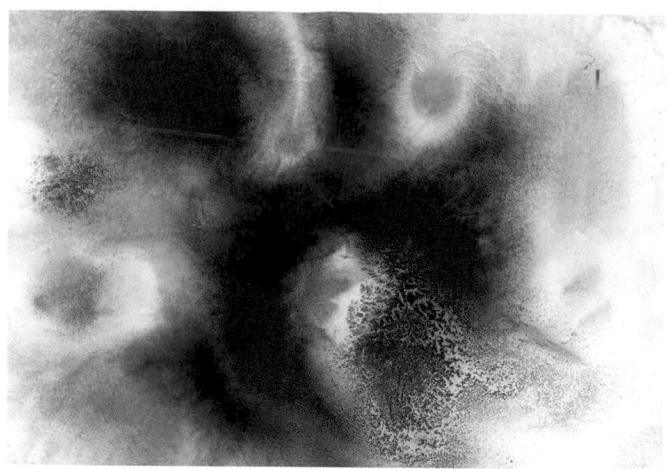

Plexiglas on Wet Paint

Try these two different techniques using pieces of Plexiglas.

Left: Press Plexiglas on top of wet paint, weigh down and let dry. Then remove the Plexiglas.

Right: Press Plexiglas onto the wet surface. Then shift it slightly to blend the paint. Let dry.

Notice how the texture is precise in the example on the left and how the colors are blended by the shifting motion on the right. Which effect do you prefer?

Ink on Wet Paper

Wet your watercolor paper, then drop several colors of ink with an eye dropper onto the paper. Tilt the paper to blend one color into another. Let dry. You can repeat the process to add more colors or another layer of colors because the first layer is staining and won't lift.

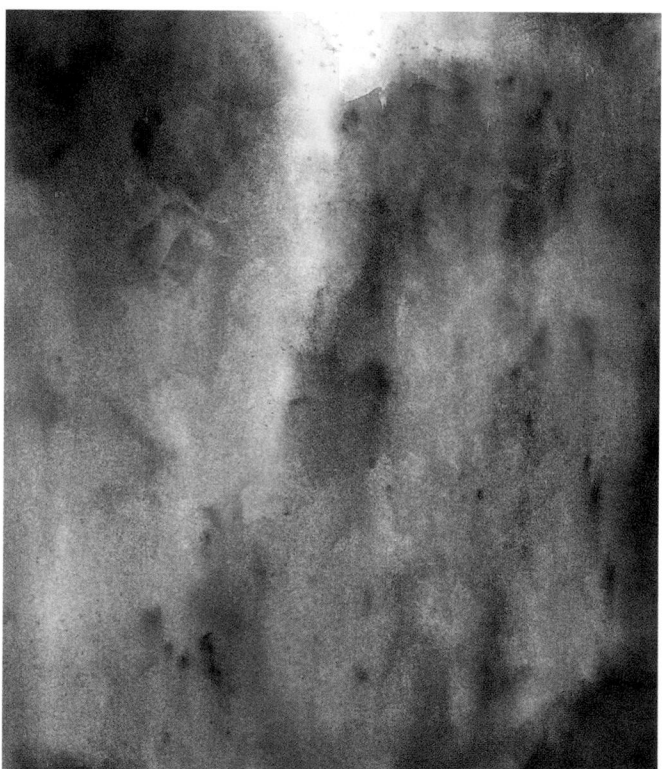

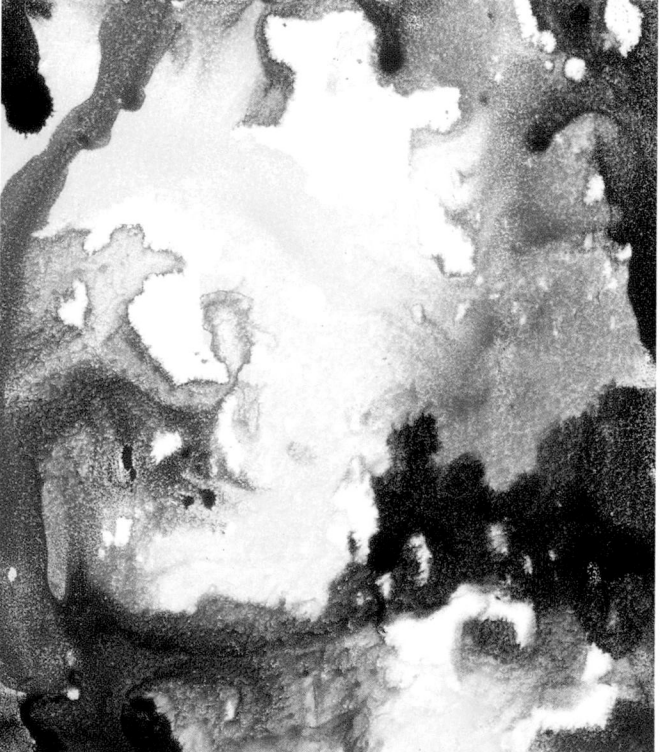

Monoprinting on Very Wet Paper

In monoprinting you manipulate paint on a non-porous surface and then transfer it to paper. The beauty lies in its spontaneity—no two prints are alike, although they remain similar. In these two examples, Plexiglas serves as the nonporous surface and is pressed onto wet paper (above) and damp paper (right).

Monoprinting on Damp Paper

Paint the surface of the Plexiglas with fairly thick paint in several colors. Turn the Plexiglas over and press into wet paper. Use a brayer to make sure all areas of the Plexiglas are pressed equally. Peel the Plexiglas away from the paper and let dry. Notice the difference in the edges, texture and color saturation when using wet versus damp paper.

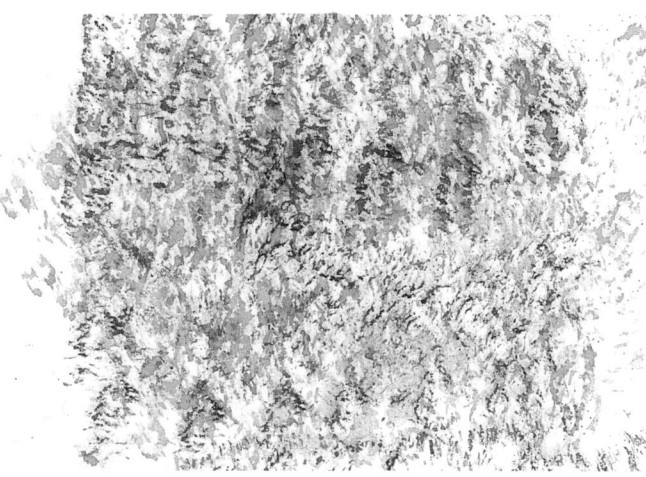

Practice Stippling

Using a stiff brush held vertically, dab the paint onto the paper's surface. When it is dry, go over it with another color and then another until you get the desired effect. This is a good method for simulating surfaces such as rusted metal, wood, brick and stone.

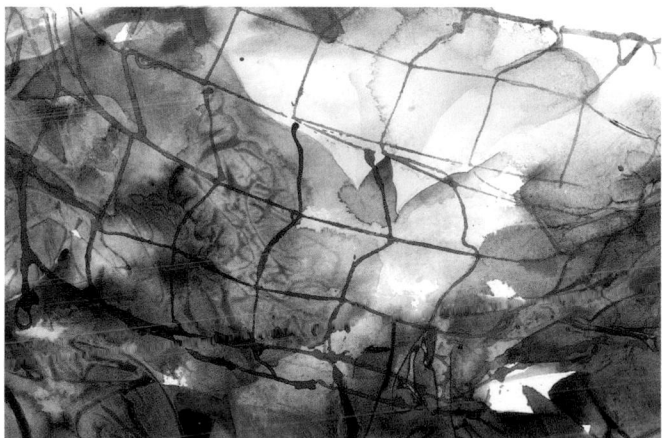

Stippling in Action

Create a tree by using your brush to stipple several layers of different colors and then, while wet, drag your damp brush through the dots to create the trunk and branches.

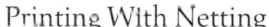

Printing With Netting

Man-made fiber materials can also be used for texture printing. Mesh netting is perfect for interesting patterns. Paint the net, then press onto a wet or dry surface.

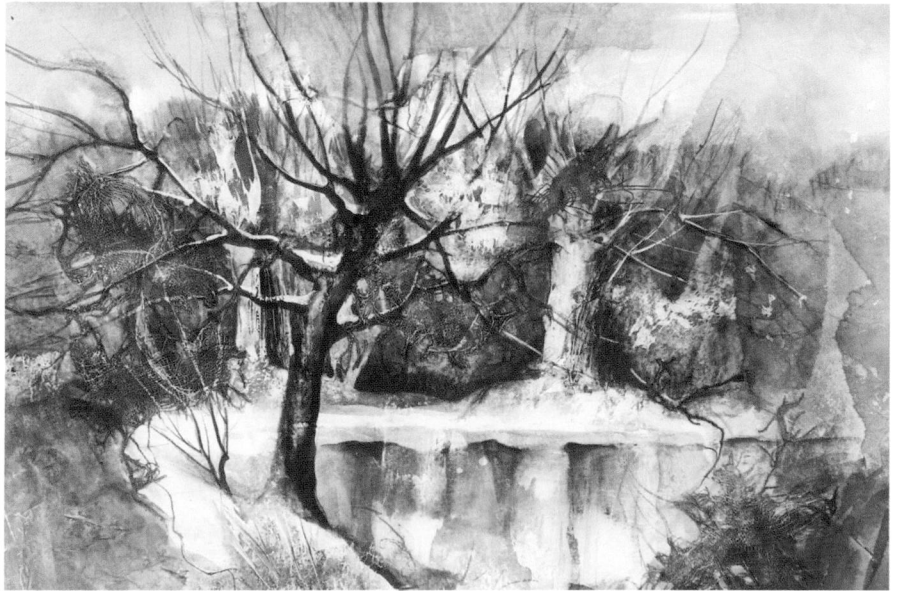

Painting With Cheesecloth

Similiar to the technique used with netting, paint the cheesecloth and press it onto a wet or dry surface to add an interesting texture to your paintings. Practice using different colors painted one on top of another for a blended effect. Also, try using paper in varying stages of wet or dryness. You can adhere the cheesecloth to the paper with acrylic gel medium for an even heavier textural appearance. In this example, the cheesecloth transforms the winter scene from a bland background to a more intricate, tactile expression complementing the tree branch pattern.

A *resist* is any material used to block a portion of a painting from accepting paint, ink or other marks. By preventing water and paint from settling into the paper, you can create interesting patterns. It also saves time to cover an area with a resist to preserve the white paper before using a wash, rather than painting around intricate shapes. Many things can be used as resists, including nonsoluble oil pastel, candle wax, crayons, glue, drafting tape and masking fluid designed specifically for this purpose. In the following examples you will see how each resist works and how each one can be employed to enhance your paintings.

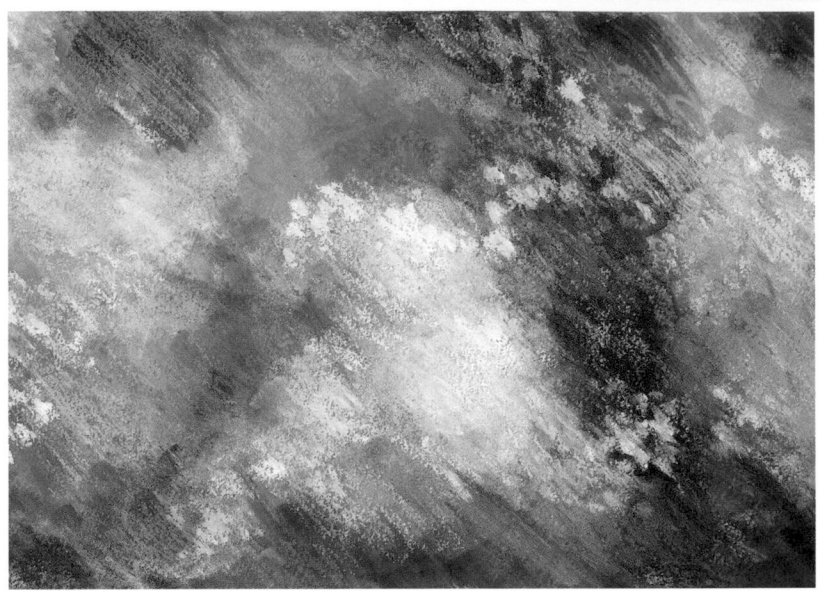

Watercolor Over Oil Pastel

Draw designs onto your paper with oil pastels and then paint over them. When dry, paint over it with other colors. You can make many layers and create any pattern with several colors. Add washes of watercolor to enhance your design. Add more oil pastel when the paint is dry, followed by more layers of watercolor washes to build up a complex composition.

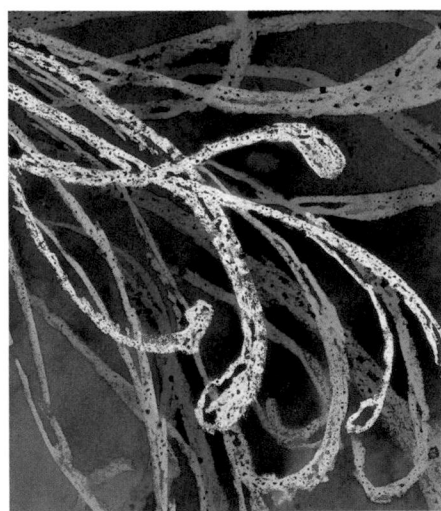

Candle as a Resist

Make patterns with white candle wax, retaining the white of the paper before painting over it. Repeat layers to retain the colors at each stage. After you have made patterns on paper with the wax, lay on a wash of color. When it is dry, add more lines of wax to preserve the color of the first wash. Add another wash with a different color. Continue building layers of wax and paint washes until your design is complete.

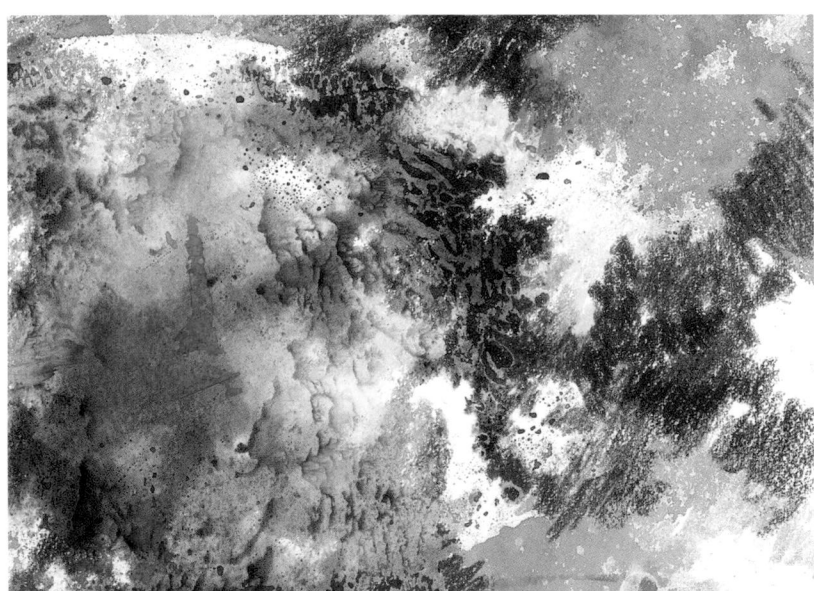

Melted Crayons and Watercolor

Make a design with crayons using various colors. Cover with wax paper and iron to blend them. You can paint over the resulting design if you wish. After melting the crayon, let it cool and add a wash layer. Repeat the process (if you wish) by adding more layers of crayon, melting and cooling, then washing over. Start with white paper or with paper already treated with a colored wash. Experiment with flat, single color washes and variegated washes.

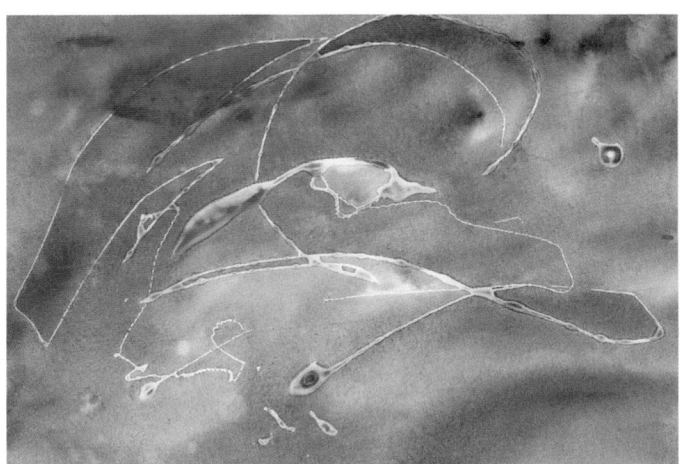

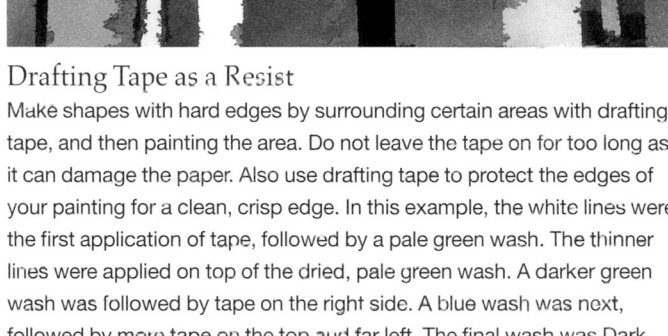

Glue as a Resist

Experiment with patterns, squiggles and droplets using white glue. Let dry and then paint over them. When the glue is dry, charge on bright and beautiful colors, letting them blend. The glue is slightly raised from the paper surface and will hold certain areas of color in "puddles." (Notice the circular green form in the center surrounded by blues.)

Drafting Tape as a Resist

Make shapes with hard edges by surrounding certain areas with drafting tape, and then painting the area. Do not leave the tape on for too long as it can damage the paper. Also use drafting tape to protect the edges of your painting for a clean, crisp edge. In this example, the white lines were the first application of tape, followed by a pale green wash. The thinner lines were applied on top of the dried, pale green wash. A darker green wash was followed by tape on the right side. A blue wash was next, followed by more tape on the top and far left. The final wash was Dark Indigo. When dry, remove all tape to reveal the multiple layers of color.

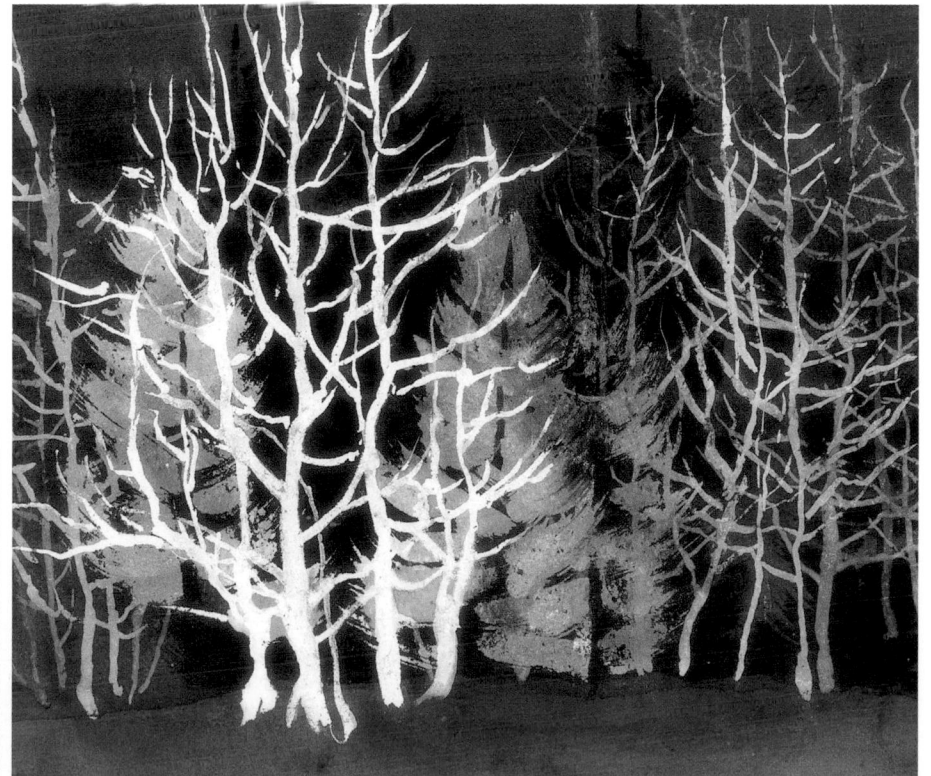

Masking Fluid as a Resist

Use masking fluid or rubber cement to resist in the areas that would be too difficult to paint around. Begin by painting the white trees (preserving the white of the paper), then lay on a light green wash. Add a bit of Burnt Sienna to the tree tones for variety. Next, paint the center pine trees with masking fluid to preserve the light green, then follow with a wash of Thalo Blue. Paint the trees on the far right and far left with masking fluid, then do a darker wash of Thalo Blue. Add a wash of Indigo in the center so the focal point (white trees) will stand out. Erase the masking fluid to reveal the colors underneath.

sprinkling and spattering

There are a variety of *sprinkling* and *spattering* techniques that will add texture to your paintings. Let your imagination run wild when coming up with different effects. You can make your paint on paper resemble natural elements such as grasses, leaves, rocks or trees, or man-made objects like masonry, barn wood or metals. The following examples will demonstrate how each texturing device works and how each can be applied to your painting.

1 Salt on almost dry paper
2 Salt on damp paper
3 Salt on very wet paper

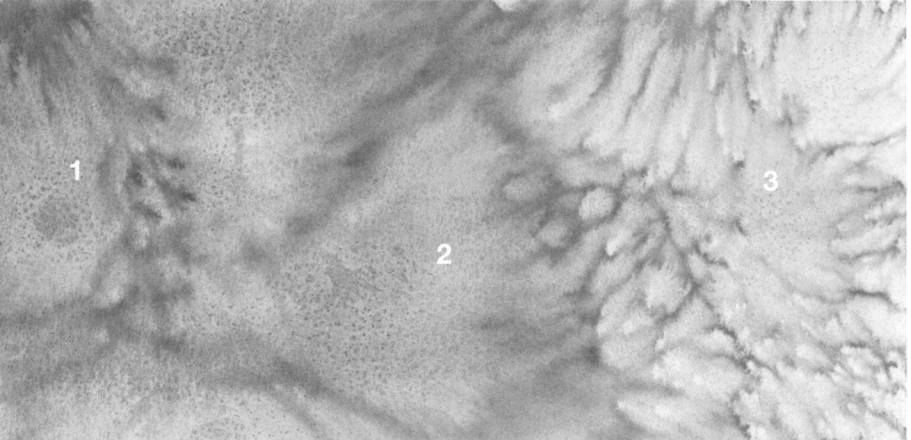

Working With Salt Patterns

Notice the different patterns created when throwing salt on wet, damp and almost dry paper.

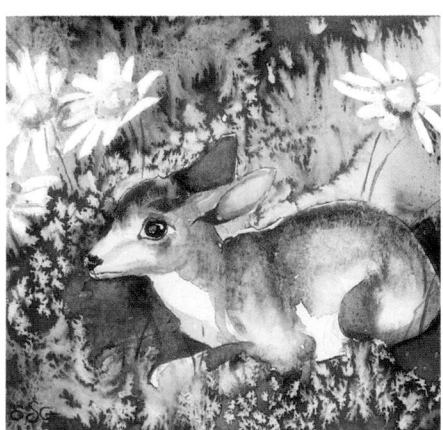

Sprinkling Salt

Sprinkle salt onto your wet painting in various stages of drying. The salt absorbs some of the paint where it's directly applied and pushes some paint aside to create many effects such as snow, foliage and texture in stone. In this painting, notice how salt forms star shapes that look like foliage. The upper corners of the paper were very wet when salt was added, creating a more fluid pattern. In the central foreground, the paper was damp, resulting in smaller star shapes. The back of the fawn was almost dry when salt was added, forming tiny dots in the fur coat.

Helpful Hint NUMBER 18

Protect the rest of your painting by placing strips of scrap paper all around the shape that you want to spatter. It is also a good idea to protect surrounding areas of your work space with newspaper because spatter sometimes goes far and wide.

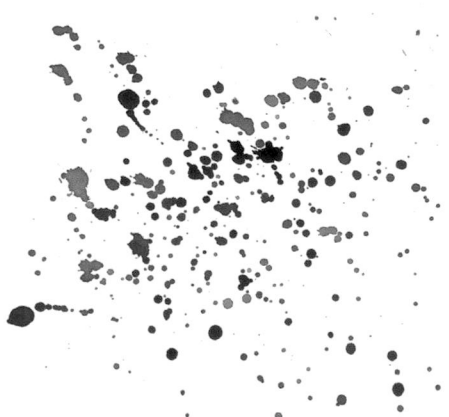

Adding Droplets of Paint

Load your bush with paint and hold it horizontally over the paper. Gently tap the handle with your other hand to create paint drops of various sizes.

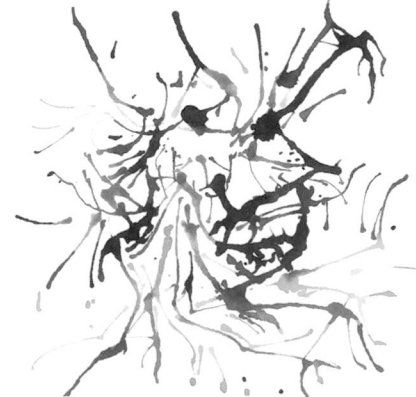

Using a Straw to Blow Paint

For a different effect, try blowing through a straw to scatter the paint droplets. Angle the straw towards the paper and practice blowing gently or strongly, tipping your paper to send the paint in the right direction. Add more water and the paint will move more easily but be less controllable.

Spattering

Using different tools, dot the paper with paint or other liquids to create interesting effects simulating rust, metal, stone, bricks, texture on leaves, wood, earth and even sparkling water by building up several layers of different colors. Try using crumpled aluminum foil, sponges, tissue paper, erasers, your finger tips, and a variety of brushes.

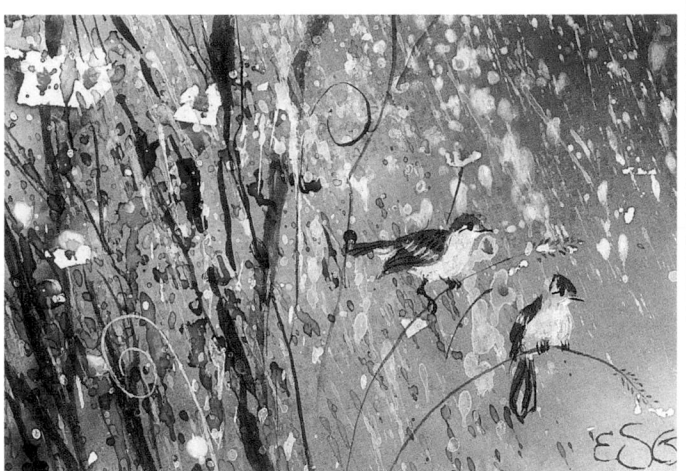

Toothbrush Spattering in Action

Load a toothbrush with paint and spatter the surface of your paper by moving your thumb across the bristles. Repeat with different colors. Try on wet or dry paper. In the small painting above, drops of masking fluid were spattered where the white flowers and birds' breasts appear. A yellow-green wash was added and allowed to dry. Loose lines were dragged across the left side of the painting to simulate leaves and stems. Dark green and Chinese White were spattered with a toothbrush for background texture. To complete the painting, the masking fluid was removed and the flower shapes and brown birds were finished.

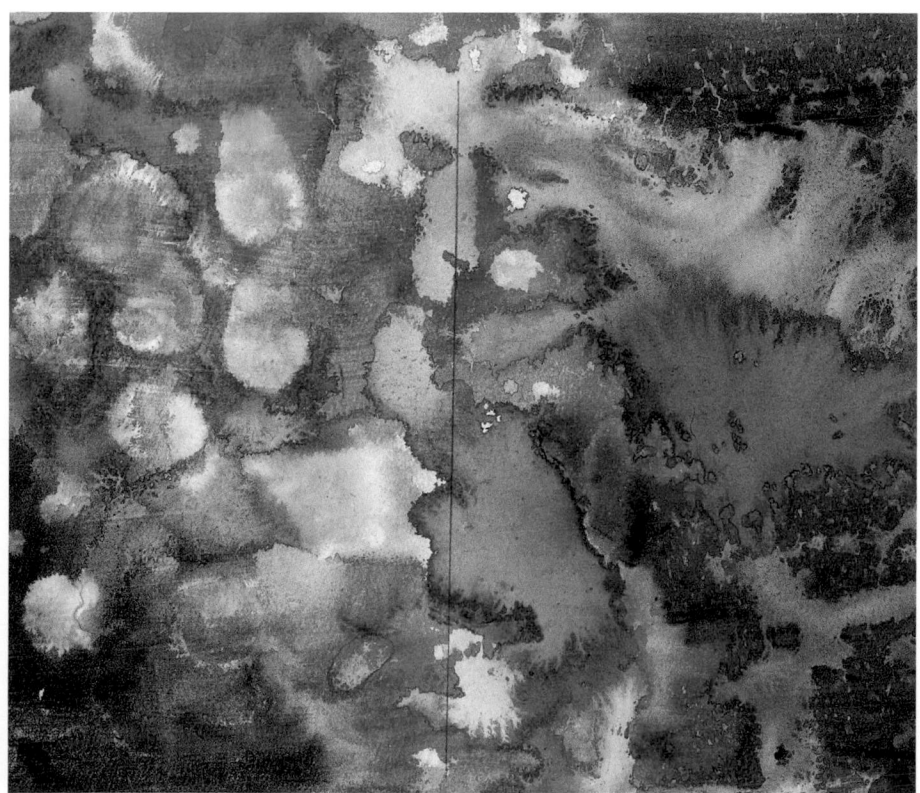

Adding Drops of Alcohol

Drop rubbing alcohol onto wet paint in various stages of drying to create different effects.

This example is divided in half. Notice how differently the alcohol works on very wet paint compared to the almost dry paint. The left side is a barely damp, variegated wash. Notice that the spotted blotched shapes are more regular in form with hard edges. On the right side, the paint is very wet. The shapes spew out in irregular and uncontrolled forms.

Cutouts can be used to create shapes by painting directly over the cutout or placing the cutout on top of a painted section and lifting out the shape. Natural elements and man-made products can also be used as *stencils,* including leaves, feathers and fiber elements. The object can be painted over directly with a brush or by using the toothbrush spatter method.

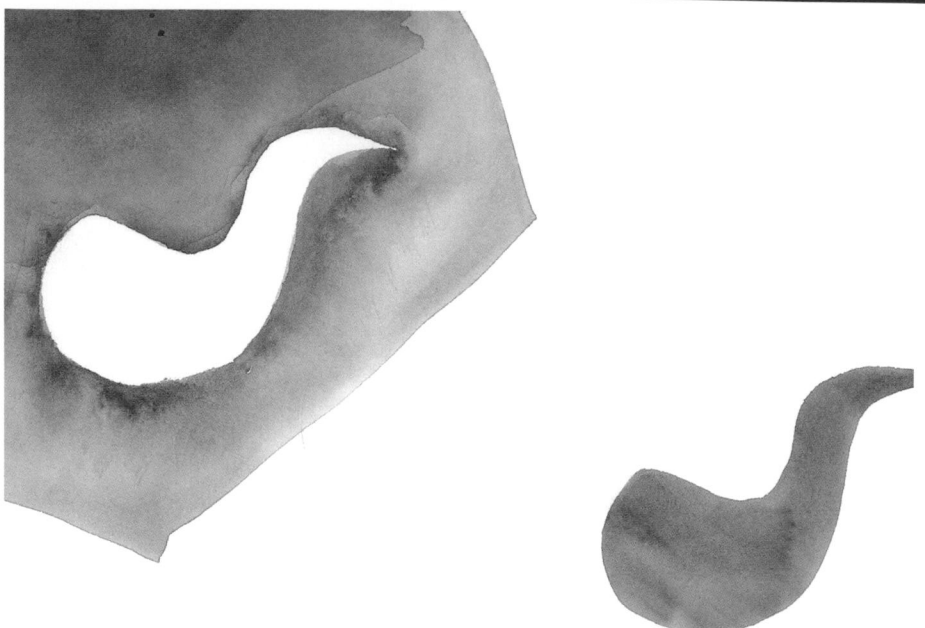

Using an Acetate or Cardboard Cutout
Cut either a positive shape or a negative shape into stiff cardboard or acetate. Hold tightly on the paper and paint around the positive cutout or within the space of the negative shape.

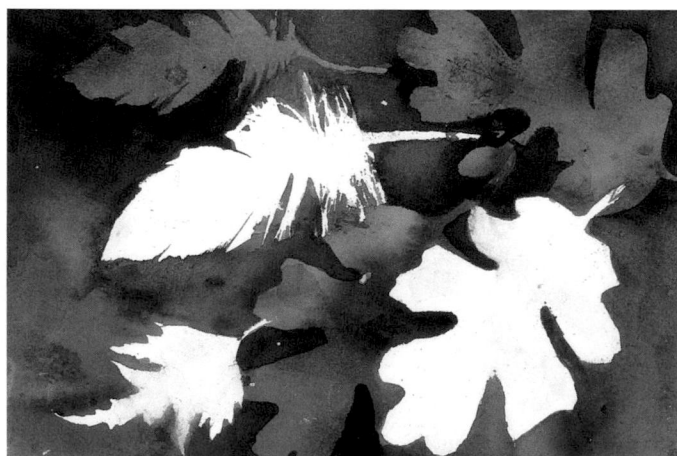

Leaves and Feathers as Stencils
Hold a leaf or feather onto the paper and paint over it past the edges and onto the paper. Lift and let dry. Repeat and overlap for an interesting design.

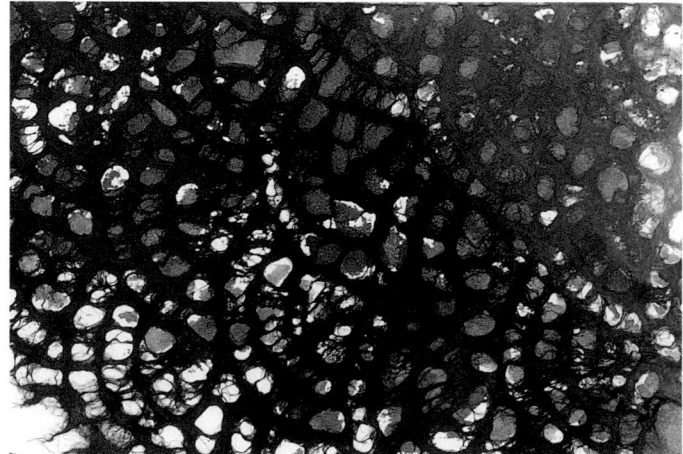

Printing With Lace Paper
Lay a piece of lace paper, or any kind of netting, onto your paper and spatter with a toothbrush. When everything is completely dry, remove the lace paper to reveal the delicate pattern or leave the lace paper on the watercolor paper as part of the design as in this example.

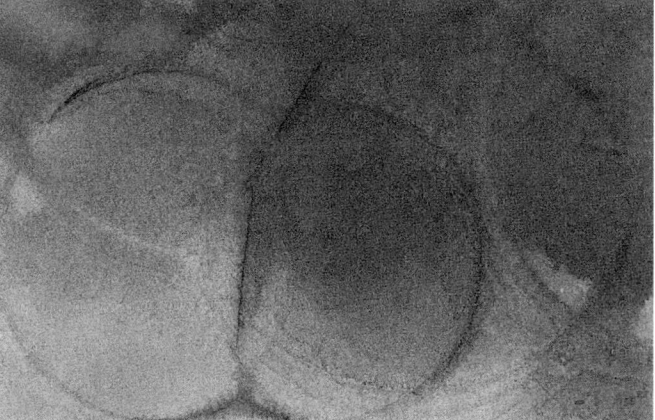

Soap Bubbles on Wet Paint

Wet your watercolor paper with a colorful wash, then have fun blowing soap bubbles and letting them fall into the wet paint. When they pop, the bubbles will leave a ghost image of their round shapes. Try a foamy mixture of soap suds for a different effect. Use this technique for abstract patterns or for creating frothy water at the base of a waterfall.

Using Colored Tissue Paper

Press crumpled, colored tissue paper on top of wet watercolor paper, then paint on top of the tissue using lots of water (and a large brush) to sink the colored dye of the tissue into the white paper. Fill the page with various colors. Let everything dry before removing the tissue paper, revealing the design. This can be used as the background for any subject.

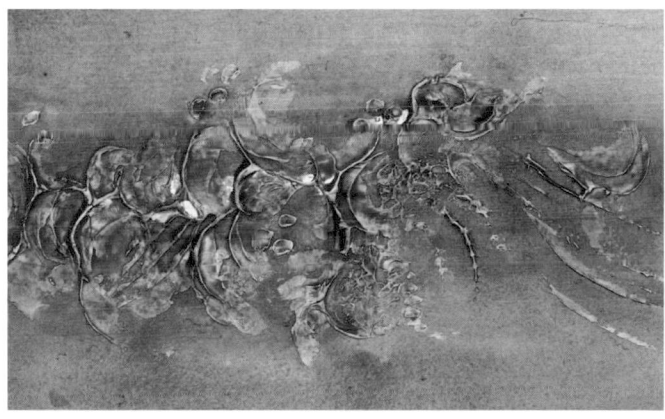

Painting Over Modeling Paste

Use modeling paste to imply depth in your paintings. With a palette knife, create intricate designs or natural patterns such as leaves or tree bark. Wash over the textured area with several layers of paint, and then rub off the highest points of the forms for a highlighted effect or add different colors to these edges.

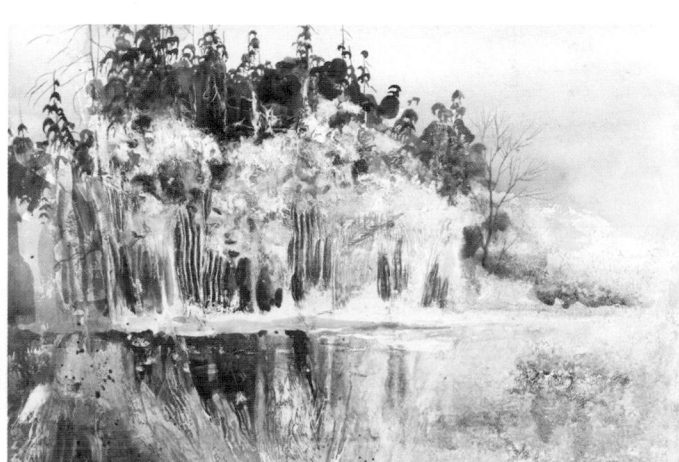

Painting Over a Gesso Ground

Spread gesso on your watercolor paper to create a heavily textured background. Make patterns with tools such as a brush handle, comb, palette knife or Plexiglas. In this small landscape example, the tree trunks were done by dragging a comb through the wet gesso. The foreground grasses were made with a brush handle. The lower right corner texture was created by pressing Plexiglas into the gesso, then removing it. When the gesso is dry, layers of paint can be added to represent trees, water and grasses.

Sometimes it's fun to think about unusual materials that can be used to create different effects on paper and paint. New ideas may come from your painter friends, workshop instructors or out of the blue. Exciting things are all around you just waiting to be discovered. Scour your house and garage for new ideas. Push the boundaries of your imagination to invent more ways to create texture and incorporate them into your paintings.

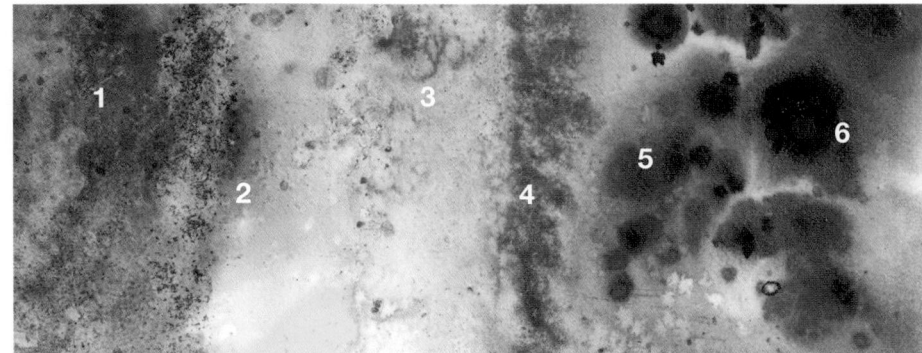

Raiding the Kitchen Pantry

Try using these texturing devices in your landscapes. Dried bread crumbs and oatmeal create marks that resemble small stones and earth textures. Salt makes excellent foliage, water sparkles or snow. Coffee can simulate rust on metal, wood rot or even stone. Be careful not to overdo it, though. The goal is for the viewer to appreciate the painting as a whole, not the texture itself.

1 Instant potato flakes
2 Dried bread crumbs
3 Oatmeal
4 Salt
5 Juice Powder
6 Instant coffee

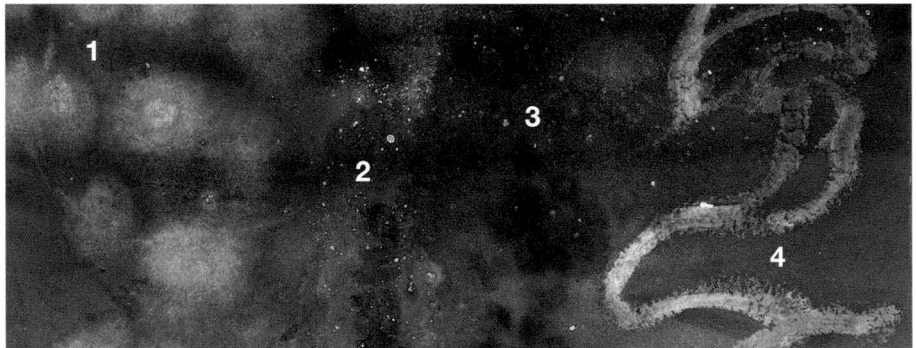

Raiding the Laundry Room

These ingredients act as resists, with qualities that push the paint aside. They can be used in any number of ways, where it is desirable to retain paint or return to a former layer of the painting.

1 Bleach
2 Detergent
3 Spray starch
4 Spot remover stick

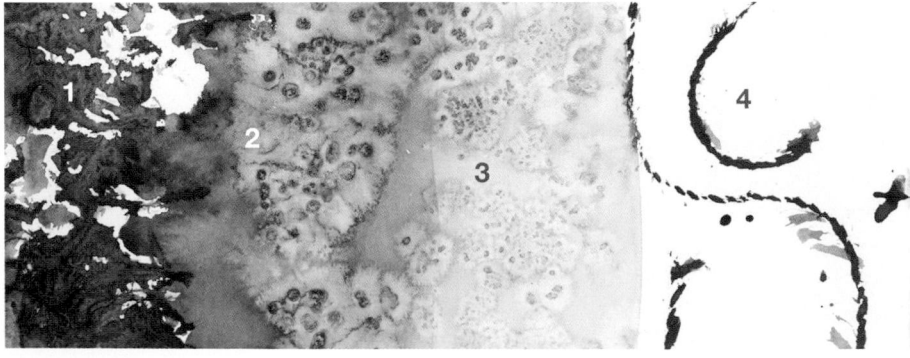

Raiding the Garden Shed

Sphagnum moss and twine are useful for making printing marks. Experiment with other materials to create different effects—fertilizer and plant food, for example—create chemical reactions with the paint to create interesting marks.

1 Sphagnum moss
2 Fertilizer
3 Plant food
4 Staking twine

Paper torture refers to methods used to abrade the surface of paper to create different effects such as sparkling water, snow or highlights by scraping and rubbing off the paint from the paper.

Don't be afraid to experiment with different materials, including various types of sandpaper, craft knives, brush handles, erasers, credit cards and combs.

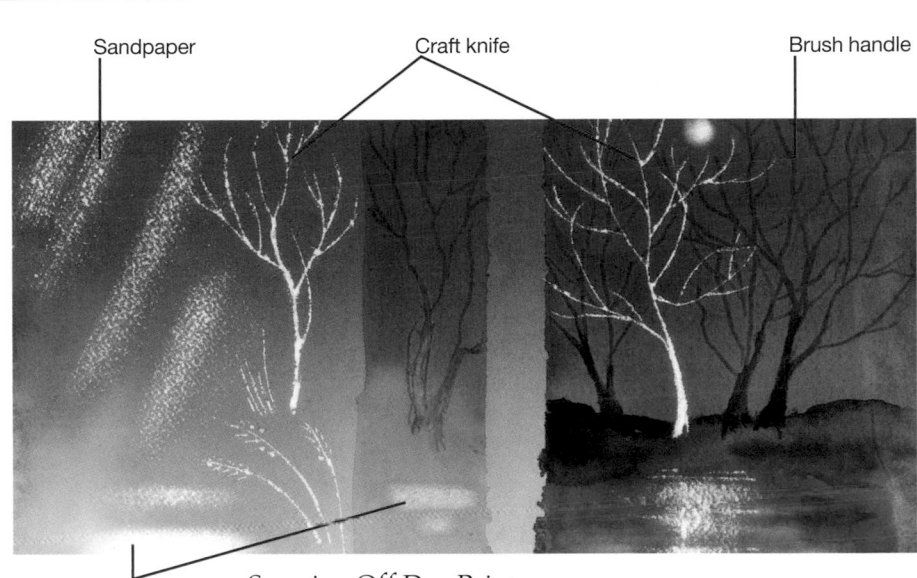

Sandpaper · Craft knife · Brush handle · Eraser

Scraping Off Dry Paint

Sandpaper: When your painting is dry, gently scuff the surface of the paper with rough or fine sandpaper to create water sparkle or highlight areas and a variety of other textures. Carefully erase over the sandpapered area to remove loosened paint. You can paint over the sandpapered area to create a darker texture.

Craft knife: Carefully cut into the painted surface or make scratches, showing the white of the paper to emulate branches, to create highlight areas on textured surfaces or reflected light on the surface of waves.

Erasers: Rub out areas of your painting with a stiff eraser to create highlights. Notice the light touch of the sandpaper on the right side of the example and the heavier rubbed out effects on the left.

Brush handle: Using the tip of the brush handle, gently gouge the paper's surface to create lines. The paint will flow back into the dents to make a darker line. Try this on wet and almost dry paper.

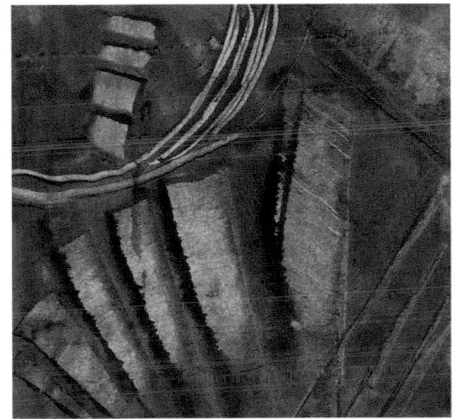

Using a Credit Card

Scrape away areas of wet paint with the edge of a credit card to make lighter shapes. Be gentle with wet paper and scrape harder on drier paper. Practice makes perfect.

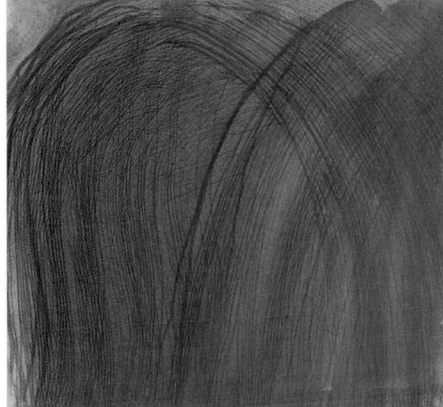

Using a Comb

Drag a comb through wet paint to simulate wood grain or to make a pretty line design.

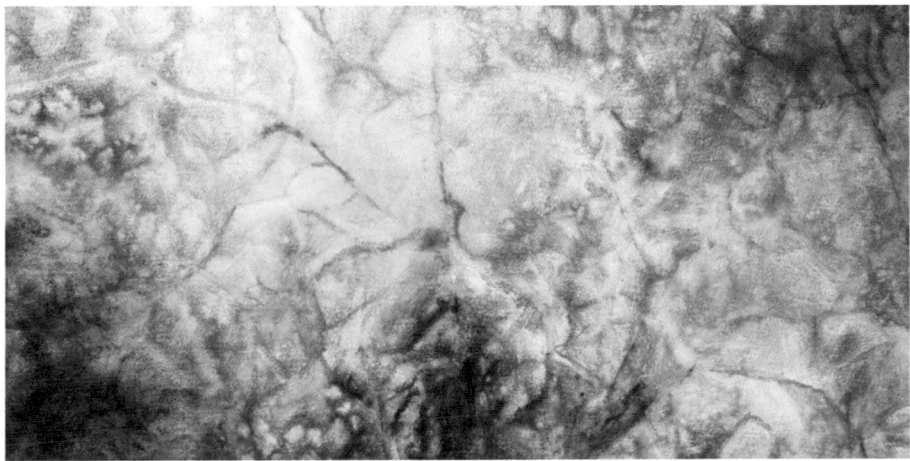

Crumple Wet Paper

Crumple wet watercolor paper to create creases. Spread it out flat and start painting. Paint will flow into the creases, creating patterns and designs. Try this on Oriental paper too.

Making Something Out of Nothing

In this exercise, you can use as many texturing techniques as you wish. The goal is to practice what you have learned and to create something out of nothing. It's exciting to begin the painting process with a blank sheet of watercolor paper and absolutely no idea of what you're going to make. By sloshing on color and adding lots of texture, pictorial content begins to emerge slowly but surely. By discovering "found" subject matter and enhancing it with negative painting, you can develop your painting to any degree of detailed completeness that you desire. The end result will be a spontaneous, original painting.

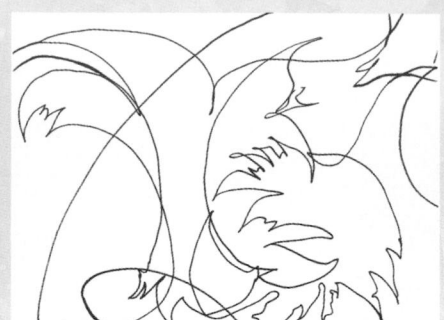

1 Create Gesture Drawings
Draw pencil scribbles on several pieces of paper without any specific subject in mind. Use large, swinging, freeform motions, as well as some that are more intricate and detailed. Go with the flow, let things happen and just have fun.

MATERIALS LIST

BRUSHES
Nos. 4 and 14 rounds
1-inch (25mm) flat

WATERCOLORS
Grumbacher: Burnt Sienna, Cadmium Yellow, Emerald Green, Sap Green

Holbein: Opera

SURFACE
11" × 15" (28cm × 38cm) sheet 140-lb. (300gsm) Arches cold-pressed paper

ADDITIONAL SUPPLIES
Pencil, Plexiglas, rubbing alcohol, salt, tissue paper

2 Drop in Colors
After looking at your sketches, turn them in all directions and choose the most interesting. If you like, combine elements from several different drawings. Enlarge your chosen drawing and copy it onto watercolor paper. Using the 1-inch (25mm) flat, drop in a selection of three or four colors (Sap Green, Cadmium Yellow and Burnt Sienna), letting them flow into each other on wet paper.

Helpful Hint NUMBER 19
Look for subject matter in simple, everyday things that most of us overlook. A single, interesting curled leaf can inspire a large abstract painting.

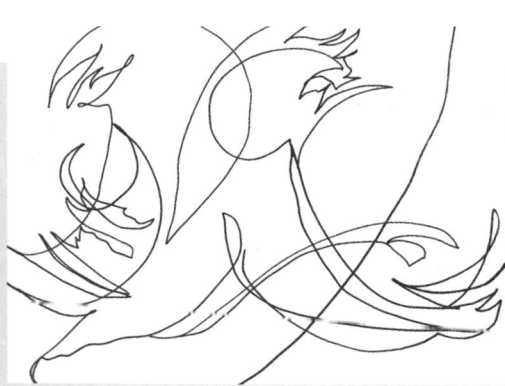

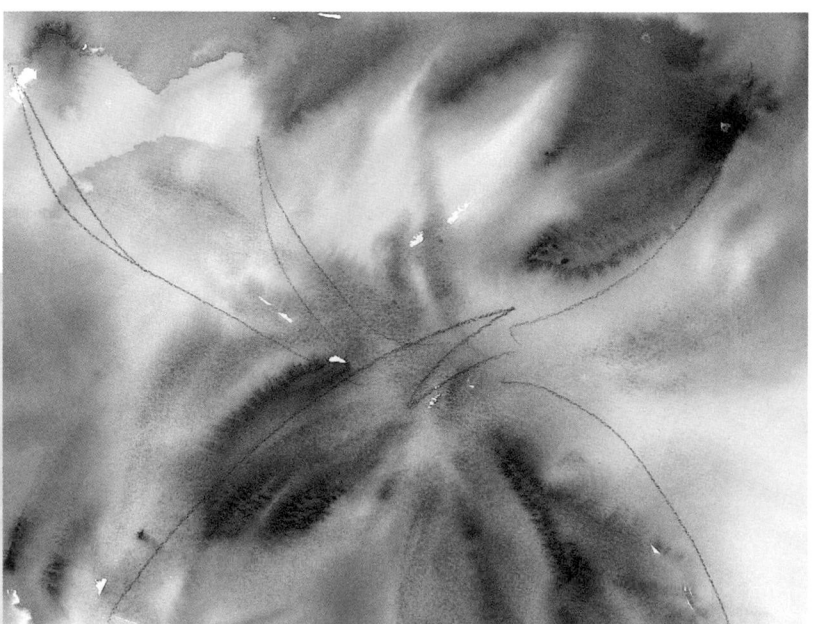

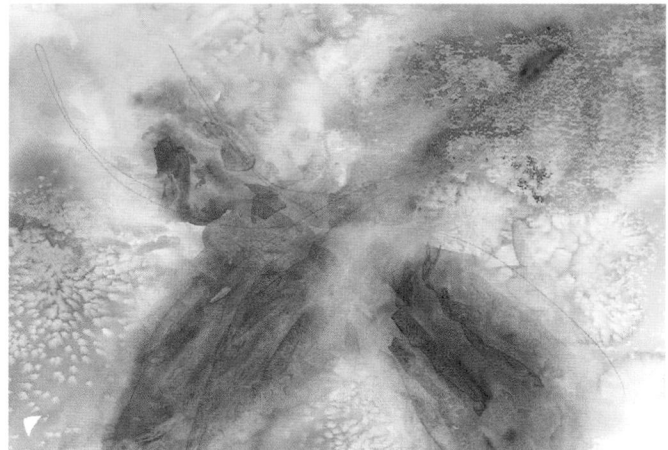

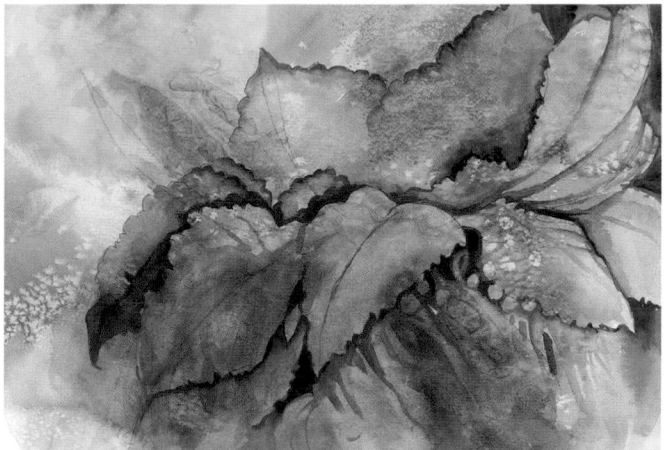

3 Add Texture

Add some texture to the paper surface while the painting is still wet. The example utilized salt, tissue paper, Plexiglas and alcohol spatter, but you can use other materials that you feel apply to your particular painting. When everything is dry, remove your texturing devices.

4 Refine the Painting

Use the resulting patterns formed from the washes and texturing effects to determine what shapes you will identify to create your composition. In this example, vague patterns become leaf shapes. Paint positively and negatively to "push and pull" different elements. Pulling your subject matter into the foreground will distinguish it from what is pushed into the background. Refine and define the painting until you are satisfied. Add detail to the leaves' veins and stems. Allow some areas to remain mysterious.

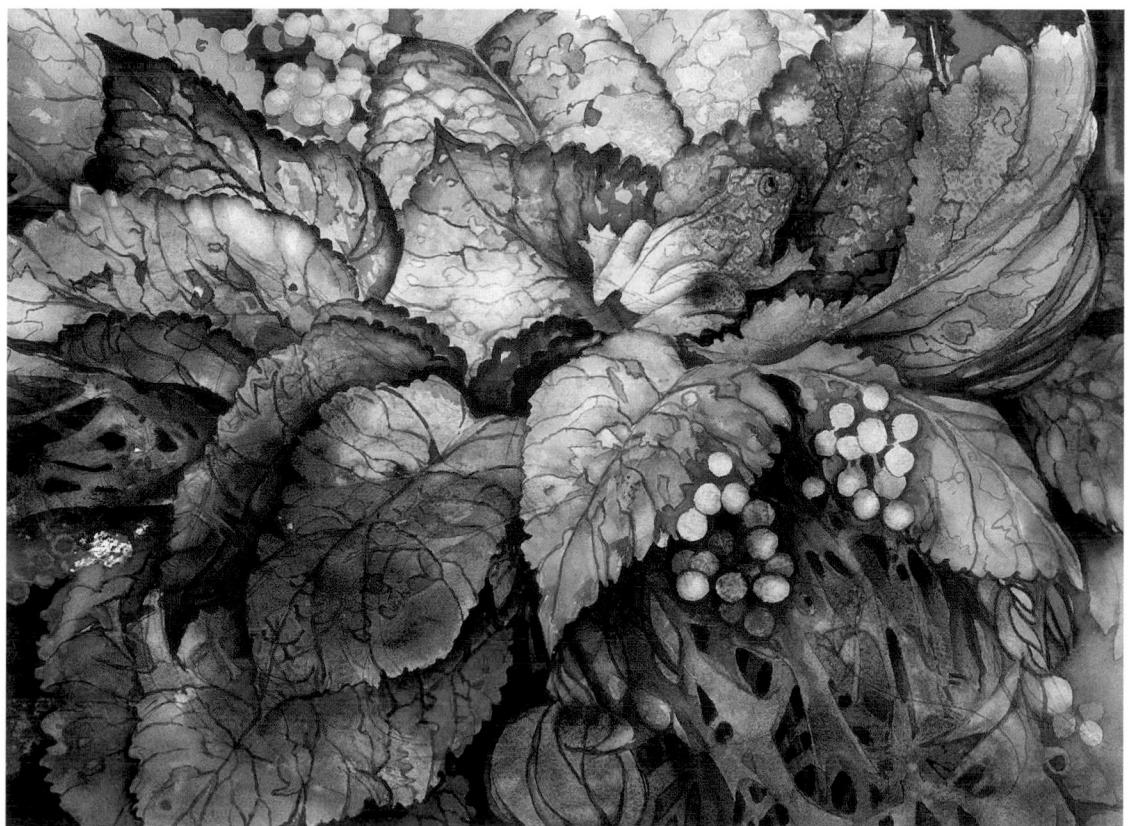

5 The Final Version

The patterns are very detailed, giving the final painting a "busy" feel in order to keep the treasure hidden. Can you find it?

Hidden Treasure
11" × 15" (28cm × 38cm)

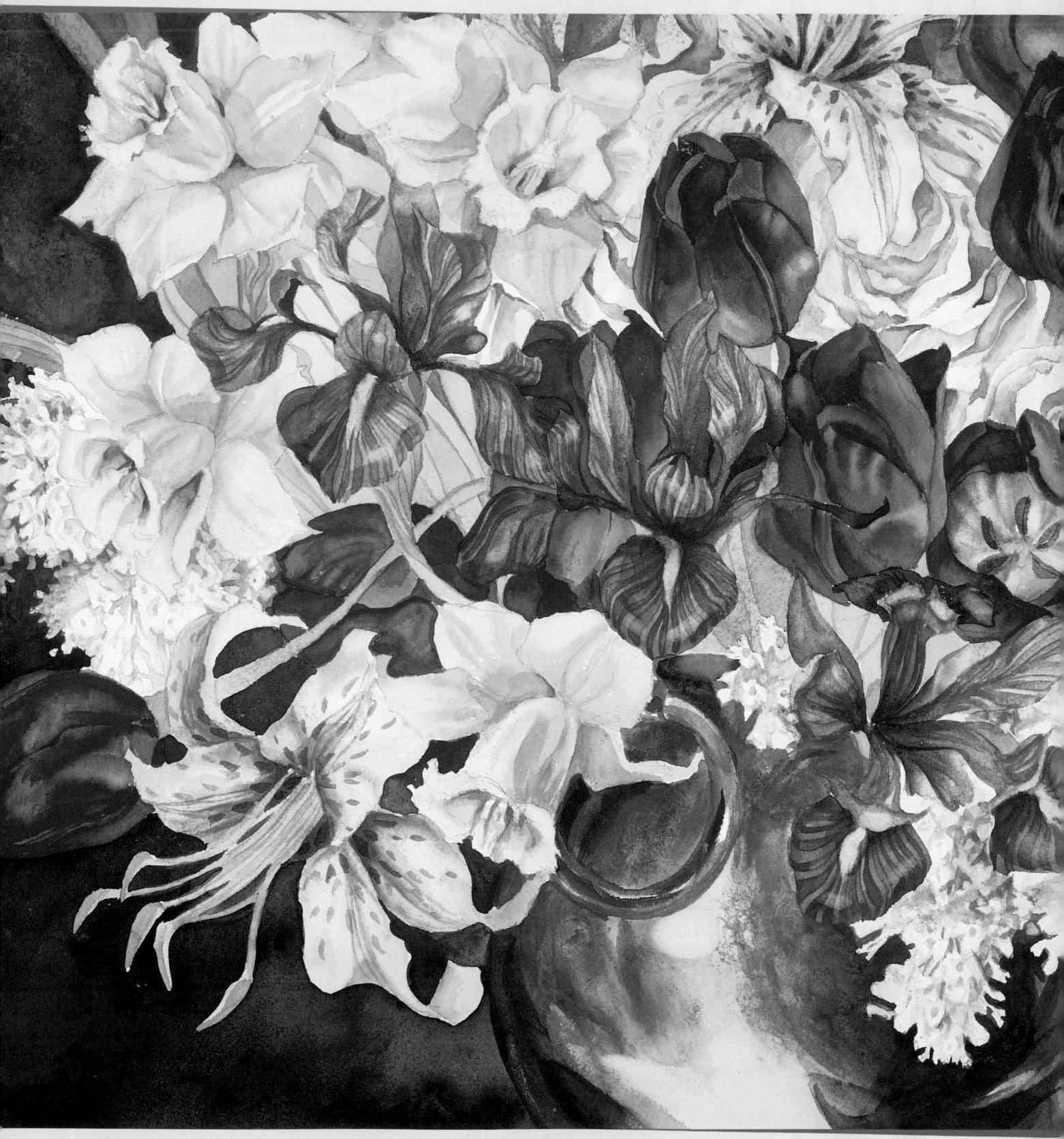

Grand Baroque
15" × 22" (38cm × 56cm)

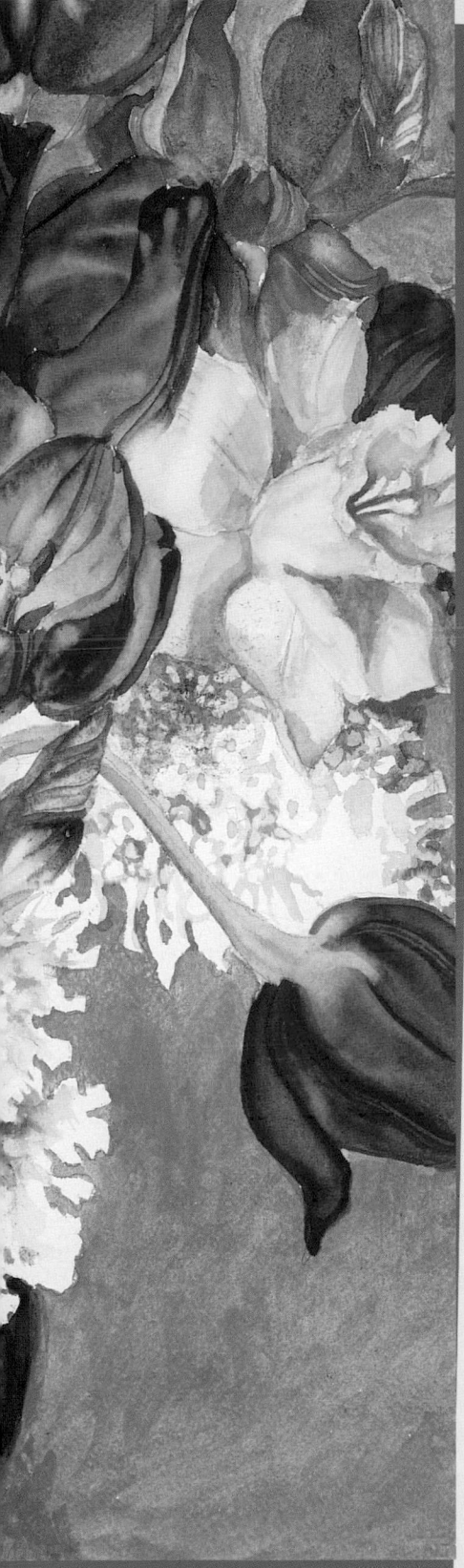

 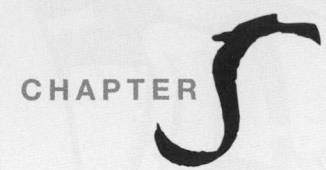

color and value

WHAT COULD BE MORE IMPORTANT IN A PAINTING FOR capturing the eye and heart of a viewer than bright and beautiful color? Color moves the spirit and delights the soul. If you are walking through a gallery of many different kinds of paintings, one or two will probably draw your immediate attention above all the rest. What is it that makes them more compelling than the others? Is it a bold splash of red that strikes the eye or the stark contrast of dark areas against light ones? Color and value are probably the most important concerns for you to consider in the planning stages and painting process. Color sets the mood of a painting. It can provide balance and visual weight through the use of lights, darks and intensity. In this chapter, you will discover ways to effectively use these powerful elements.

The *color wheel* is a basic tool that illustrates the many relationships between colors. By studying colors in this wheel format, it's easier to understand where a color belongs in relation to others. Also, the color wheel will help you improve on your ability to visualize color mixing.

PRIMARY COLORS:

On a standard color wheel, the three *primary colors* (red, blue and yellow) are placed equidistant from one another. In theory, these three colors, along with the addition of black and white, can be combined to produce any color. The primaries are the foundation of color—they cannot be made from any other colors.

SECONDARY COLORS

On a color wheel, *secondary colors* are located halfway between two primary colors. Between the primary colors red and yellow lies the secondary color orange; between red and blue lies violet; and between yellow and blue lies green.

INTERMEDIATE COLORS

Intermediate colors, or tertiary colors, are produced by mixing a primary color with a secondary color next to it on the color wheel. Examples include: mixing red (primary) with orange (secondary) to produce red-orange (intermediate), or mixing red (primary) with violet (secondary) to produce red-violet (intermediate).

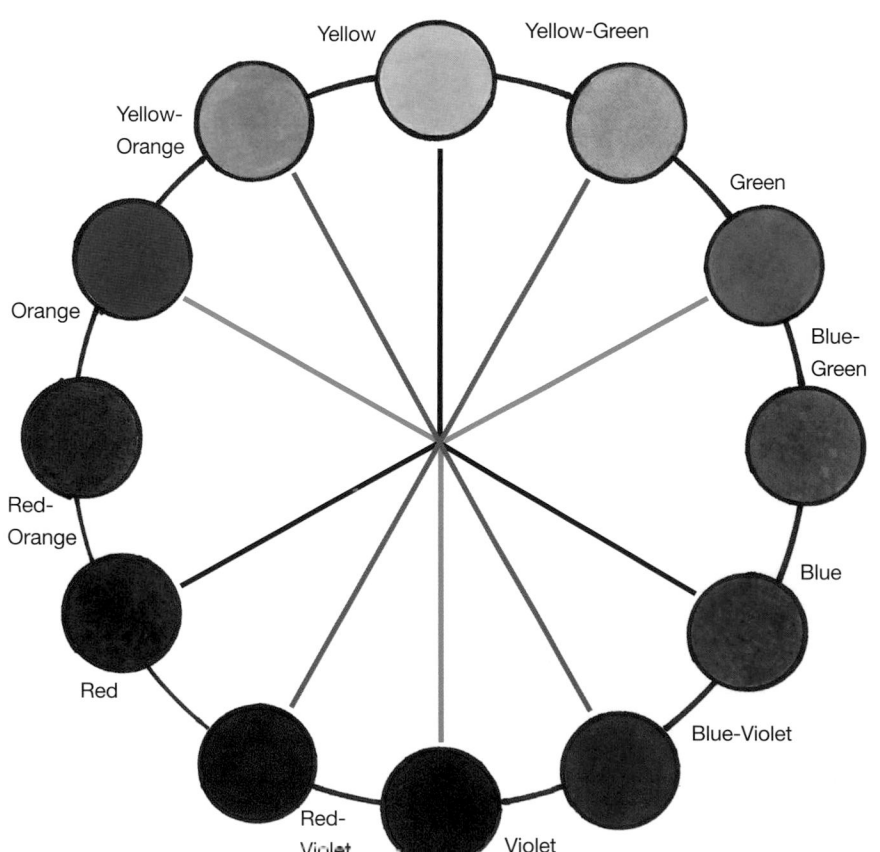

The Color Wheel

Primary
Secondary
Tertiary

Helpful Hint NUMBER 20

If the colors in your painting look boring, add a small shape or two and incorporate a jarring, surprise color such as red or purple. Even if you think the new color doesn't make logical sense, it might work well within the composition. You never know!

There is more to color relationships than simply the primaries, secondaries and intermediates. By understanding their relationships to each other, you will be on your way to creating aesthetically pleasing color groupings in your compositions.

ANALOGOUS COLORS

Colors closely related along the color wheel are considered *analogous*. Analogous colors can be defined as any three adjacent primary, secondary and tertiary colors. For instance, the colors red, violet and red-violet are analogous. By using such closely related colors together, an artist can assure color unity within a painting or color schemes.

TRIADS

A *triad* is a group of three colors equally distant from one another on the color wheel. The three primary colors, for example, form a triad. Also, the three secondary colors create a triad.

To form a triad, the colors must be at equally distant positions on the color wheel.

The Color Wheel

COMPLEMENTARY

Complementary colors are located opposite one another on the color wheel (such as red and green, blue and orange, yellow and violet). The two colors adjacent to the complement are *near complements*. Mixing two complementary colors can produce a range of grays or neutral browns.

MONOCHROMATIC

Monochromatic colors can be varying shades of a single color or several colors that are all very close in *hue* (another word for color).

In choosing my colors, I select not by brand name, but by the properties of the individual paint and how it behaves on paper. For example, Davy's Gray by Grumbacher is very different than the Winsor & Newton version. Grumbacher's is dark and almost green—it's wonderful to use in mixes with Sap Green for foliage. On the other hand, the Winsor & Newton product is very light and lovely for other uses, such as creating atmospheric fog, misty effects or sunstruck stone textures. Another example is Cobalt Blue, which varies greatly in its consistency because of the amount of filler used by the individual manufacturer.

Conversely, some differently named colors by other companies can be very similar once on paper: Vermilion by Grumbacher is much like Bright Red by Winsor & Newton, and Permanent Rose by Winsor & Newton is similar to Thalo Crimson by Grumbacher. Therefore, it is not necessary to have every color by every manufacturer. Experiment with different brands and select the few that suit your painting needs.

Don't be afraid to branch out and try different color combinations. For a luscious violet, glaze Opera over Cobalt Blue. Then, try it over Manganese Blue to see the difference. Or, brighten Burnt Sienna with a glaze of Opera. Try mixing and then glazing Opera and Viridian for a gorgeous gray.

It's always fun to experiment with other colors.

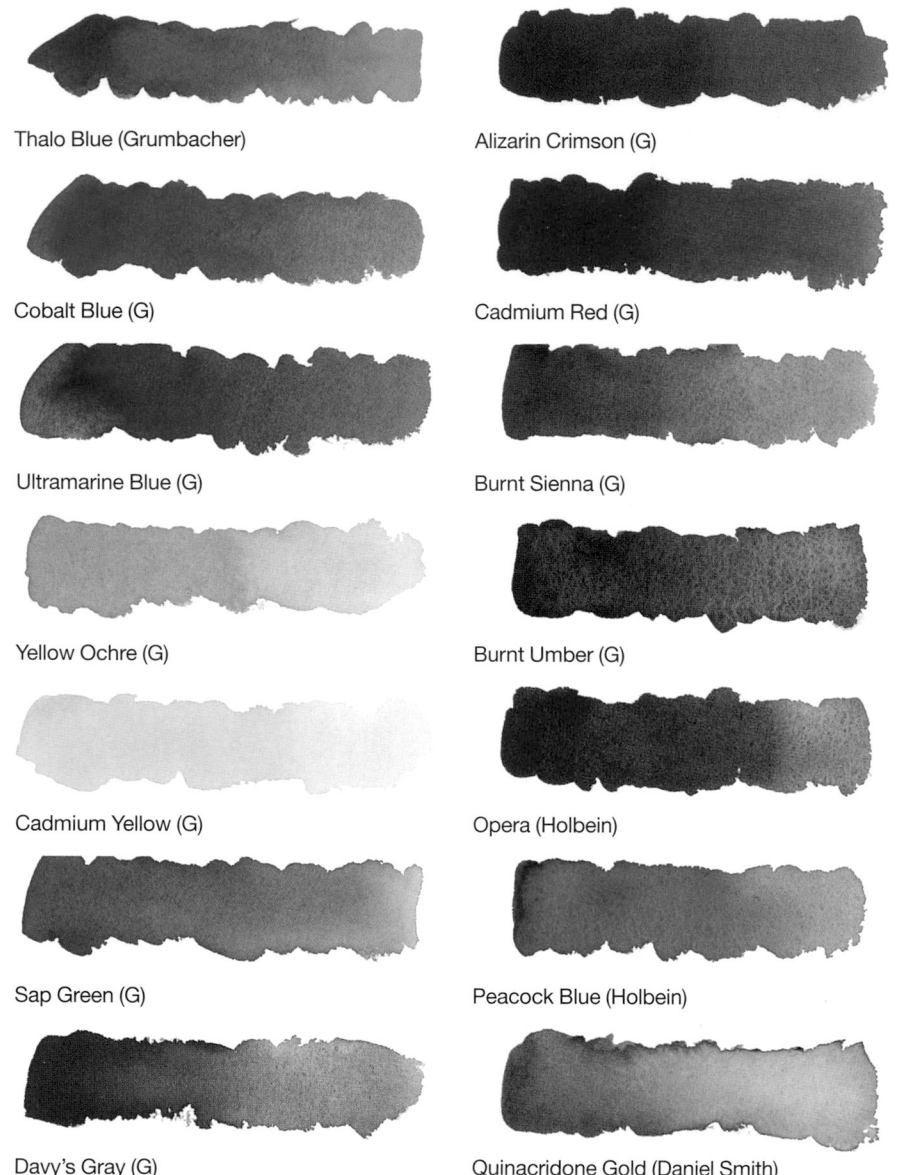

Thalo Blue (Grumbacher)

Alizarin Crimson (G)

Cobalt Blue (G)

Cadmium Red (G)

Ultramarine Blue (G)

Burnt Sienna (G)

Yellow Ochre (G)

Burnt Umber (G)

Cadmium Yellow (G)

Opera (Holbein)

Sap Green (G)

Peacock Blue (Holbein)

Davy's Gray (G)

Quinacridone Gold (Daniel Smith)

Elizabeth's Palette

My choice of colors is an ever-evolving palette that has developed over the years. It changes according to the particular needs of each painting. I'm always trying new combinations that I discover by accident or hear about from others, but my working palette usually consists of the following colors: Thalo Blue, Cobalt Blue, Ultramarine Blue, Yellow Ochre, Cadmium Yellow, Sap Green, Davy's Gray, Alizarin Crimson, Cadmium Red, Burnt Sienna, Burnt Umber, Opera, Peacock Blue and Quinacridone Gold. The last three colors are excellent for mixing or glazing. Other brands may be substituted, except for Davy's Gray.

Making freeform collages offers great freedom to use color and shape. Use these studies to reinforce the principles of color and design. Make them small or large patterns that are simple or complex. Practice color relationships and see how color choices affect the mood and arrangement.

To begin, scan through the pages of magazines for colorful pictures and advertisements and randomly tear out colors that might look good together. For fun, add some random surprises (such as clashing colors or irregular shapes) that you wouldn't think were compatible.

Tear the sheets into smaller pieces of different sizes and then sort them into piles of color and shade. Tear the page away from your body for a colored edge. Tear towards your body for an edge showing the white paper.

Arrange and rearrange the pieces on a sheet of paper until you have a pleasing design. Don't forget to incorporate the white of the paper as a design element.

Use some edges cut by scissors for definition and variation. Then, glue the pieces onto the white paper. The result can be a pretty collage in itself or the beginnings of an idea for a larger painting.

The two design examples on this page are quite different in mood and sentiment because of the way color has been manipulated. The same colors have been used, but the results differ.

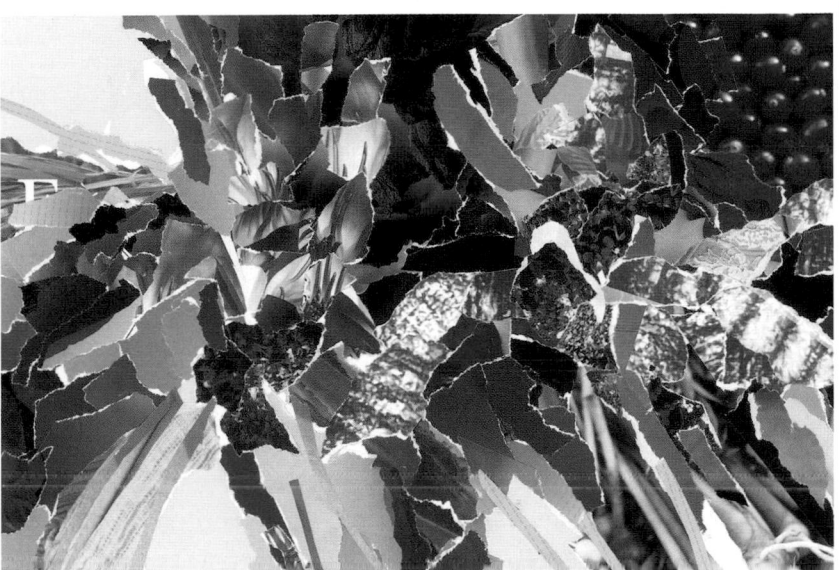

Create a Pleasing Design
Here a soft color blend of pinks merge into purples with some browns and yellows to temper them. The complex composition has a feeling of delicacy and intracy. The red in the top right corner is balanced with red at the bottom left, spicing up the other colors. Cover up the red and the design is less appealing.

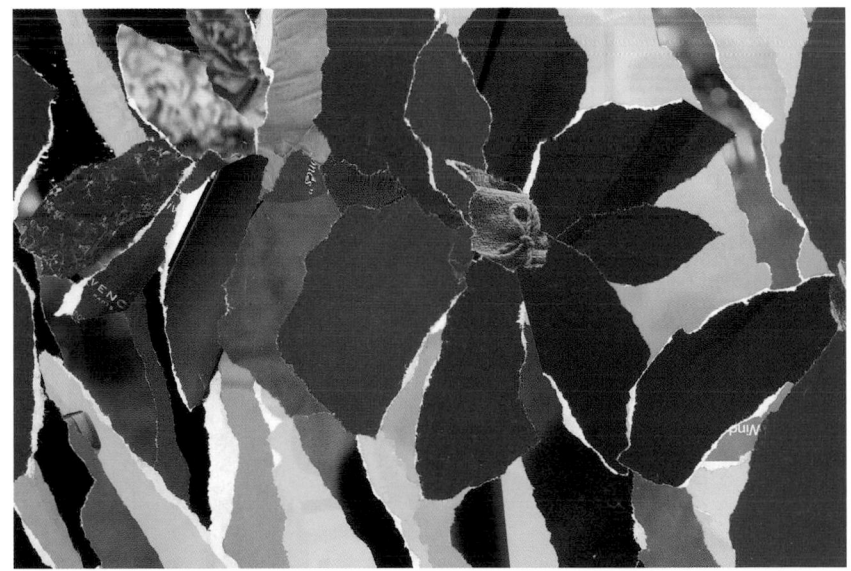

Another Design
In this example, the large red flowers are the dominant shapes, immediately attracting the viewer's eye. It is a bold and commanding arrangement. The simplified red shapes are made even more important by the variety of complementary greens in the leaves. Notice how the purple adds a zing to the piece.

color schemes in composition

Earlier in the chapter, you learned about different color relationships by studying the color wheel (see pages 86–87). Now put some of those relationships into action.

It is important for the artist to create mood and feeling in a painting. An understanding of the following color schemes will help you avoid color mistakes and give meaning and sensitivity to your compositions.

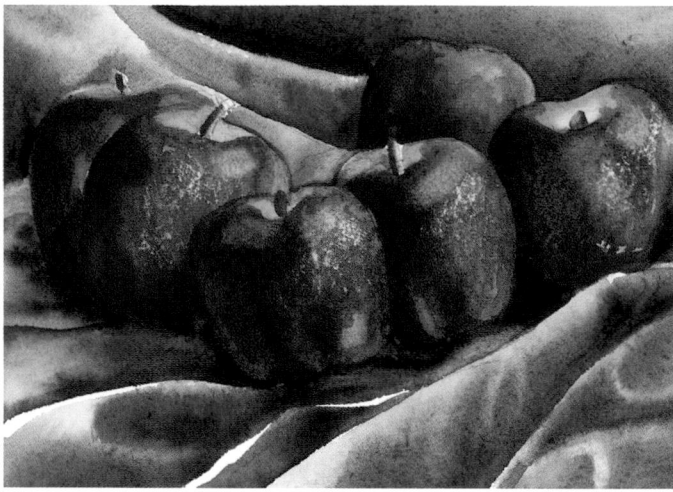

Complementary Colors

Complementary colors create a strong pattern because there is a strong contrast between them as they compete for attention. Here, red dominates because it is brighter and the greens sink into the background because they are dulled by neutrals.

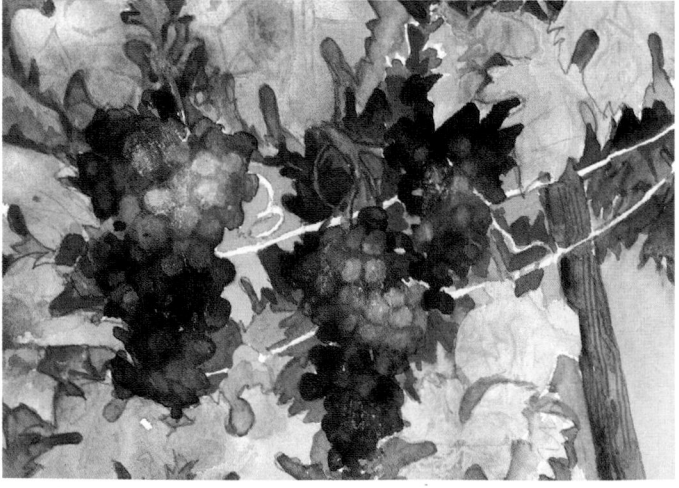

Triadic Colors

Triadic colors are equidistant from each other on the color wheel and form a triangle. Here, a variation of purple, yellow-green and orange is used with a warm netural. Purple dominates because it is the brightest and darkest color, attracting the eye first even though the greens cover more area.

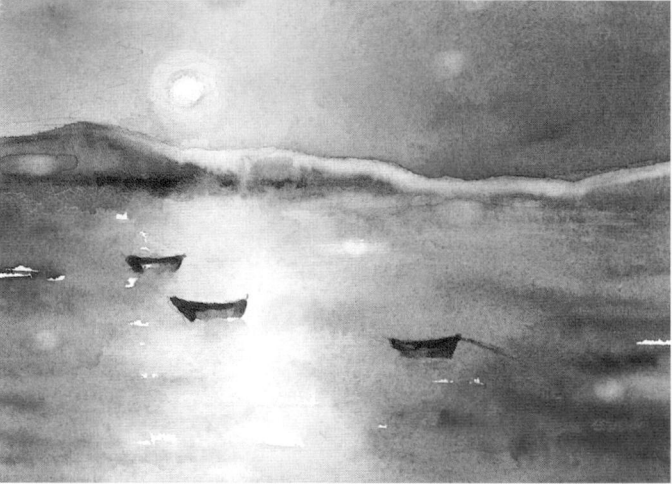

Analogous Colors

Analogous colors are two or three colors next to each other on the color wheel. Varying the degree of intensity of any color will alter the mood. Here, warm colors are used with a warm neutral for the darks. Orange is dominant, yellows are subordinant, while the variation of the hues adds interest. The darkest dark neutrals act as the focal point.

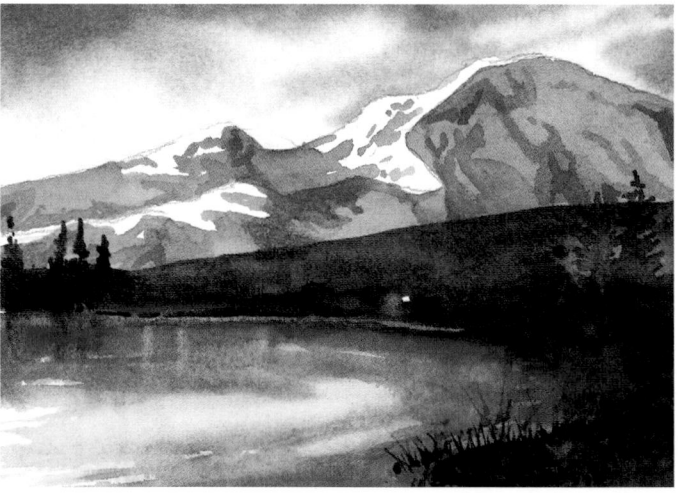

Monochromatic Colors

A monochromatic color scheme uses different values of a single color. With no contrasting or competing colors, the scene can be peaceful. Or, it can be quite powerful if full color intensities are used. Here, blues range from very light to very dark values. Cool neutrals are used for the darkest darks. Using the same blue, but varying the intensity, ensures unity.

analyzing color relativity

Every color is influenced by the colors surrounding it. The following chart features the same blue rectangle in the center of many different colored squares. Even though it's the same blue rectangle, it appears different from one example to the next because of its relationship to the color around it. When placed on top of reds and pinks in the second to last row, the blue rectangle pops forward. When surrounded by varying shades of blue and green, the same blue rectangle sinks into the background. More differences occur in the first and second rows when the blue rectangle is surrounded by yellows and browns. The viewer can sense the difference in value, temperature, mood and dominance in each example.

Understanding color relativity will help you in guiding the viewer's eye around your painting and directly to the focal point.

Helpful Hint NUMBER 21
While flipping through magazines, keep an eye out for interesting design ideas. An advertisment might suddenly strike your eye as especially appealing. Clip it out and save it for future reference. Make a note explaining why it grabbed your attention. Is it an unusual color combination? Is there a beautiful pattern between lights and darks? Collect your favorite examples in a notebook, which can serve as a design lesson book for reference.

Same Blue, Different Backgrounds
Cut out squares of color from magazine advertisements. Put a smaller rectangle of one color on top of each one. Notice how the blue squares in this example seem to change in value, importance and mood in each case.

color splash exercises

The experimental color splash method is a quick and easy way to put colors onto paper. These playful and fun exercises will help you to understand how colors relate to one another. Also, you'll learn how color placement, combined with different brushstrokes, can affect the sense of mood, rhythm and speed in your compositions.

Make small, quick statements with wet paint and large brushes (a no. 10 or 12 round) on Arches 140-lb. (300gsm) cold-pressed paper. Don't concern yourself with detail or subject matter. Instead, concentrate on what happens as colors merge and blend together depending upon how you apply them. Bright, strong colors denote energy and power, and the abrupt, disjointed movements of your brush can enhance this feeling. Use softer, loose color and brushstrokes to create serenity and calmness. Experiment to see what you can discover about the exciting nature of color.

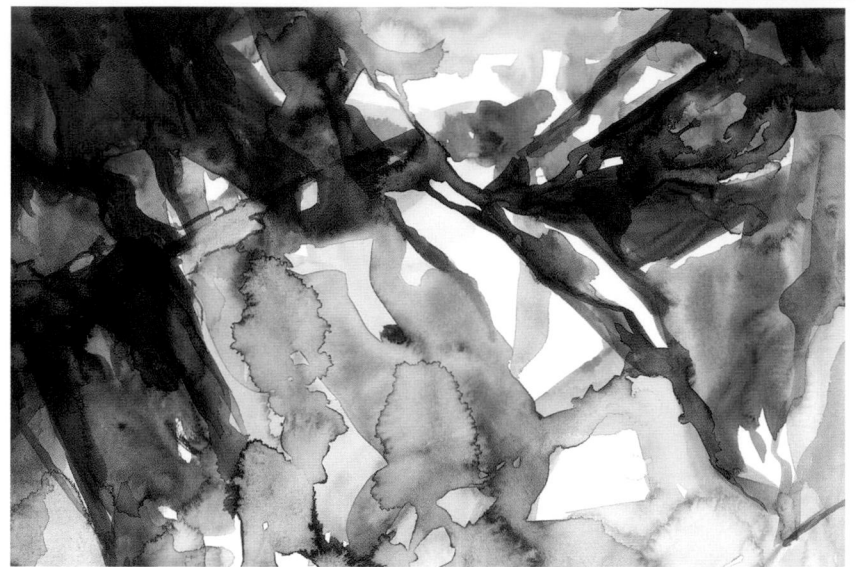

Comparison: Fast Tempo
Make a small color splash study using bright primary colors (blue, red and yellow) on a diagonal structure to show energy and fast tempo.

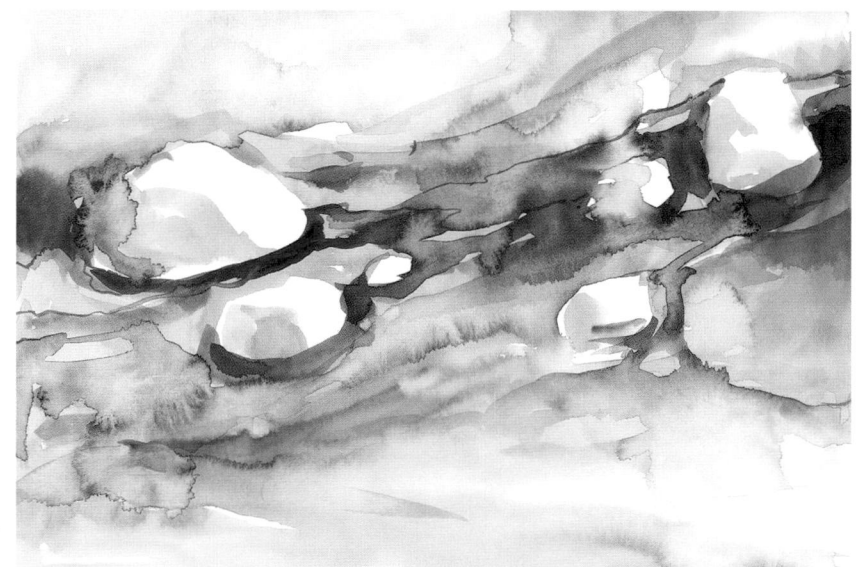

Comparison: Calm Tempo
Make another sample using the same colors diluted and mixed as neutrals on a horizontal plane to show calmness. Primaries mixed together create soft browns and grays that play a neutral role in unifying the sections of a painting. If you add more water, they become even softer.

Helpful Hint NUMBER 22

Don't try to paint like someone else. There is no "right" way to paint. Each artist is unique.

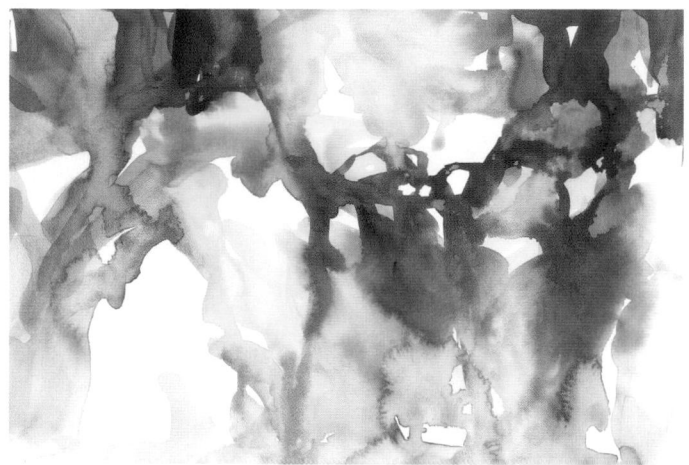

Comparison: Vibrancy

Make a color splash sample choosing three variations of the primaries that are bright and dark in value. The result is a strong and commanding statement.

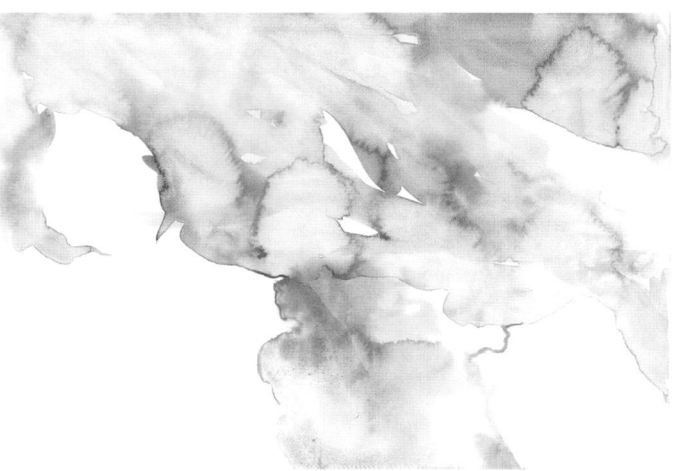

Comparison: Dullness

Use the same colors, mixed as neutrals and diluted, to create a different mood reflecting a gentler and duller feeling.

Comparison: Opposition

Choose three colors that clash. The example uses purple, green and orange. These triadic colors clash placed next to each other on the format and their values are equally intense. To create a more harmonious balance, one color must dominate in size, intensity or value. The other colors would play subordinant roles.

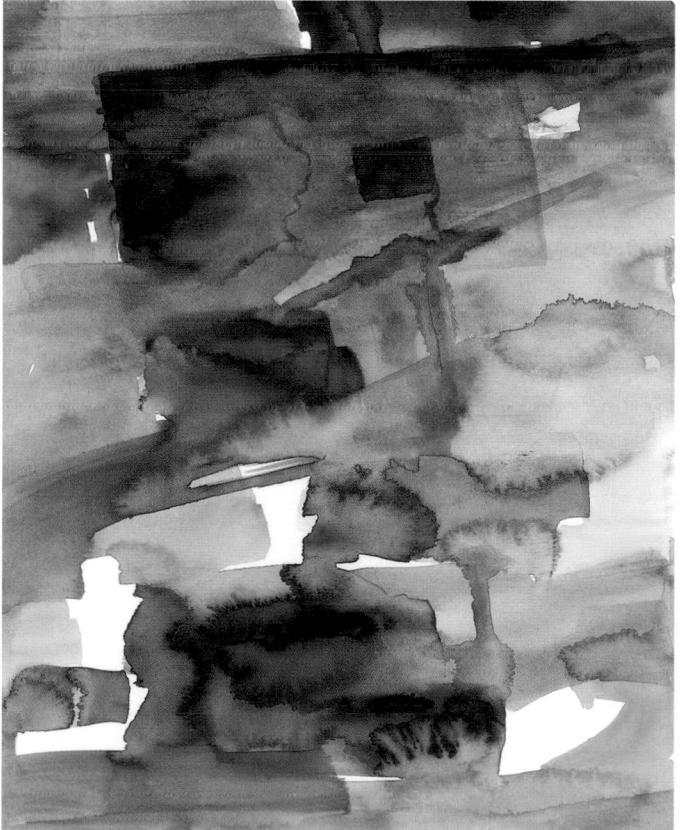

Comparison: Unity

Using the same colors, find unity by blending each color into its neighbor. In this example, the purple is dominant and the colors are more blended.

Value refers to the lightness and darkness of a color. Value forms the pattern in your painting and creates the mood or emphasis. Think of it as the strength or intensity of your colors. A "high key" painting is one with mostly light values and a "low key" painting has mostly dark values. Strong paintings have an entire range of values from the lightest lights to the darkest darks. A strong value pattern is even more important than the most beautiful color arrangements or the most advanced mastery of the techniques because the value pattern will almost always attract the viewer's eye before anything else. It is the balancing of the lights and darks and their relationships to one another that creates spatial dimensions, depth, contrast, volume and strength.

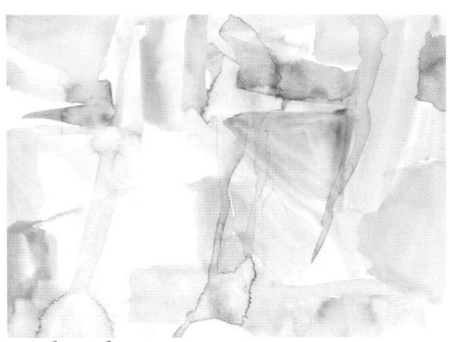

High Values
Make a small color splash in three different colors, using very light tones or "high key" values. The result is a soft and delicate statement.

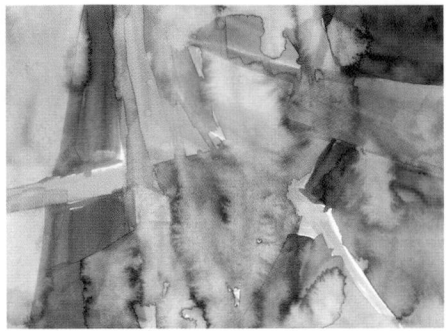

Medium Values
Using the same colors, make a similar color splash in medium values. There is more body and strength in this example.

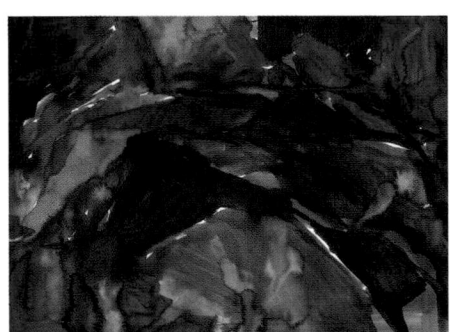

Low Values
Make another color splash, this time in all dark, or "low key," values. Notice how using the same colors at their fullest intensity creates a very commanding and powerful result.

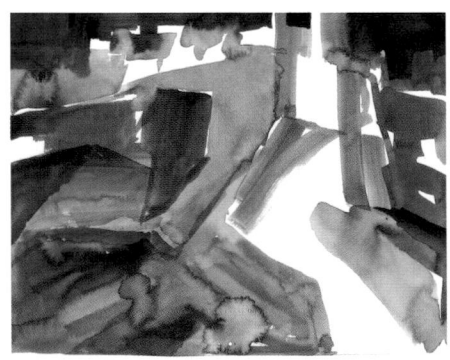

Create Eye Flow
Make a "low key" sample in all dark values, leaving a pathway of connected lights that allows the viewer's eye to travel around the picture.

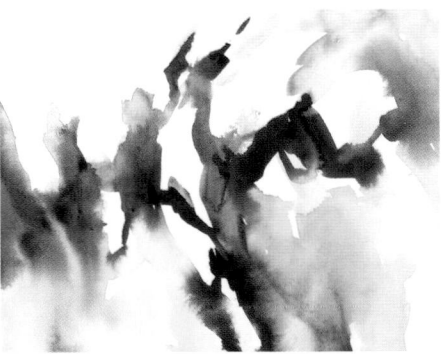

Emphasize Dark Values
Make a small study of pale pastels in the background. Charge in darks to show off the dark values.

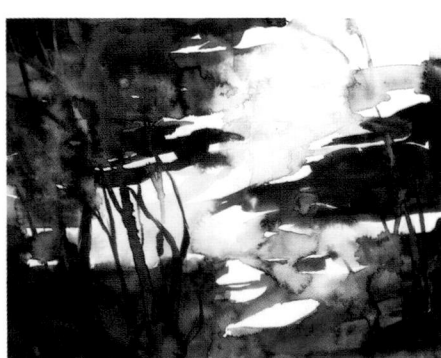

Emphasize Light Values
Make another small study of the darkest dark shapes, reserving traveling lights to show off the light values.

using value

A *value ratio* is one of the most important things that affects the success or failure of a painting. By using a combination of intuitive and intellectual choices, we can arrange a pleasing design. It is almost natural for us to decide not to put all the darks on one side of a painting and all the lights on the other—that would just "feel" uncomfortable.

Using a value ratio according to the composition principles, you create the underling abstract structure upon which your painting is based. The success of your painting depends on it.

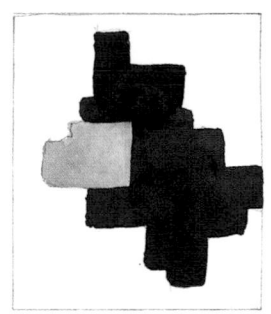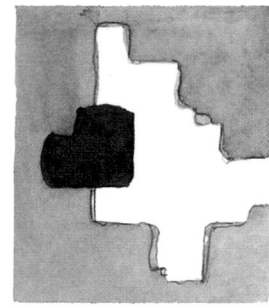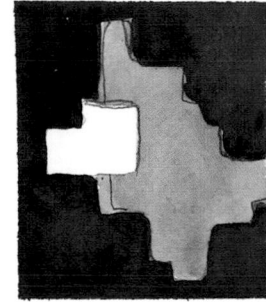

Value Exercise
Use three shapes: small, medium and large. Use three values: light, medium and dark. Make three different combinations. Notice how the "mood" (or emotional tone) varies from one example to the other. Keep this concept of value in mind when you plan a more complex painting. It will help you establish the mood you seek.

Lightest lights	Mid-tones	Darkest darks

Value Bar

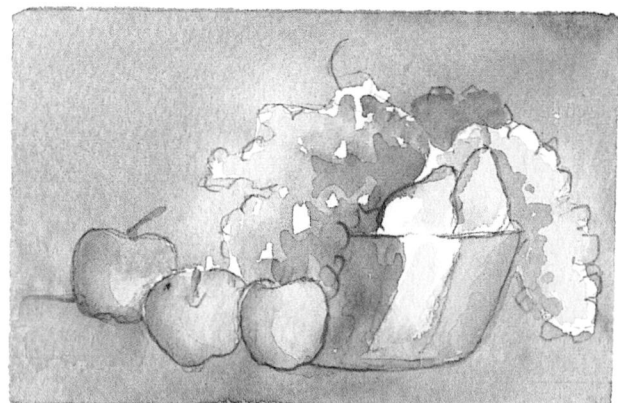

Comparison: Boring Value Pattern
This painting uses only mid-tones. It has only flat surfaces and shallow spaces.

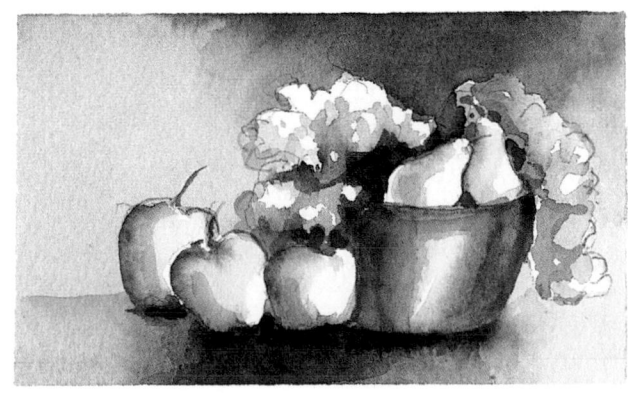

Comparison: Interesting Value Pattern
This painting uses the full range of values. As a result, the forms are manipulated to move forward and sink backward, giving the painting dimension, richness and depth.

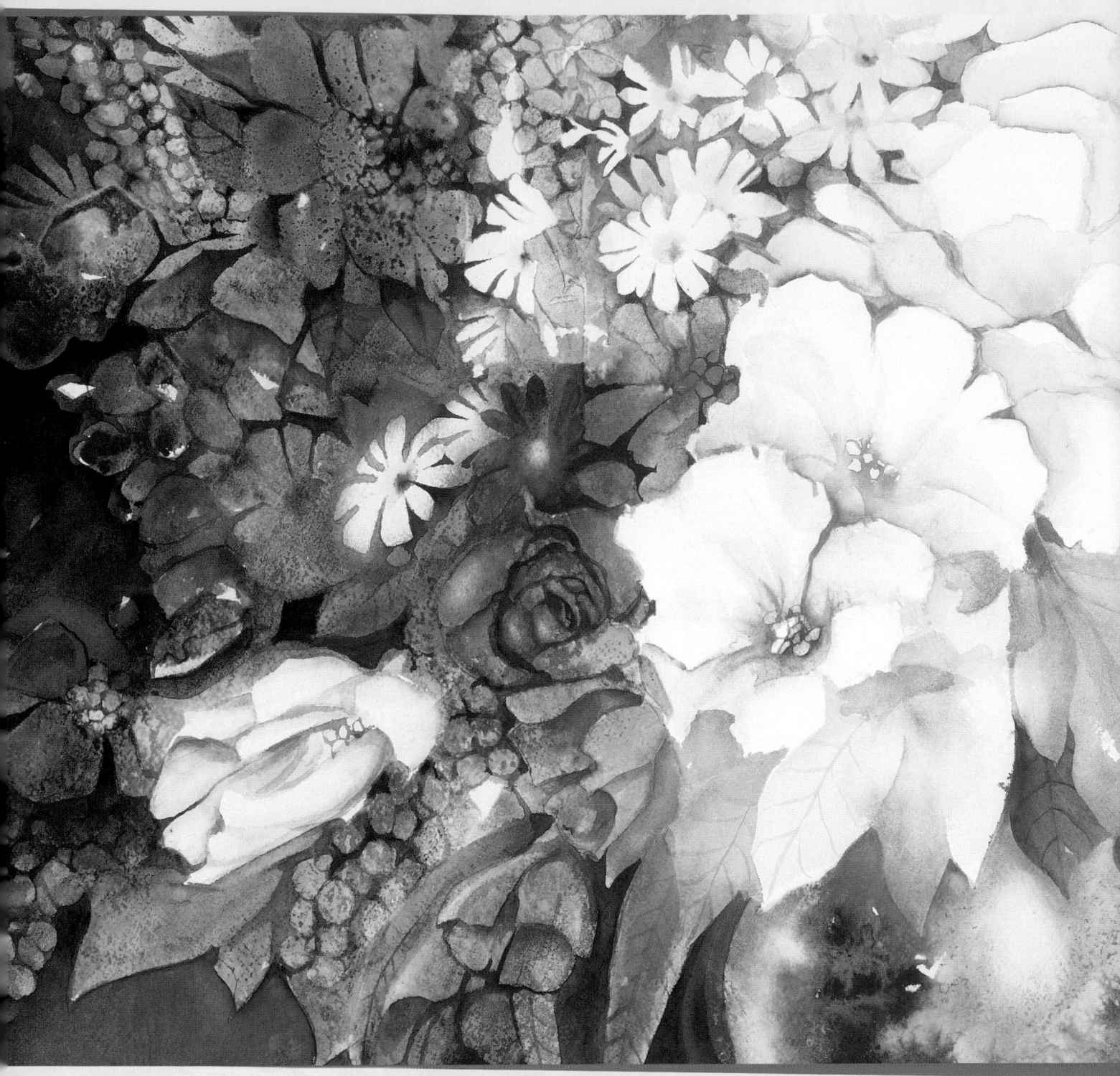

Angelique
15" × 22" (38cm × 56cm)

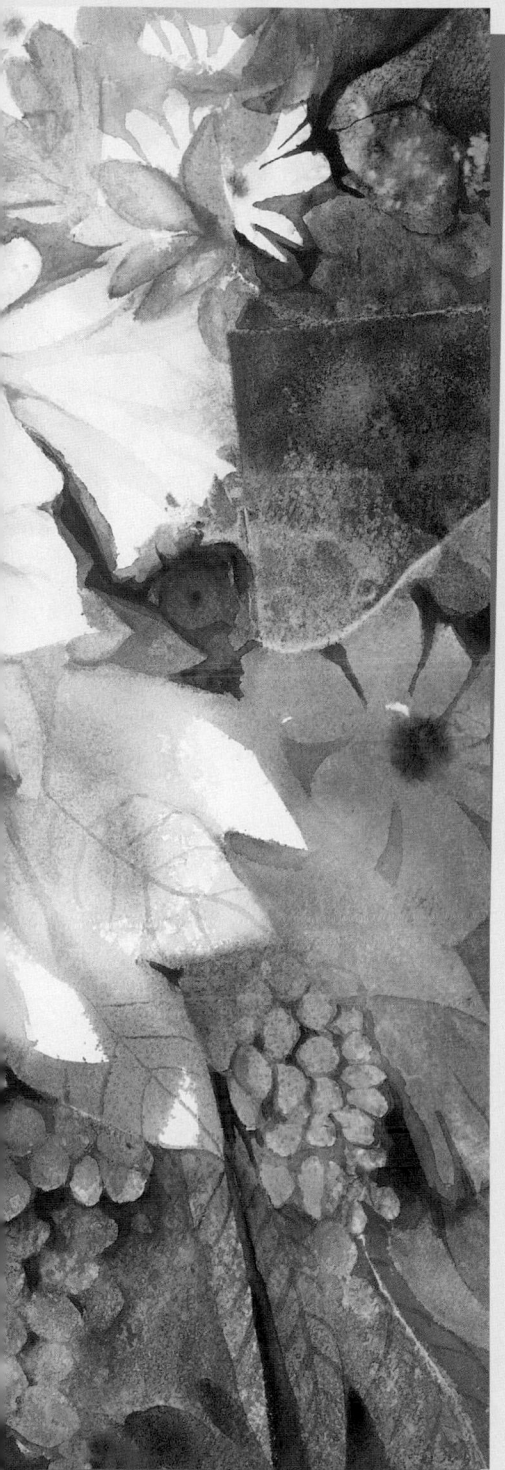

 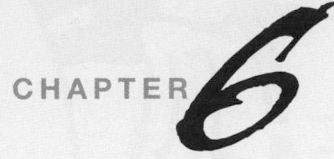

painting demonstrations for captivating creativity

IN THIS CHAPTER YOU WILL FIND BASIC, INTERMEDIATE AND more complex, larger painting demonstrations that combine techniques so that you can practice the knowledge and skills you gained in the previous chapters. You will be working on both wet and dry paper, as well as on Oriental paper. Also, you will be working with different concepts such as negative painting, glazing, rubbing out, layering and edge control. This chapter references a variety of materials, including masking fluid, drafting tape, salt and many more "tricks of the trade." If you prefer, practice on small sheets of paper, doing only some of the instructions. Or tackle the complete, step-by-step demonstrations to create finished paintings.

You can do these exercises over and over again, using different combinations of color, paper and technique. Try combining some of the lessons described in one demonstration with those in another. The possibilities are as limitless as your desire, drive and imagination. Soon you will be creating exciting, innovative expressions that reflect you and you alone. The goal is to learn new ways of painting, to build your repertoire of skills, and to have fun doing the exercises.

Paint an Apple Using Masking Fluid

Bright red. Crisp. Crunchy. This demonstration will show you the techniques to paint these adjectives to describe the surface of a beautiful, red apple.

MATERIALS LIST

BRUSHES
No. 8 round

No. 2 detail

WATERCOLORS
Grumbacher: Alizarin Crimson, Cadmium Red, Cadmium Yellow, Thalo Yellow Green, Thio Violet

Winsor & Newton: Winsor Red

SURFACE
140-lb. (300gsm) Arches cold-pressed paper

ADDITIONAL SUPPLIES
Eraser, masking fluid, pencil, Plexiglas, stiff bristle brush, toothbrush

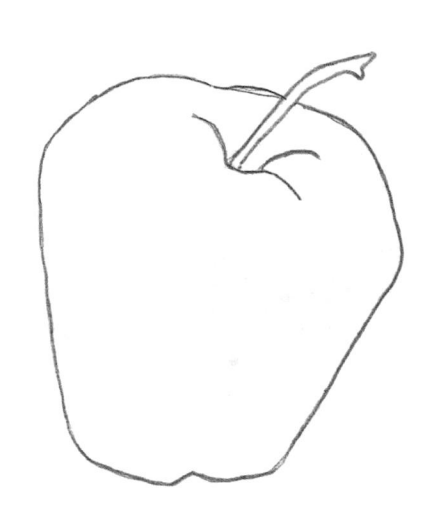

1 **Draw the General Form**
With the pencil, lightly draw the general apple form on watercolor paper and spatter masking fluid with the toothbrush. Let dry.

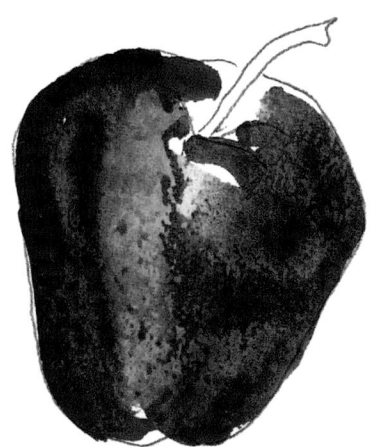

2 **Add Colors and Plexiglas**
Using the no. 8 round, run together washes of Cadmium Red, Winsor Red, Alizarin Crimson and Thio Violet. Press Plexiglas into the wet paint for texture. Weigh it down until it is dry.

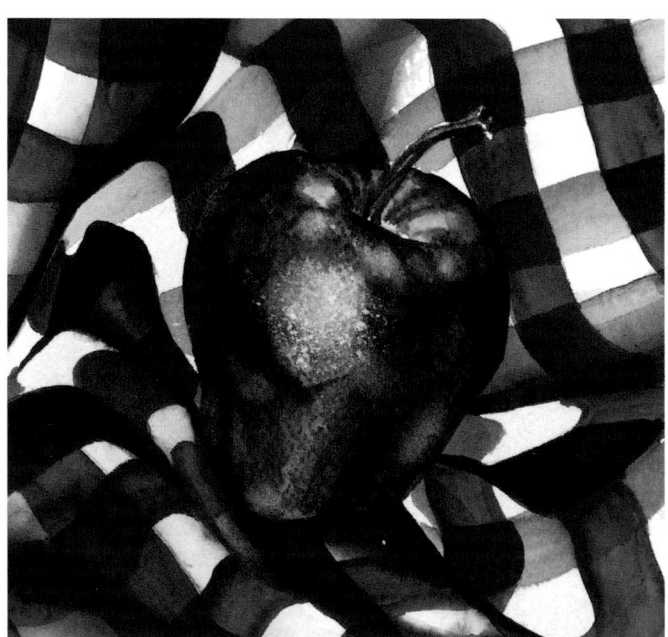

3 **Apply Finishing Touches**
Lift the Plexiglas and add washes of Cadmium Yellow and Thalo Yellow Green. When dry, use your bristle brush to rub out highlights and erase the masking fluid. Add hints of lines, stems and other details with the no. 2 detail. A red, plaid napkin serves as a background.

Paint Peaches Using Wet-Into-Wet

Soft. Fuzzy. Delicate matte hues. You will learn to paint these words in this demonstration by using opaque colors, layering with wet-into-wet and employing the rubbing out technique.

MATERIALS LIST

BRUSHES
No. 8 round

No. 2 detail

WATERCOLORS
Grumbacher: Alizarin Crimson, Cadmium Orange, Chinese White, Indian Red, Thio Violet

Winsor & Newton: Naples Yellow

SURFACE
140-lb. (300gsm) Arches cold-pressed paper

ADDITIONAL SUPPLIES
Pencil, stiff bristle brush

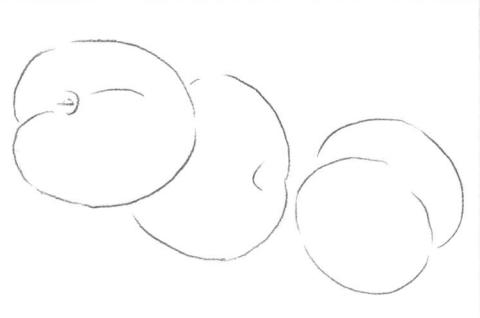

1 Draw the General Shapes
With a pencil, lightly draw circular shapes onto your watercolor paper for the placement of the peaches.

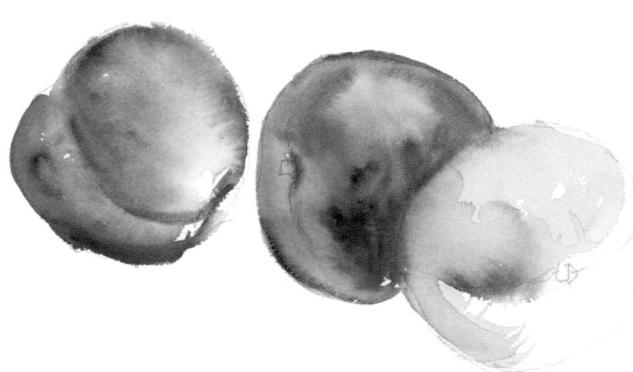

2 Add Colors
Cover the peach shapes with a fairly thick wash of Naples Yellow using the no. 8 round. Then, surround the shapes at the edges with Cadmium Orange. Add splashes of Indian Red and Alizarin Crimson by dropping in paint and letting it bleed into the other colors to give the peaches a fuzzy effect. Let dry.

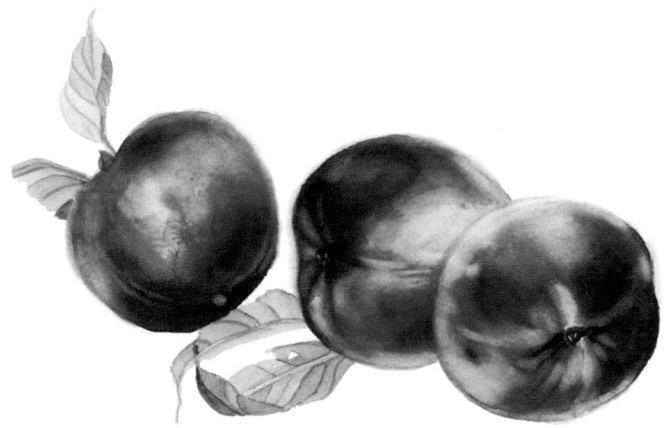

3 Apply Finishing Touches
Add Thio Violet for the darks and shadow areas. Gently rub the edges with your bristle brush to soften. Add Chinese White to the highlights to make them look soft instead of shiny. Add stems with the no. 2 detail brush.

Paint Pears Using Blended Colors

Granular. Slightly bruised. Pitted. In this demonstration you will learn how to describe the surface texture of pears with the use of paint, various brushstrokes and texturing devices.

MATERIALS LIST

BRUSHES
No. 8 round
No. 2 detail

COLORS
Grumbacher: Indian Red, Raw Umber, Sap Green, Thio Violet, Yellow Ochre
Holbein: Opera
Sennelier: Brown Pink
Winsor & Newton: Naples Yellow

SURFACE
140-lb. (300gsm) Arches cold-pressed

ADDITIONAL SUPPLIES
Pencil, Plexiglas, stiff bristle brush

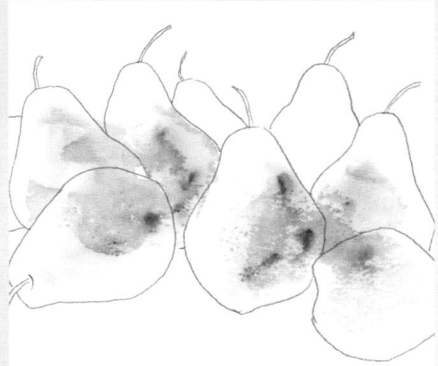

1 **Draw the General Shapes**
After drawing the pear shapes on your paper with a pencil, spread Brown Pink into the center of each pear and dot with Raw Umber using the no. 8 round. (A mixture of Sap Green and Yellow Ochre is a good substitute for Brown Pink.) Lay Plexiglas into the wet paint and let dry.

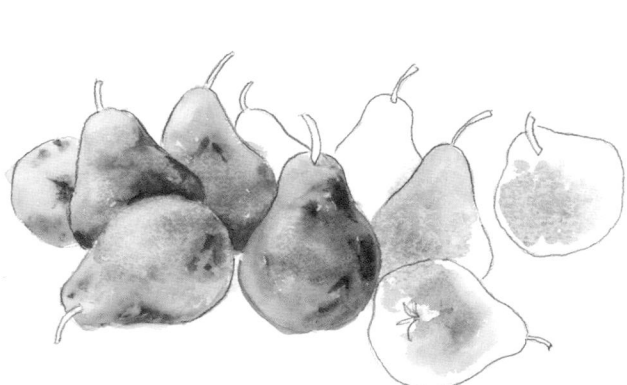

2 **Add Colors**
Remove the Plexiglas. Add Naples Yellow around the edges of the pears and blend into the center of each form with the no. 8 round. While wet, add touches of Indian Red, Opera, Sap Green and Yellow Ochre. For the shadows add a hint of Thio Violet.

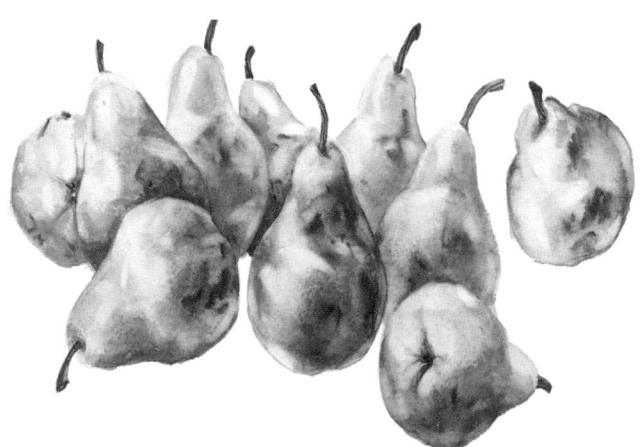

3 **Apply Finishing Touches**
Rub out highlights with your bristle brush and add stems and bruise markings with Raw Umber using the no. 2 detail.

Paint Grapes Using Tissue Paper

Moist. Mottled. Dewy. You will learn to paint these descriptive words by using color, texturing devices, glazing and painting positively and negatively.

MATERIALS LIST

BRUSHES
No. 8 round

No. 2 detail

WATERCOLORS
Da Vinci: Permanent Rose
Grumbacher: Burnt Sienna, Indian Red, Sap Green, Thalo Yellow Green, Thio Violet, Yellow Ochre

SURFACE
140-lb. (300gsm) Arches cold-pressed paper

ADDITIONAL SUPPLIES
Bristle brush, pencil, Plexiglas, sandpaper, tissue paper

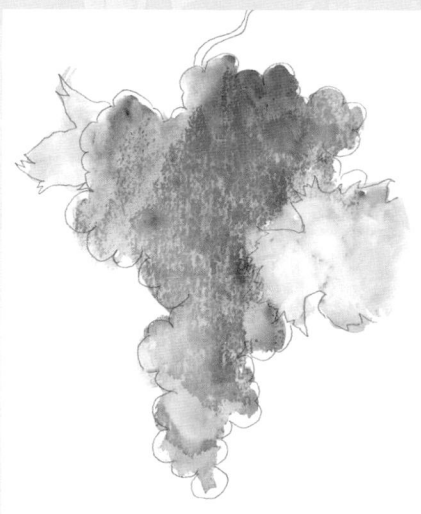

1 Draw the Forms, Add Color
Draw the grape forms (clusters, not individual grapes) and leaf shapes with a pencil. Using the no. 8 round, cover the grapes with washes of Indian Red, Burnt Sienna, Permanent Rose and Thio Violet, and wash Sap Green, Thalo Yellow Green and Yellow Ochre in the leaf areas. Blend the colors by tipping the page. Press Plexiglas on top of the grapes and crumpled tissue onto the leaves for texture. Let dry.

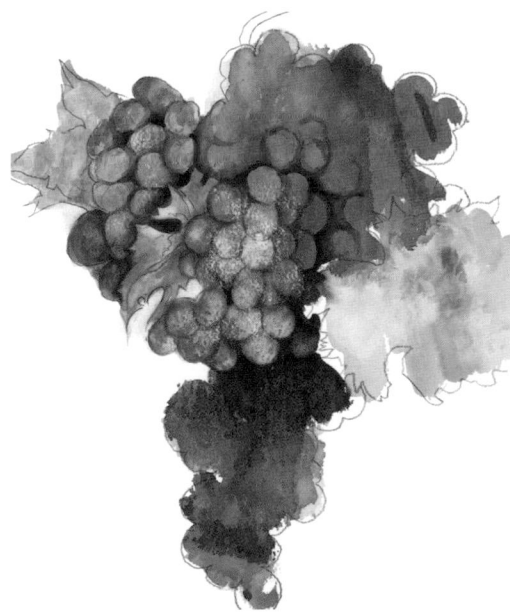

2 Paint Positively and Negatively
Remove the tissue paper and Plexiglas. Deepen the colors with another glaze, painting both positively and negatively. Develop clusters and darken by painting negatively. Paint sections and reapply Plexiglas as needed. Paint, lift and repaint for your desired result. Use sandpaper and the bristle brush to rub out paint and create texture.

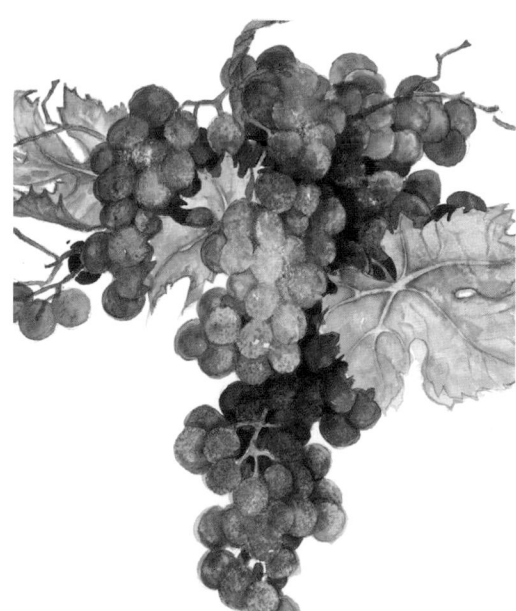

3 Apply Finishing Touches
Add the final details of stems and leaf veins by lifting paint and using the no. 2 detail.

Watercolor on Top of a Latex Ground

This is the first of five full demonstrations that move through a series of steps, from the planning stages to the final painting. Sometimes it's hard to visualize how we can start with a vague idea and eventually end with a completed composition. It can be a daunting prospect, but by taking one small step at a time the process becomes more manageable.

Here is a good exercise for reclaiming paper from a previously failed painting. The best part of this demonstration, though, is that it allows you to be daring—you can rub out any mistakes and start over at any time. For a similar effect, try gesso instead of acrylic latex.

MATERIALS LIST

BRUSHES
Nos. 4, 8 and 14 rounds

1-inch (25mm) and 2-inch (51mm) flats

COLORS
Grumbacher: Burnt Umber, Raw Umber, Sap Green, Yellow Ochre

Winsor & Newton: Brown Madder, Indigo

SURFACE
22" × 30" (56cm × 76cm) sheet 140-lb. (300gsm) Arches cold-pressed paper

ADDITIONAL SUPPLIES
Cardboard, gesso, off-white acrylic latex paint, pencil, scrubber brush

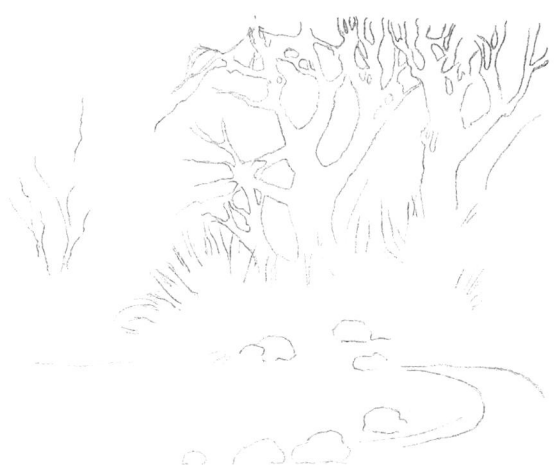

1 Prep the Surface and Identify the Subject
With the large 2-inch (51mm) flat, cover the entire paper with acrylic latex paint in sweeping strokes and various directions. Generously apply thick paint so brushstrokes show. Add drips, dribbles and spatter for background texture. Lightly scrape over the top of some droplets with a piece of cardboard to flatten them. Leave small patches of paper showing through to fully absorb the watercolor. After the background has dried, use a pencil to loosely draw in the general tree forms, branches, grasses and rocks. Nothing should be rigidly planned at this point. Everything will change several times during the painting process.

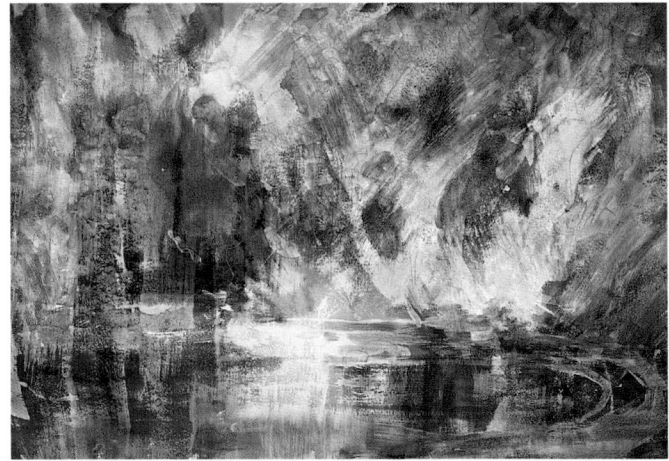

2 Add the First Layer of Color
Load the 2-inch (51mm) flat with a mixture of Sap Green and Yellow Ochre, the 1-inch (25mm) flat with Indigo, and the no. 14 round with Brown Madder. Starting at the top left corner, drop the colors into each other with quick, loose strokes. Use sweeping strokes in all directions, alternating colors as necessary. Cover the entire paper and don't worry about runbacks, puddles or hard edges (these can be useful later or changed). Tilt the paper in different directions so the paint blends. The paint will stay on the surface of the paper, so you can manipulate it easily. Let everything dry.

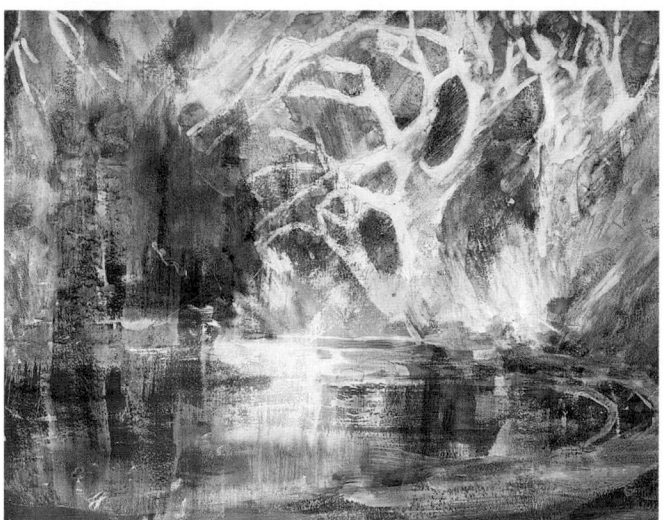

3 Identify the Trees

Begin developing the tree shapes by rubbing out branches and trunks with your scrubber brush. The pencil lines visible through the paint will act as general guidelines. You don't have to be precise or detailed at this point.

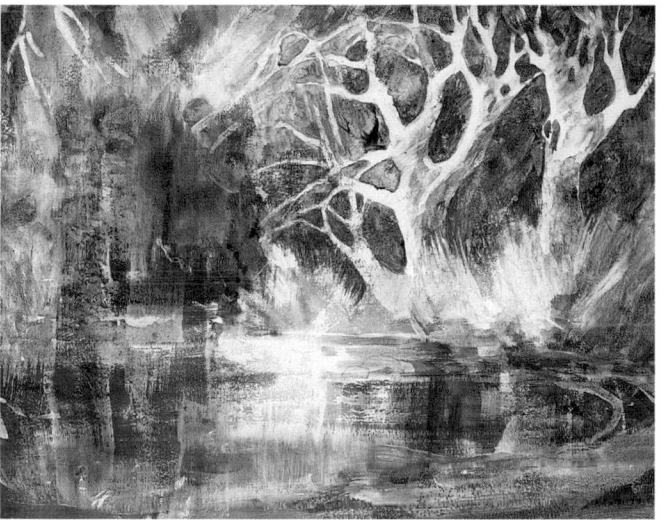

4 Give the Trees Volume

Paint negatively behind and around the tree trunks and branches using the same colors that appear in the background of the area where you are painting. Blend out the far edges with water. This process will slowly bring the trees forward, giving them depth and form, and enriching the background colors.

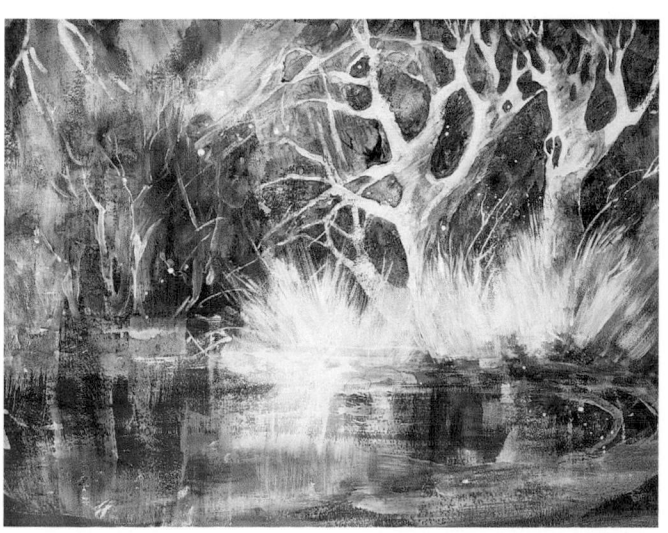

5 Add More Gesso for Detail and Texture

Spread out the bristles on the 1-inch (25mm) flat with your thumb and forefinger, then dip lightly into the gesso. Gently swipe the brush across sections of the painting, such as the grass and parts of the background, to create a scumbled effect. Use the no. 4 round to spatter gesso here and there. Add small branches for detail. Place vague tree shapes in the blue area on the left.

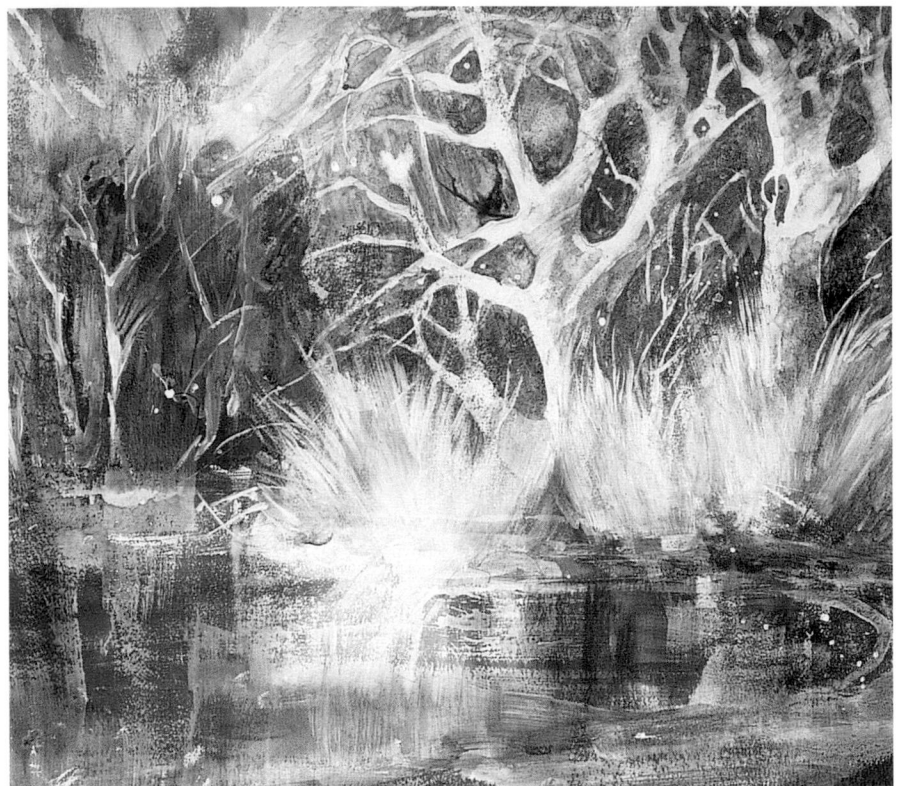

6 Glaze Over the Gesso

When the gesso is dry, paint back into some of the areas such as the grasses and tree branches by glazing over sections using the same colors as before. Add dark twigs and branches for further detail.

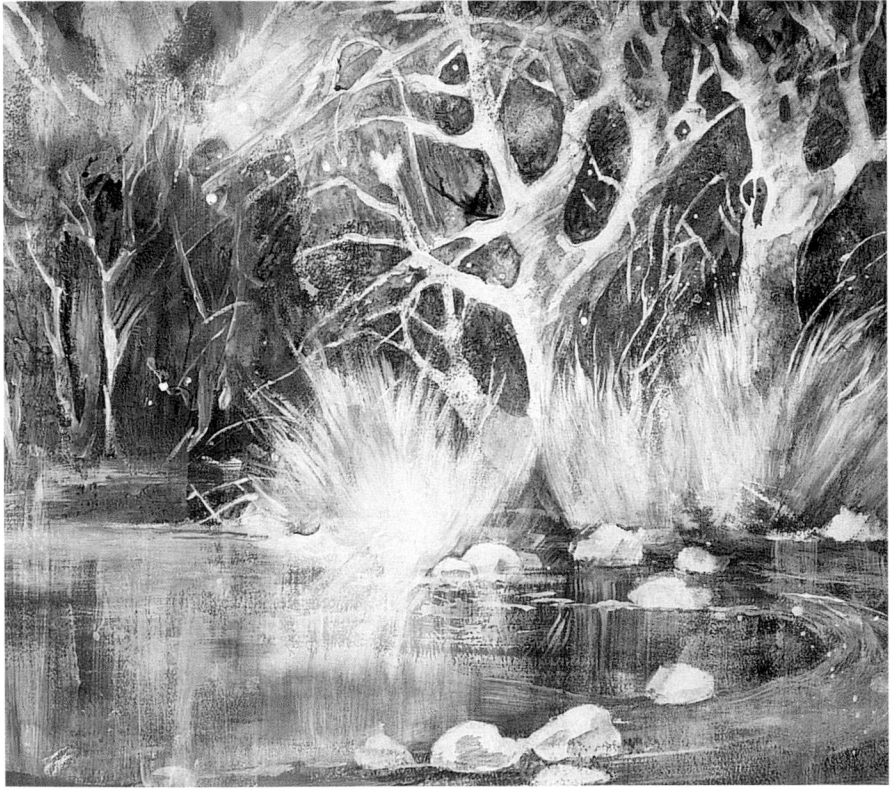

7 Develop the Rocks and Water

Rub out the rock shapes with the scrubber brush. Slant the 1-inch (25mm) flat and scumble lightly over the water in both horizontal and vertical sweeps to create the look of light reflections in the water. Make a curve on the right side of the paper to help draw the viewer's eye into the painting. Glaze over the scumbling with the colors of the water. Work paint into the rocks to help build form. Keep reworking the shapes until they are satisfactory.

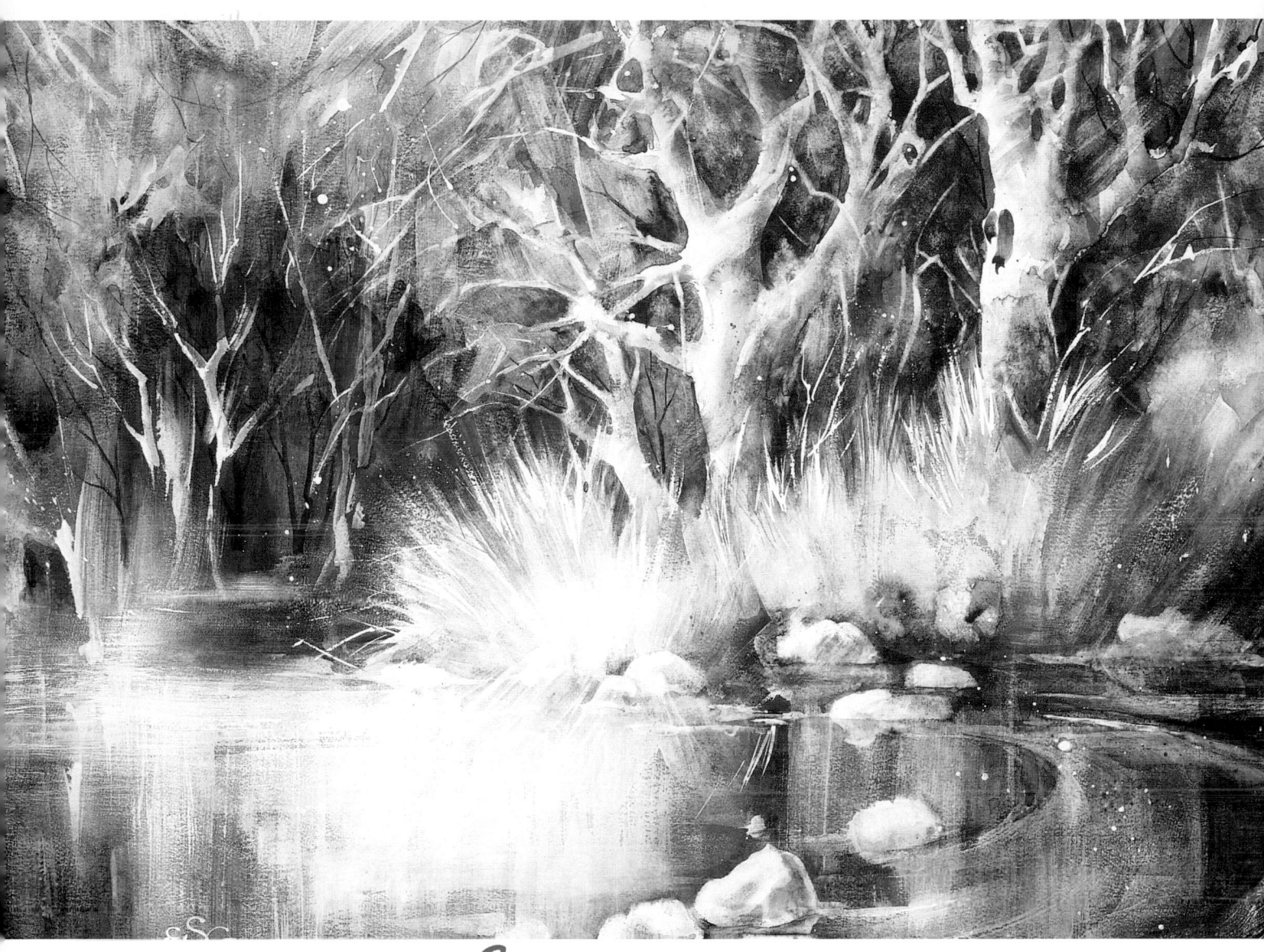

8 Final Version

Continue refining and defining all areas of the painting. Repeat the process of rubbing out, applying gesso and glazing over as many times as you wish to achieve the final effect you want.

November Morning
22" × 30" (56cm × 76cm)

Helpful Hint NUMBER 23

Don't worry about the results. Your picture may not turn out as you hoped. The important thing is to enjoy the process. At the very least, you learn from the experience.

Acrylic Leaf Printing

Printing with leaves is an interesting way to use natural materials to create intriguing patterns using the principles of design and elements of composition. This demonstration allows you to practice the techniques of direct printing, tracing, stenciling, layering and glazing.

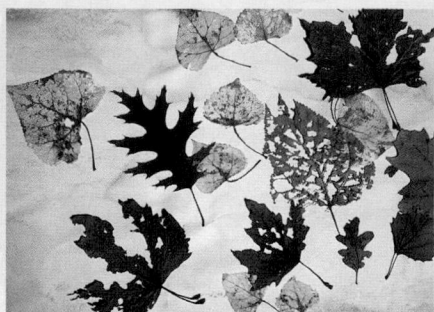

Collect and Press Leaves

In autumn, accumulate fallen leaves of interesting and varied shapes. Over several weeks, dry and press the leaves under weights until they are ready to use as printing material.

MATERIALS LIST

BRUSHES

Nos. 4, 8 and 14 rounds

1-inch (25mm) and 3-inch (76mm) flats

No. 1 detail brush

WATERCOLORS

Daniel Smith: Quinacridone Crimson, Quinacridone Gold

M. Graham & Co.: Cobalt Blue, Dioxazine Purple, Hooker's Green, Thalo Blue, Titanium White

SURFACE

22" × 30" (56cm × 76cm) sheet 140-lb. (300gsm) Arches cold-pressed paper

ADDITIONAL SUPPLIES

Acrylic gloss gel medium, gesso, newspaper, paper towels, pencil, Plexiglas, small hand roller

1 Plan the Format

Make several thumbnail sketches to determine a pleasant flow of dark and light shapes across the page. Choose the most interesting composition and use it as a guide for the next few steps until the design begins to take shape.

2 Prepare the Background

With the 3-inch (76mm) flat, coat the paper with loose, sweeping strokes of gesso to create texture. Let dry. Load several large rounds with different colors. Work across the page, changing colors often and working one color into another. Continue until the entire page is covered. The painting will become darker as layers build up, so this first step can be fairly light. Paint the entire page with a half-and-half mixture of acrylic gloss gel medium and water to even out the luster on the surface.

3 Print the Leaves

Use newspaper as the surface to paint the leaves on. (Allow them to dry after use. Leaves can be used over and over again.) Choose a leaf with an interesting shape and paint one side of it with gesso. To show more veins paint the back of the leaf, or use the front for a smoother effect. Place the wet leaf on the painting (paint side facing down), cover with a paper towel, and then roll over it several times. Lift off the leaf and set it aside. Use the no. 1 detail to fill in the edges and veins to better define the shape. Continue printing across the page, using the general flow of your thumbnail to suggest placement. Choose leaves that vary in size and shape as you progress.

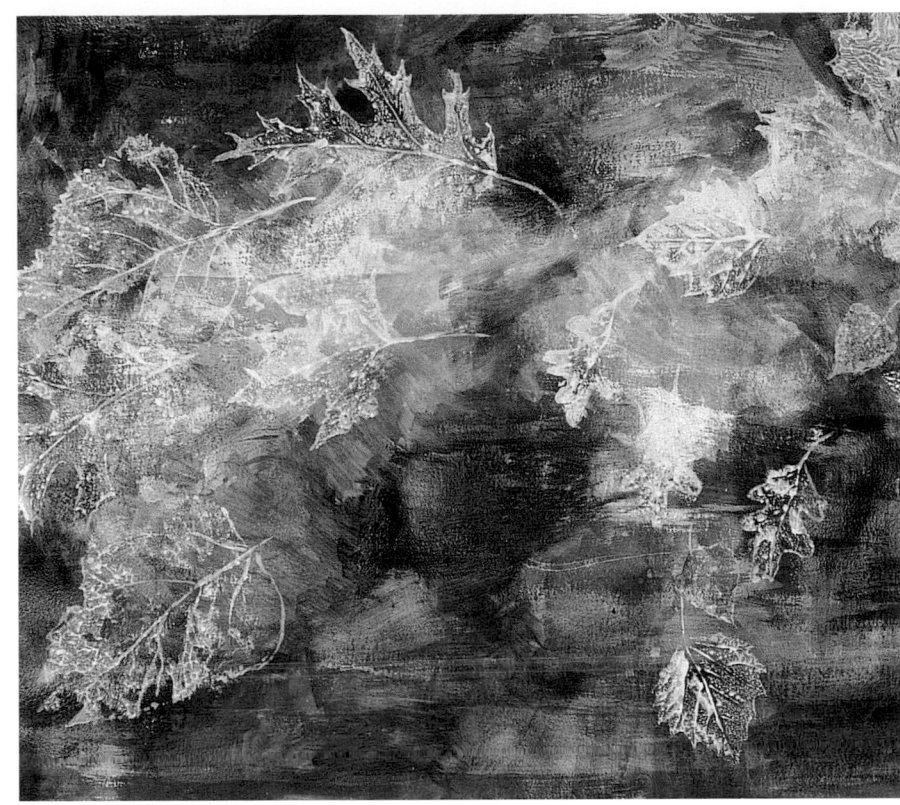

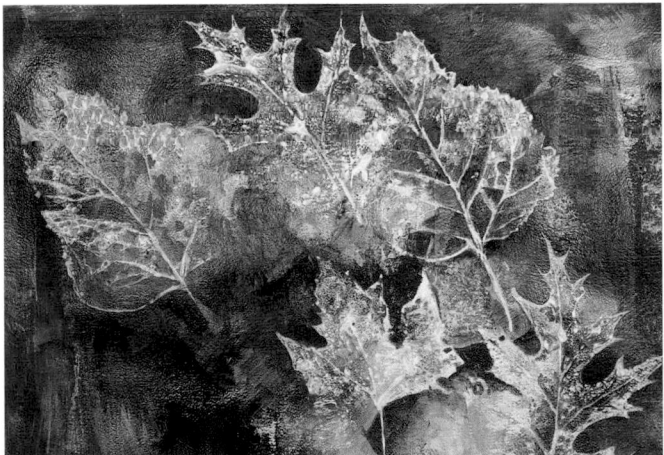

4 Further Identify Shapes

Paint around the outside of the leaf edges with a dark mixture of the color that appears in the background behind where you are working. Blend the far edge into the background with water. Continue around the entire leaf, bringing it into the foreground. Paint into the leaf using the leaf printing process as a guide to the leaf texture. If you cover too much of the pattern, either re-print the leaf or paint a piece of Plexiglas with white acrylic and press it on top of the over-painted area to regain the original texture. Continue around the entire page until your first layer of leaves is complete. When dry, add another coat of the gel medium mixture.

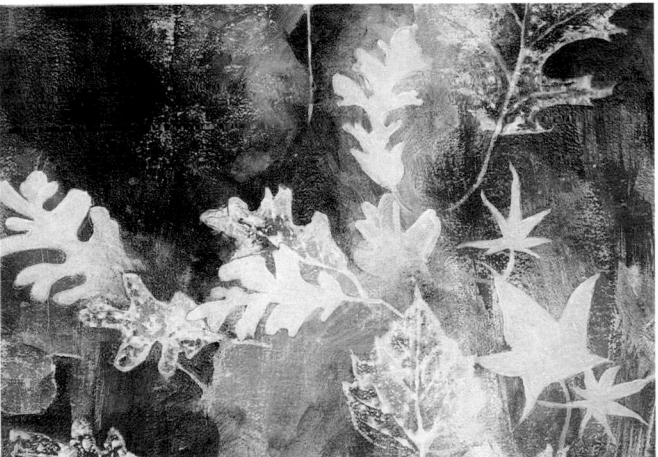

5 Add More Leaves by Tracing

Place several interestingly shaped leaves along the flow of the leaves already printed, filling in gaps and sometimes overlapping other leaves to create a new layer. Trace around the edges of these leaves with pencil and then paint them in with gesso. In some places, soften the edges to blend into the background. Apply a second coat if it doesn't look rich and luminous as it dries.

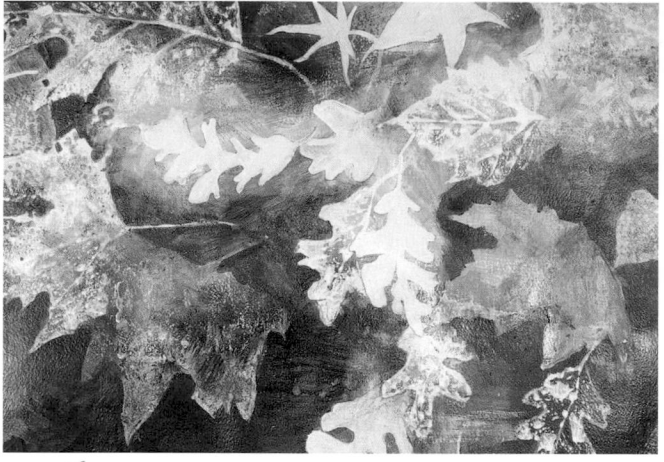

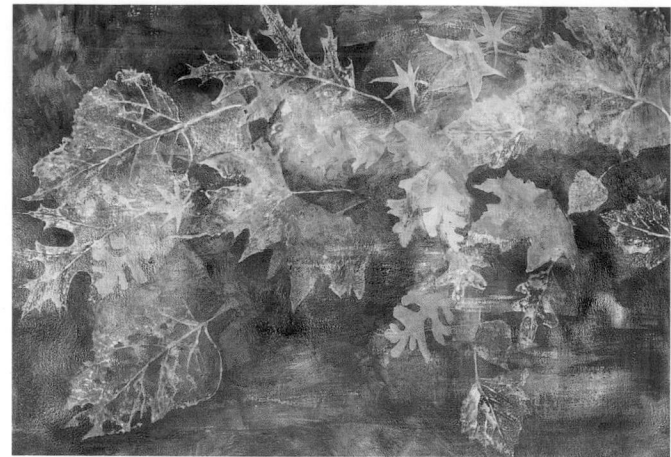

6 Add More Leaves by Stenciling

Place a leaf with an interesting shape on top of the water-color paper where the shape will add to the design of the composition. Paint over the edges of the leaf onto the painting in the same colors as the background behind it, blending the far edge into the background. Continue around all of the edges and then lift the leaf and set it aside. You will have a negative print of the leaf. Some edges will be hard and some will be soft, disappearing into the background. If you want more hard edges, paint into the leaf with gesso and texture by pressing Plexiglas over the newly painted area. Continue filling in the design with this stenciling method until you are pleased with the path of the leaves across the painting.

7 Glaze Over All the Leaves

Make washes of all of the colors you have been using and glaze over the leaves. Use colors that are similar to the background in some areas and colors that contrast in others. For variety, change colors within the leaf. Cover the entire page, blending colors into the background to enrich it. Let everything dry. If you want to add texture or veins and stems, work back into the leaf with gesso and re-glaze when it's dry. When you are satisfied with this initial glazing layer, coat the entire painting with your half-and-half mixture of water and gloss gel medium.

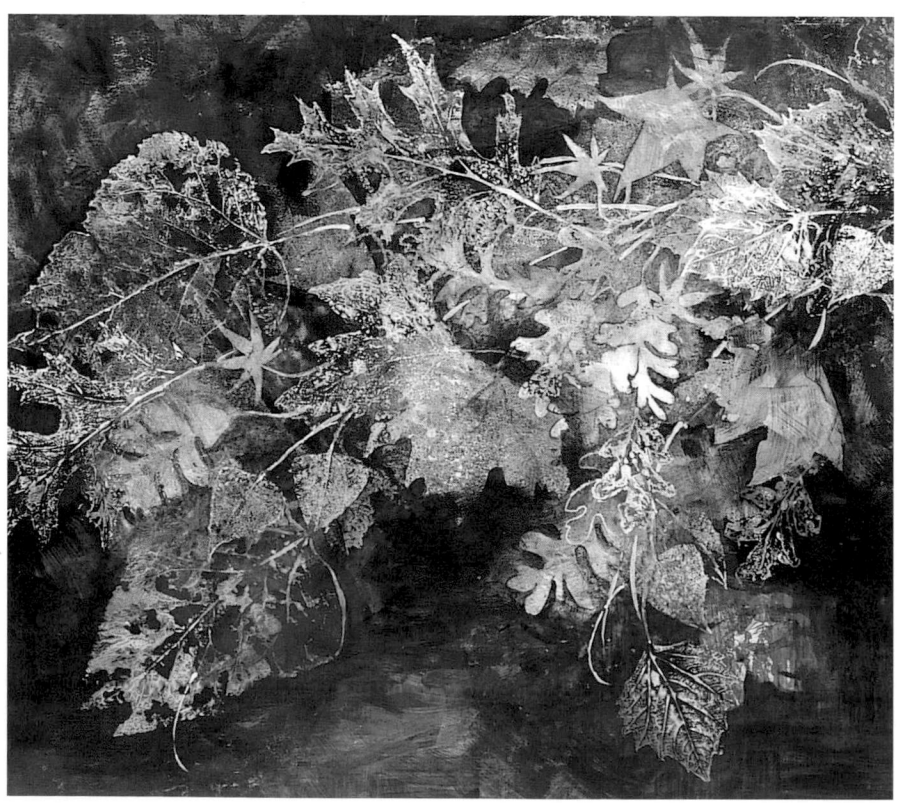

8 Add More Layers

Continue printing, tracing and stenciling leaves, and applying glazes for several more layers. Apply a coat of gloss gel medium every two or three layers. Gradually, the painting will get darker with successive layers. Work until you are pleased with the general design.

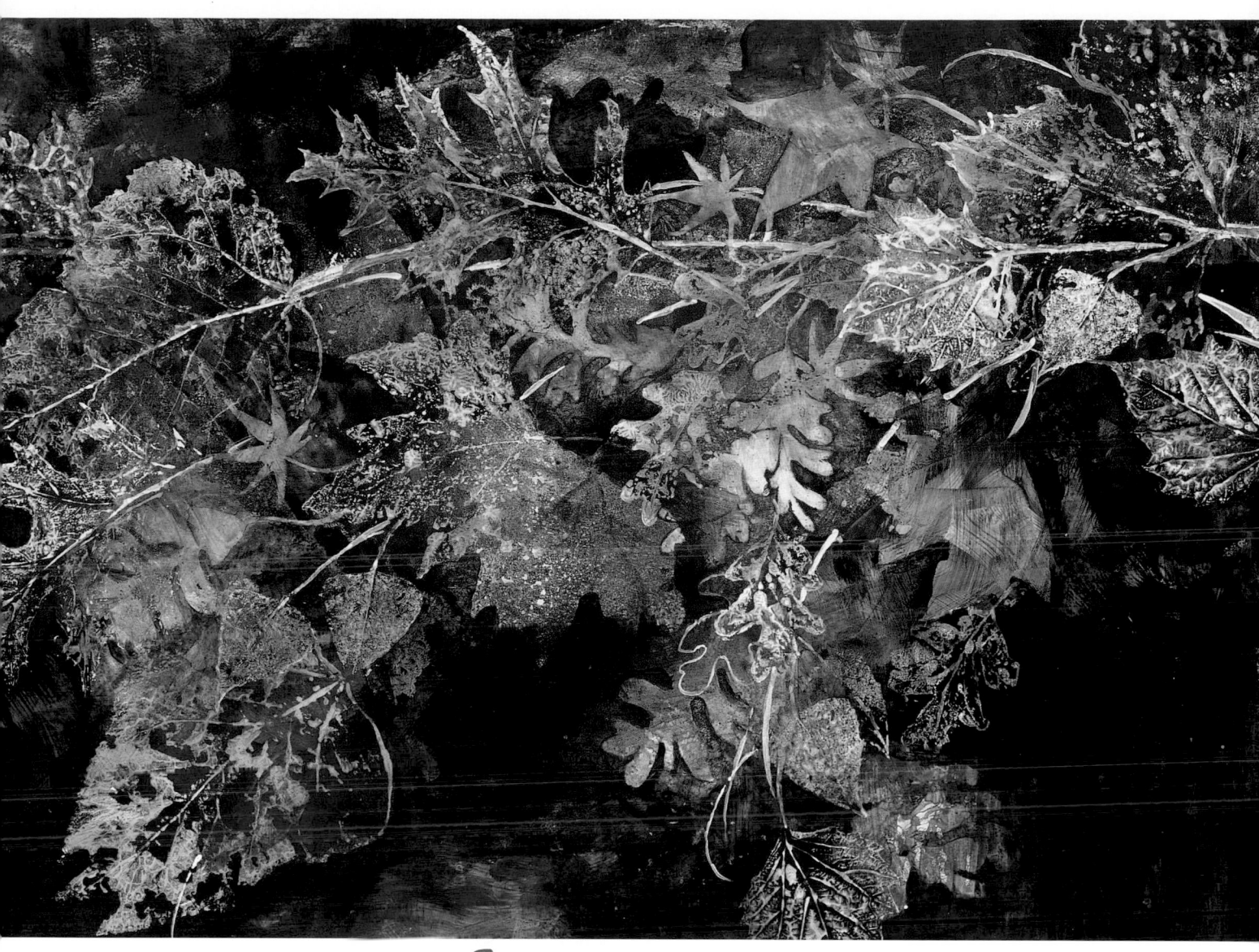

9 The Final Version
Add strength to your horizontal design structure by adding twigs and branches with gesso and glazing until the painting is complete.

Autumn Splendor
22" × 30" (56cm × 76cm)

Helpful Hint NUMBER 24

Unlike the dry, leftover watercolors on your palette that can be reused by adding water, acrylics are unusable when they dry out. If you still have unused paint at quitting time, cover your palette with plastic wrap and freeze it. You can use it during your next painting session after it thaws. Don't forget to thoroughly wash out your brushes. If acrylic paint dries in them they are ruined.

Combining Application Techniques

Sunflowers assume a forlorn look at the end of summer when their heads droop and the large, lush green leaves turn to brown. This is the mood that I tried to capture in *Sad Sarah*, who weeps sunflower seed tears. In this demonstation, you will practice combining several techniques, including glazing, overlapping, dropping in, rubbing out and using Plexiglas. Use these techniques alone or in combinations; you can apply them to any painting.

MATERIALS LIST

BRUSHES
Nos. 8 and 14 rounds

No. 1 detail

WATERCOLORS
Daniel Smith: Quinacridone Gold, Sap Green

Grumbacher: Alizarin Crimson, Burnt Umber, Cadmium Yellow, Raw Sienna, Raw Umber, Van Dyke Brown

Holbein: Opera

SURFACE
22" × 30" (56cm × 76cm) sheet 140-lb. (300gsm) Arches cold-pressed paper

ADDITIONAL MATERIALS
Books (for weight), newsprint, Plexiglas, scrubber brush

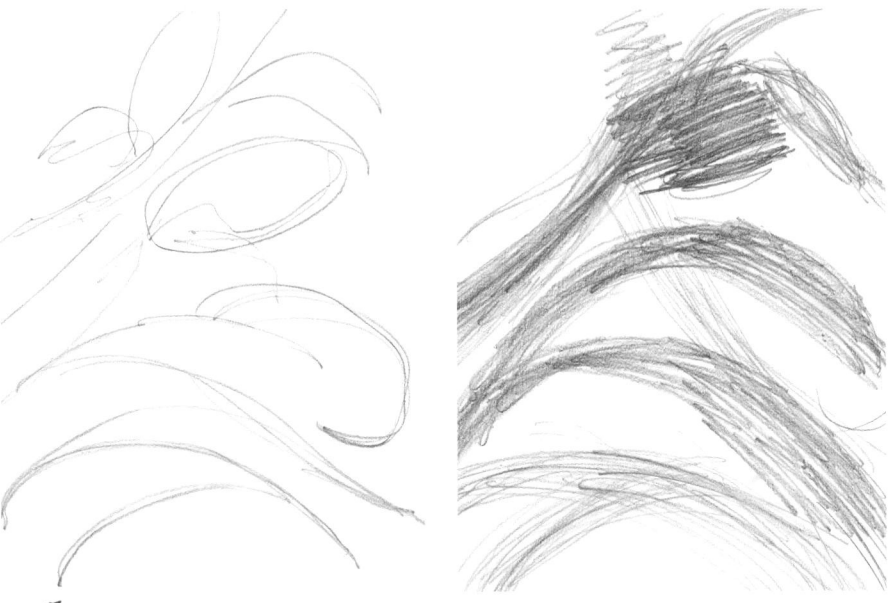

1 **Plan the Format**
Make several rough gesture drawings with loose and swinging lines to determine the general feel of the design structure. In this case, it's a vertical thrust with a pyramidal base. Show movement and counter movement in your drawing. Then draw several similar thumbnails to establish an interesting value pattern.

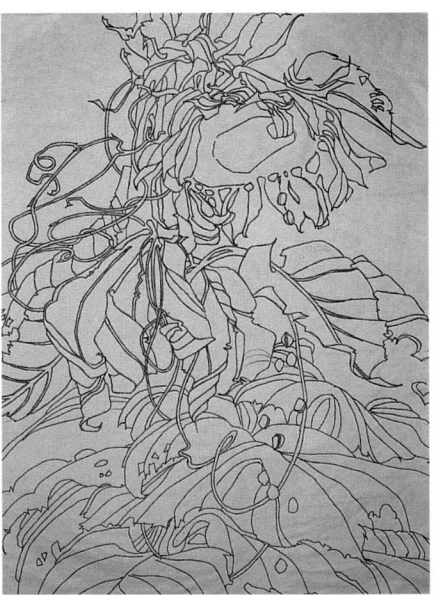

2 **Make a Line Drawing**
Make a detailed line drawing on a sheet of newsprint cut to the same size as the 30" × 22" (76cm × 56cm) watercolor paper. Use lots of twists and swirls to represent the crumbling, curling and drying stems, petals and leaves. Trace your drawing onto the watercolor paper.

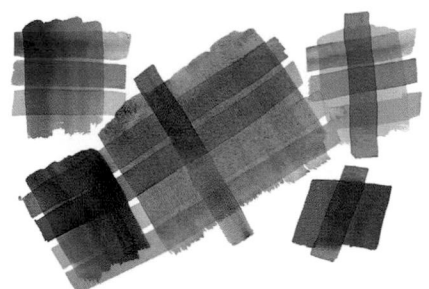

3 Choose the Colors

Make a sample of your glazing colors on another sheet by painting a square of Raw Sienna. When it is dry, paint stripes of other colors such as Sap Green, Opera and Quinacridone Gold over the square. Try other colors to find out which ones you prefer. Transparent colors usually work best.

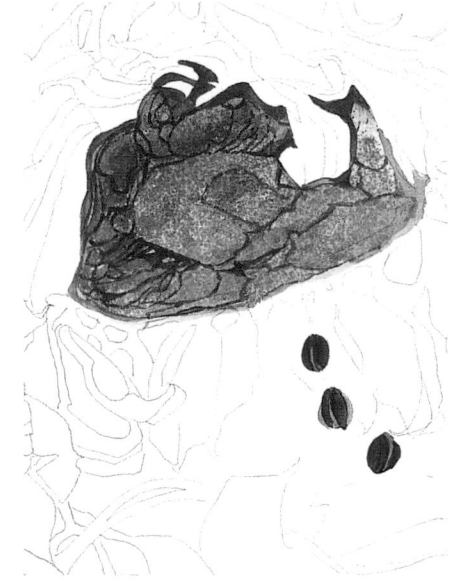

4 Begin the Sunflower's Head

Paint the seed area of the sunflower with Raw Sienna and a little Burnt Umber. While it is wet, press a piece of Plexiglas onto the paint and hold it down with a weight. When it is dry, lift off the Plexiglas to produce a nice texture.

Next, paint seed shapes onto the textured area, outlining them in Burnt Umber. Carry the shapes to the edges bordering the petals. Add Raw Umber in the darkest areas. Glaze some areas lightly with Alizarin Crimson and others with Cadmium Yellow. Don't try to be realistic. Let the texture be your guide.

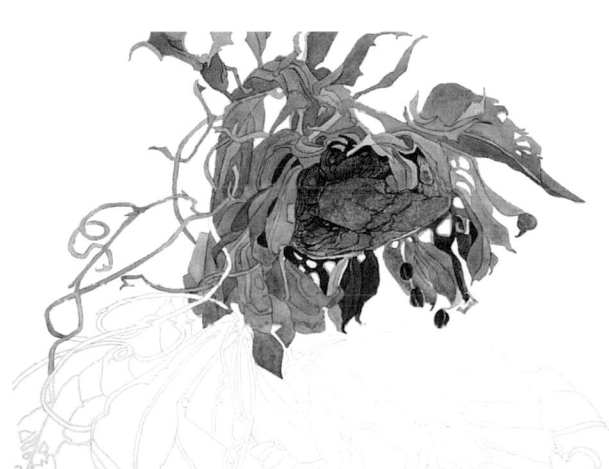

5 Add Surrounding Flowers

Fill in the surrounding petals and leaves with Raw Sienna. Glaze over the leaves with Alizarin Crimson in some places, Cadmium Yellow and Opera in others. The appearance of the flower head will change a little as you make adjustments to balance all the parts of the painting. Later, you may want to add extra petals and stems.

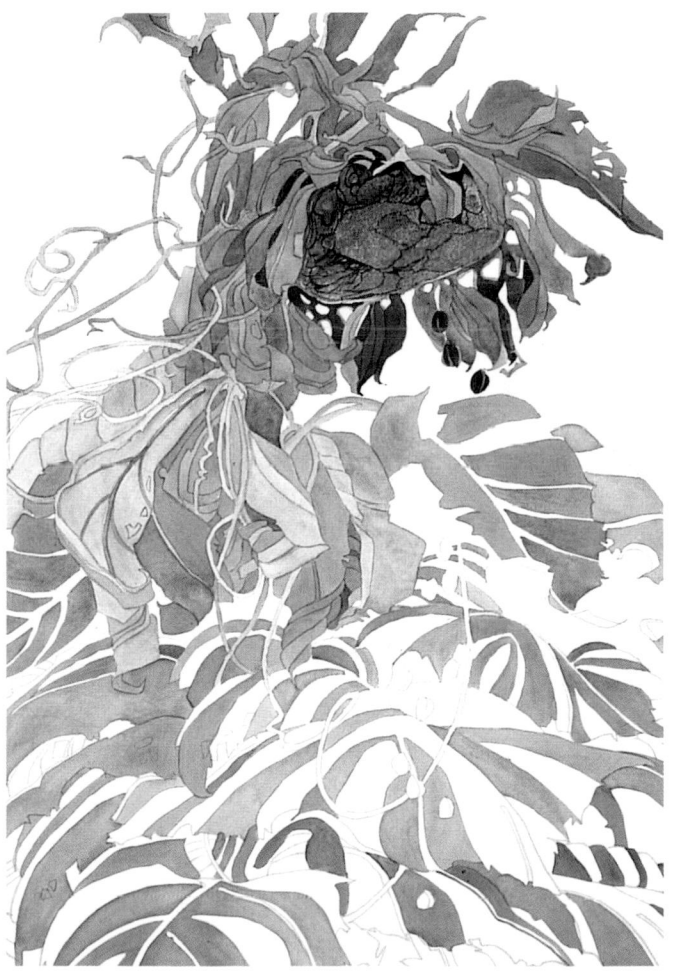

6 Begin the Body of the Plant

For the initial layer use only browns. Try Raw Sienna, Raw Umber and Burnt Sienna. Paint the shapes within each leaf, alternating section by section. The leaves will be striped like zebras. Cover the entire page, changing the brown colors from leaf to leaf for variety. Let dry.

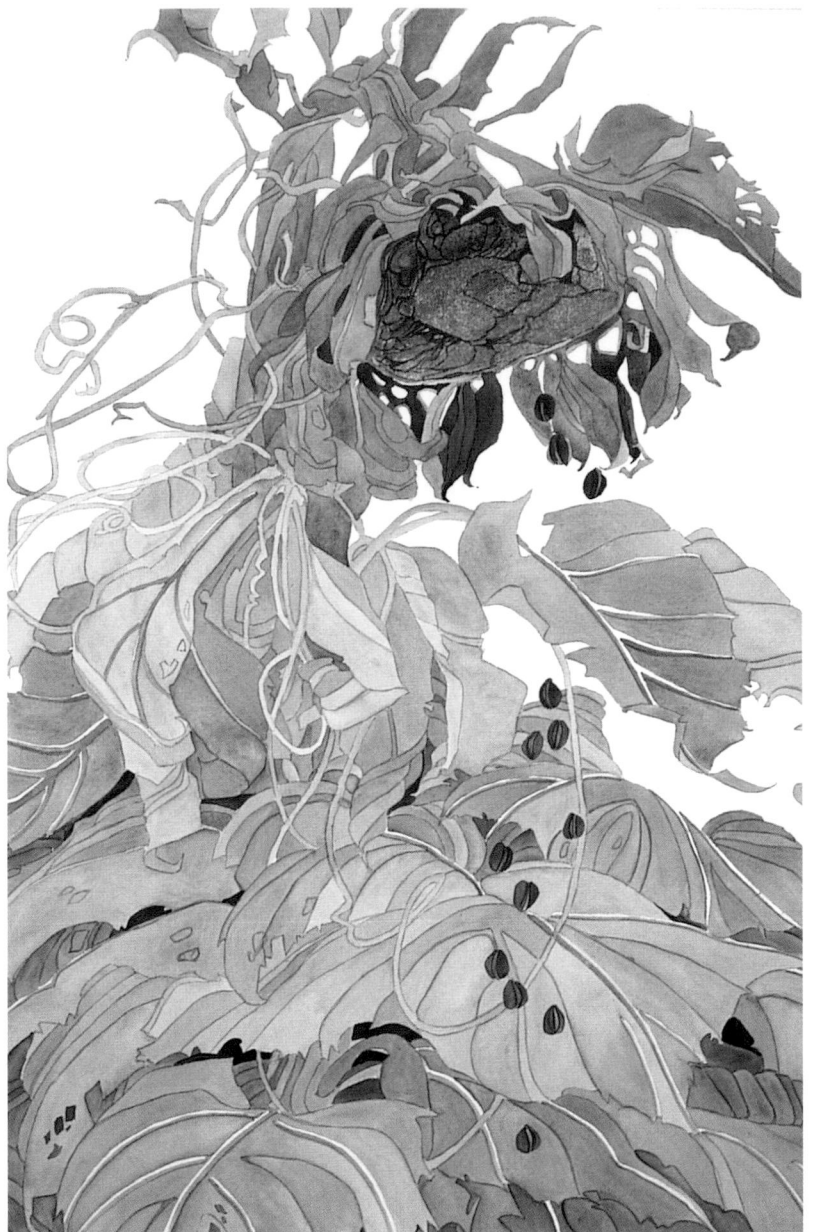

7 Finish the First Layer of Leaves

Paint the in-between spaces of the leaves, slightly overlapping the previously painted sections to give the effect of veins. The first section must be entirely dry before you overlap so that the edges remain sharp and don't run. Paint close to the dry edge, leaving thin white lines to create sparkle and to help the eye follow the flow of the design. When all the leaves have been painted, move around the painting adding Van Dyke Brown for the darkest darks. Create a "push and pull" effect of sinking some areas into the background and bringing other areas forward to add a range of values to your pattern of movement. Go back over areas where washes are uneven. Clean up rough edges.

8 Start the Glazing Process

Choose a color and begin glazing at the center of a leaf section. Gradually wash toward the edges so there is less paint and more wash on the far edge to give the leaf form. In some cases, glaze only parts of the leaves. Don't go over the same area a second time until it's completely dry or the sharpness of the vein lines will blur. If colors fade as they dry, add another glaze to enhance the vibrancy or glaze over with a third color. You can layer on washes indefinitely. Add more paint and less water to leaves in the background to push them back and give depth. Lift paint in the lower leaves by wetting and gently scrubbing with a stiff brush to bring the leaves into the foreground.

Helpful Hint NUMBER 25

If a wash in a large shape within a leaf is not smooth, paint a thin line around the irregularity to make a hole in the leaf or an extra vein. If a wash mixture looks undefined, paint a dark shape with hard edges in that area or rub out a white area for sparkle.

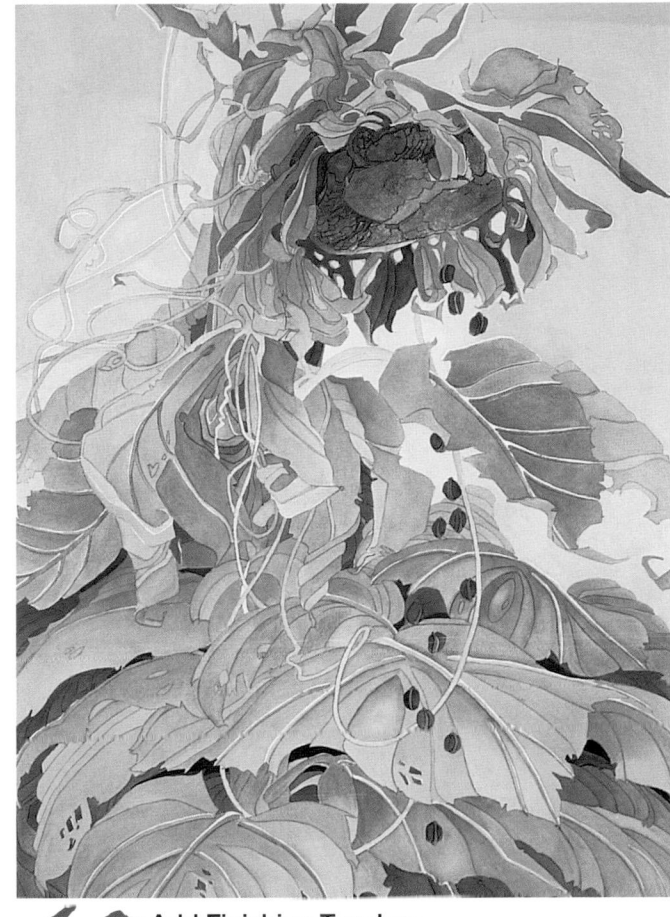

10 Add Finishing Touches

Refining, defining, tidying up edges and re-doing some of the washes will help balance all sections of the painting. Some sections can be wet and blotted to lighten and others can be further glazed to darken for the best result. Use the no. 8 round and paint in and around the stems and leaves to fill in the shapes that form the background.

9 Choose the Background Color

The background color establishes the dominant mood of the painting and must harmonize with the many shades of browns. Test several colors that might complement the subject. Two options are presented here: blue and yellow. Since browns are warm, yellow seems to be the best choice.

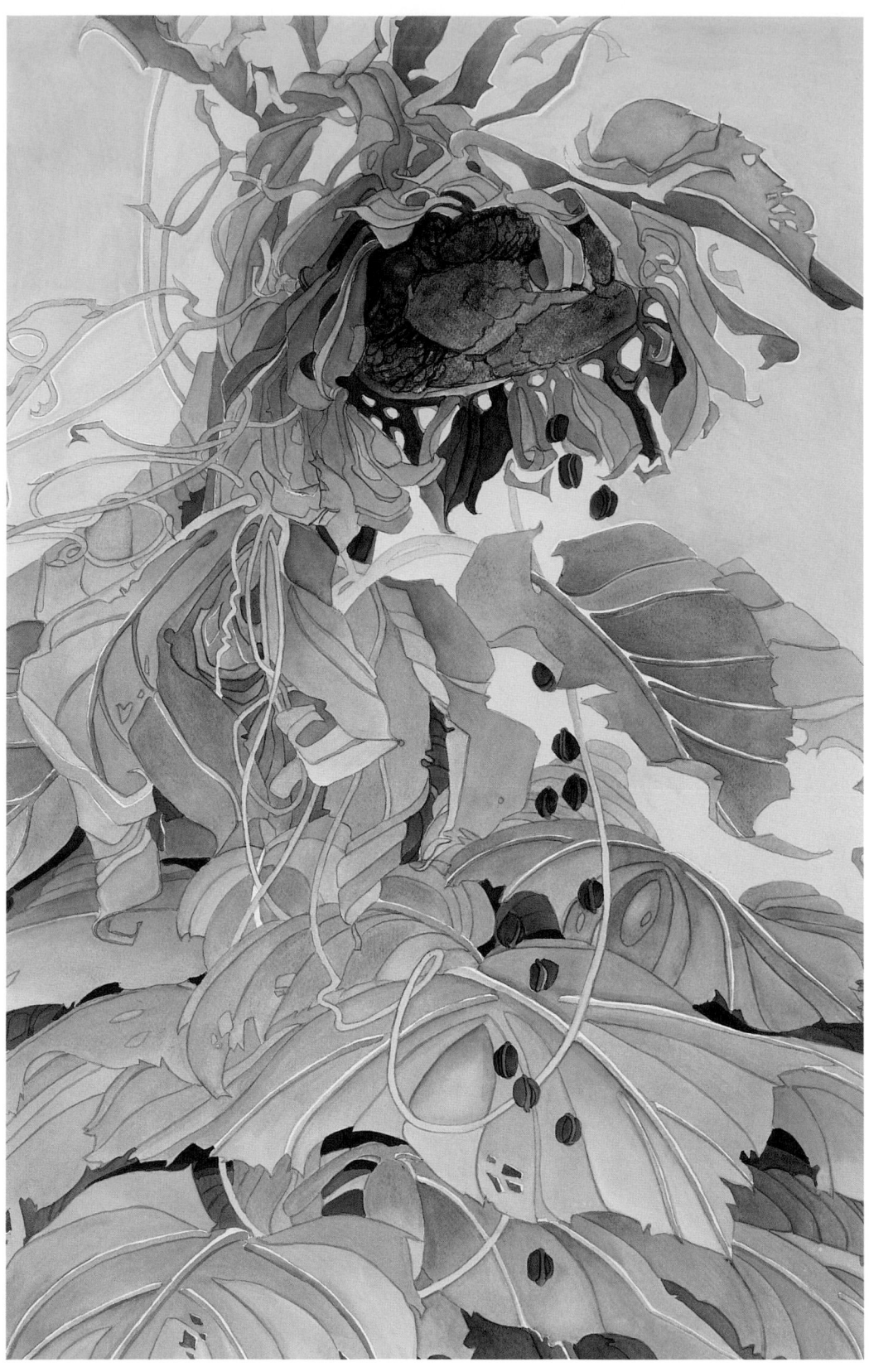

11 The Final Version

Sad Sarah
30" × 22" (76cm × 56cm)

Working With Oriental Papers

Oriental papers are available in a wide variety of textures and patterns ideal for watercolor painting. The papers lend themselves beautifully to the ethereal look that is characteristic of the medium. The delicacy and softness of the technique, combined with the natural fibers of the various papers, are especially excellent for developing floral paintings that range from vague color spills to hard-edged definition. In this demo, you will be practicing wet-into-wet, drybrushing, positive and negative painting, layering and edge control.

MATERIALS LIST

BRUSHES
Nos. 4 and 8 rounds

1-inch (25mm) flat

No. 1 detail

WATERCOLORS
Daniel Smith: Quinacridone Gold

Grumbacher: Burnt Sienna, Cadmium Red, Cadmium Yellow, Chinese White, Sap Green, Thalo Blue

Holbein: Opera

M. Graham & Co.: Quinacridone Violet

Winsor & Newton: Permanent Rose

SURFACE
8" x 10" (20cm × 25cm) Unryu Oriental paper

ADDITIONAL SUPPLIES
Bond paper, glue, pencil, Plexiglas

1 Practice First
Practice on small squares of paper to get the feel of how wet paint reacts, travels across and dries on this very absorbent Unryu Oriental paper. Place the squares on Plexiglas and wet them down. Control your edges, keeping them loose (soft) or making them sharp (hard), to create an ethereal floral effect. Add loose splashes of paint with a lot of water in some places, and tighten edged shapes with more paint and less water in others. This gives the fresh feeling of lost and found edges upon which to build the painting.

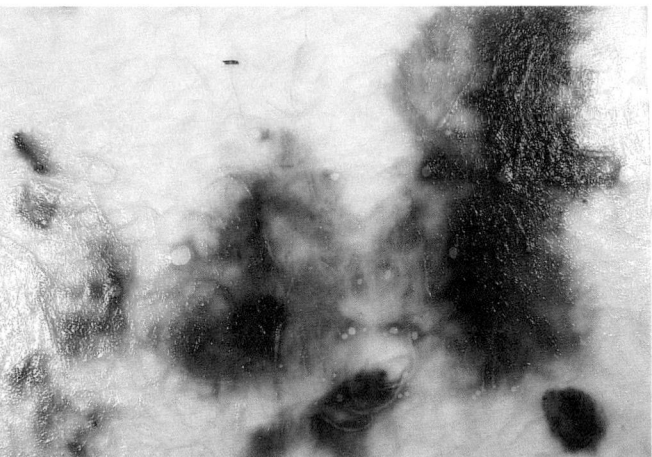

2 Get Started
Place your paper on top of a nonabsorbent surface (Plexiglas on glass works well). Using the 1-inch (25mm) flat, load the paper with clean water so that it is thoroughly saturated and sticks to the surface board. Tilt the board so the excess water runs off and then blot all around the edges of the paper. With the no. 8 round, charge in the flower colors, letting them blend freely together.

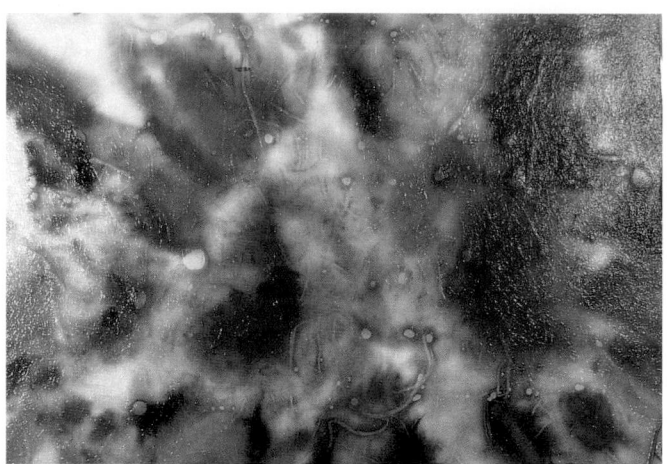

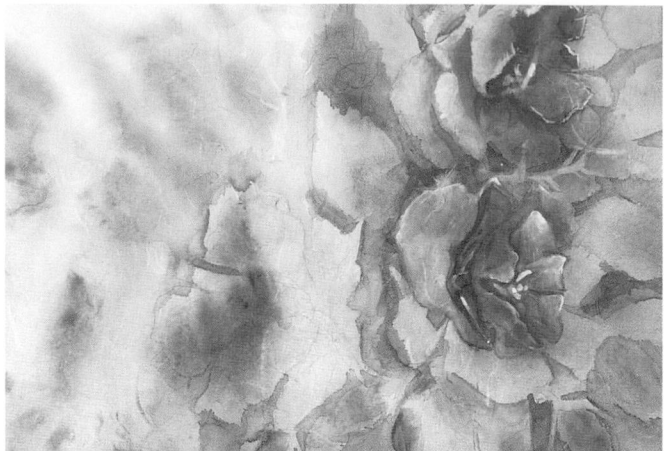

3 Cover the Paper With Paint

While the paper is still wet, switch to your leaf colors and begin painting green splotches in and around the red. Vary your greens by mixing blues and yellows and add a little Burnt Sienna and Quinacridone Gold for a diversion from the greens. Do not try to make actual leaf shapes. At this stage everything will be blurry and formless. Add extra paint to the flowers if some areas are fading. Let everything dry completely.

4 Develop the Flower Forms

Carefully pull the dried paper off the Plexiglas. Look at both sides of the paper and choose the one with the most potential. Lightly draw pencil lines around the edges of the flower petals to define their shapes. Paint into the areas behind the blossom forms with a damp brush loaded with greens for the leaves. It will take a little practice to get just the right amount of dryness so that the colors are controllable. Practice with the brush fully loaded with watery paint so that the brushstroke flows and leaves an irregular, soft edge. For controlled, hard edges, practice with an almost dry brush. Wash out the far edge of your shape with water to blend it into the background.

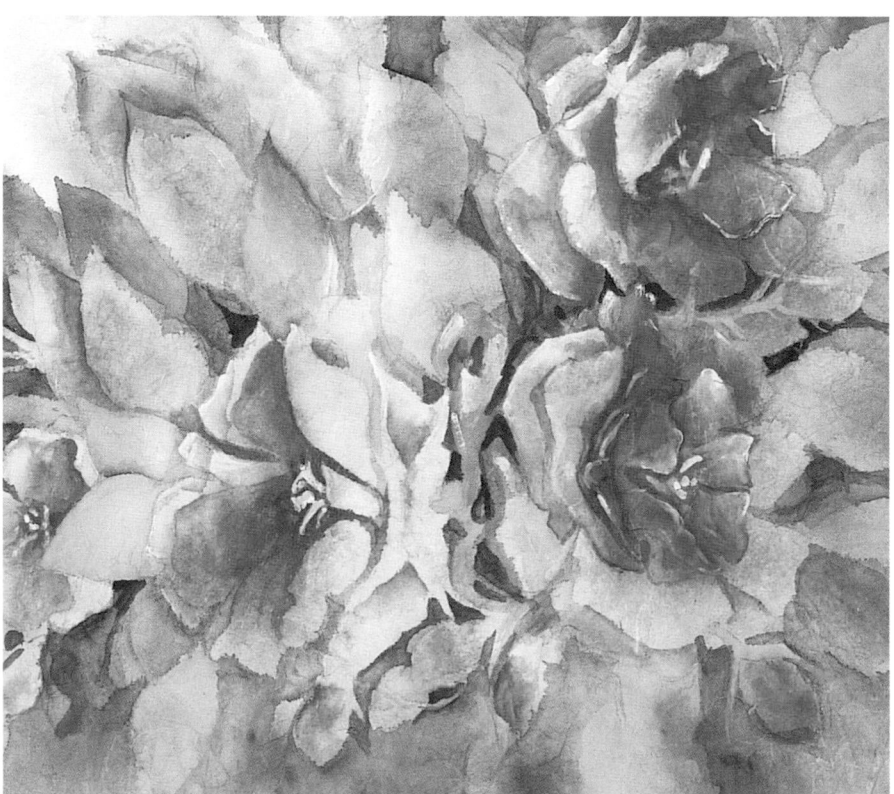

5 Fill in the Format

Continue as in step 4, identifying flower petals, leaves and clusters of buds. Paint both positively (by coloring in the actual petal or leaf) and negatively (by coloring the background around the petals and leaves). Use more water with the paint for loose edges and less water for hard edges. Don't worry if you lose some of the edges you intended to keep. The shapes will continue to change as you paint and will end up differently than what you planned. Fill the entire format so that the shapes flow across the page.

6 Add Depth by Layering Negatively

Create more stems and leaves by painting behind the existing ones with colors similar to the background (blues and greens). Add positive leaves in some places as well. Keep some edges soft and blurry by using a lot of water and some edges sharp, especially near the focal point, using an almost dry brush. Since you cannot regain the white of this delicate paper by rubbing out, use Chinese White to redefine some of the lost edges that are important to regain. Also, use Chinese White to lighten areas that became too dark and for highlighting petal edges.

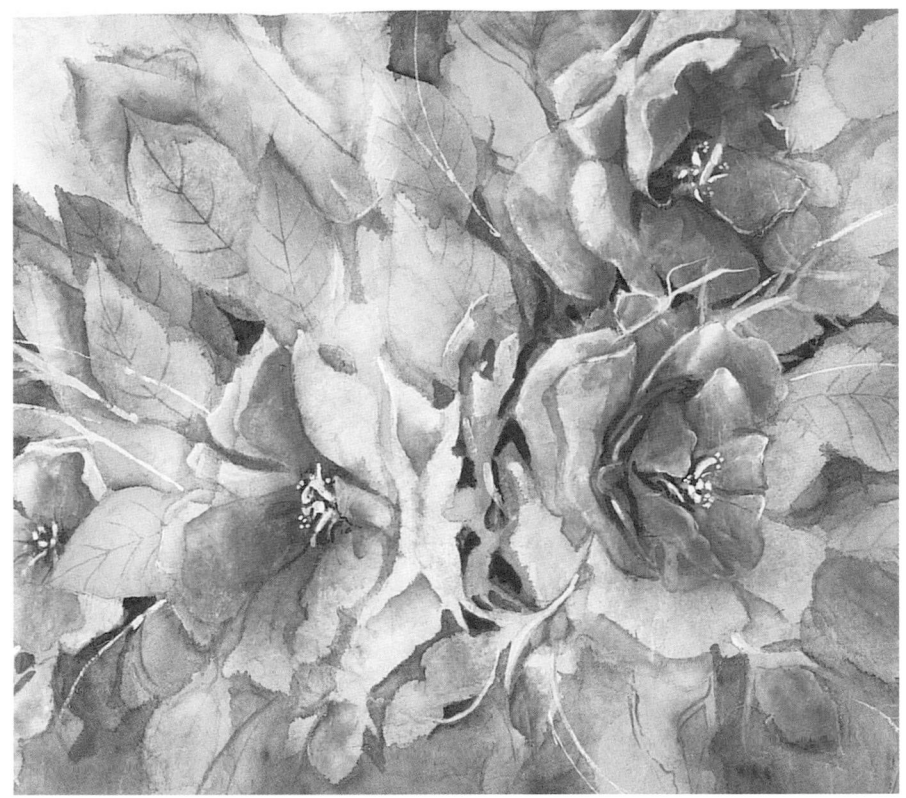

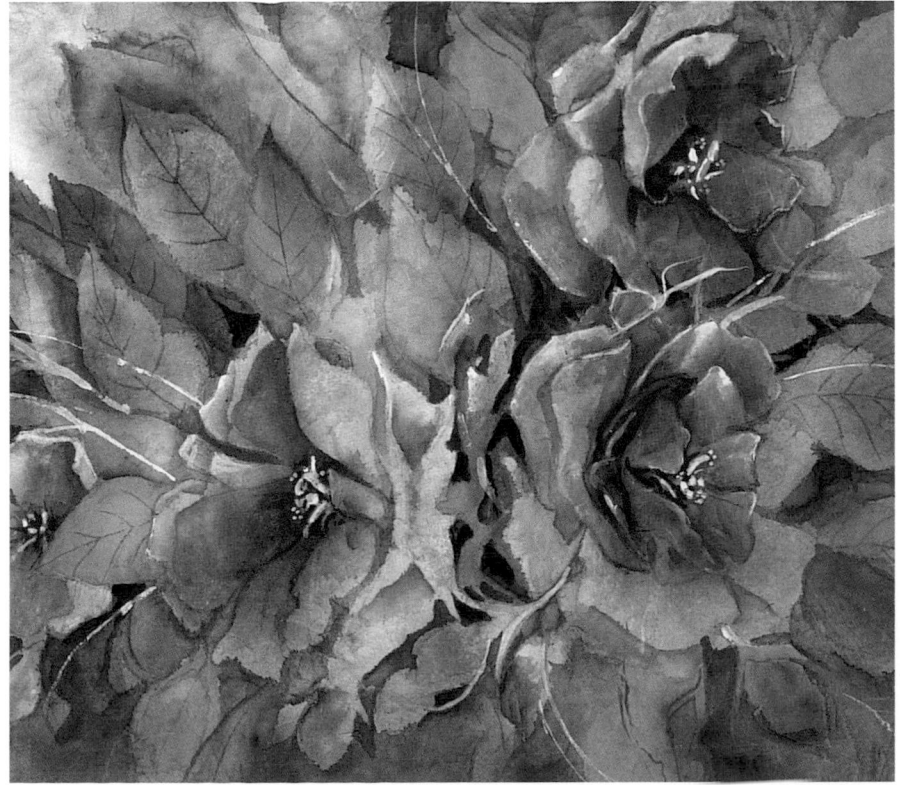

7 Add Details and Balance

Using the no. 1 detail, paint positively, adding stems and veins in directions that help designate the flow of the painting across the page. Add deeper color to the flower centers and around the petals at the focal point. Define some of the edges and add more Chinese White for highlights. You can keep the general feel loose or make it tighter with more hard edges. Maybe you want a combination of both.

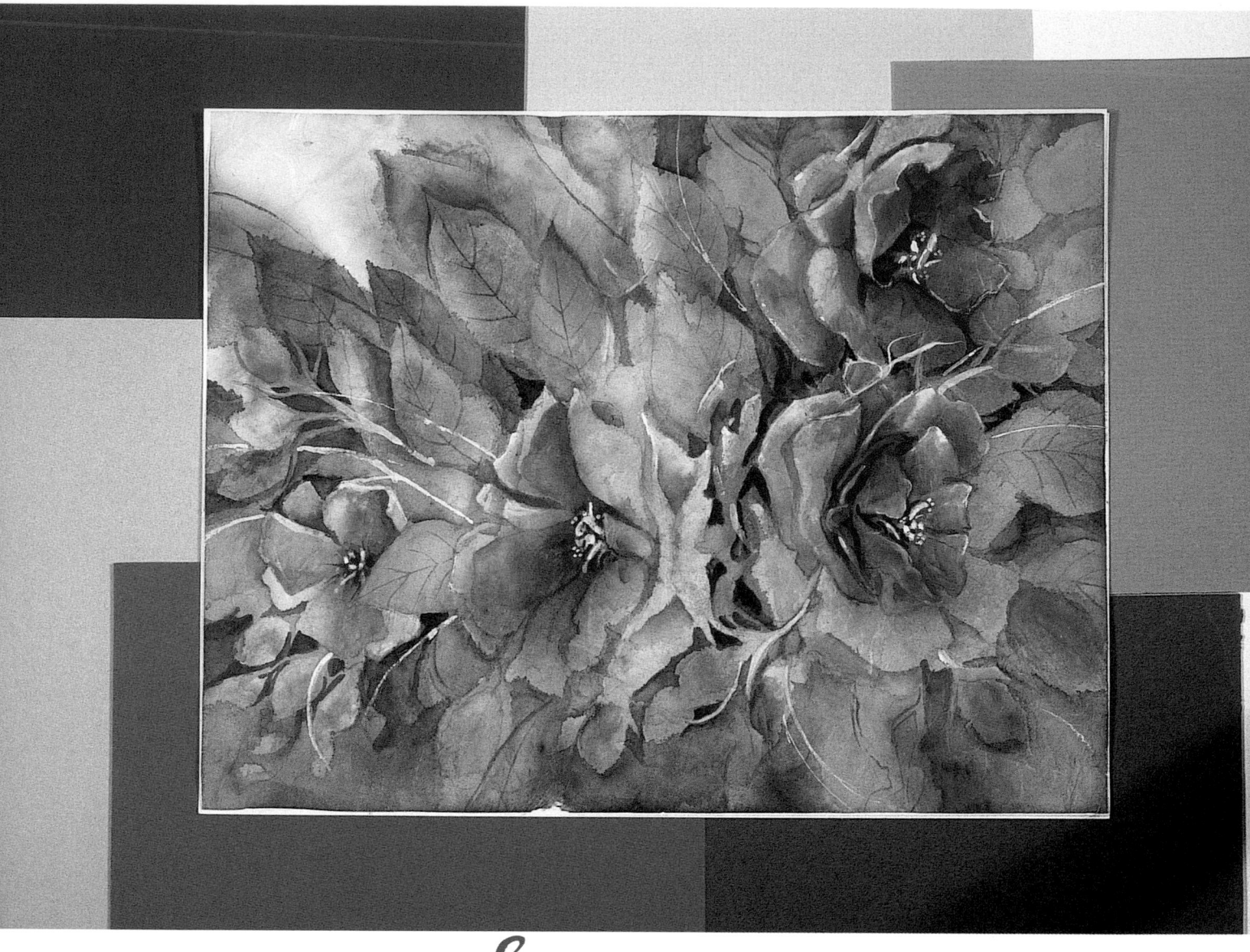

8 Mount Your Painting

Tear a piece of white bond paper to match the size of the finished painting. Glue it lightly to the back of the painting; this will show through making the colors appear brighter. Try several different colors of precut mat board to see which color best suits the mood you choose to express. Depending on the size of the painting, you can use your finished piece in a number of ways—from greeting cards to small framed paintings.

Ikebana
8½" × 11" (22cm × 28cm)

Helpful Hint NUMBER 26

Of all the choices of Oriental papers available, my favorite is Unryu because of its heavy fiber texture and natural look. When working with this paper, you'll notice that the fibers sometimes retain paint and sometimes resist it, resembling twig veins and branches.

You can tear some of the edges of the paper for added interest or to conform with the leaf edges or flower bud shapes. Practice on small 5" × 6" (13cm × 15cm) pieces to see how the paper and paint work together.

Using Masking Fluid in a Layered Painting

Repeated subject matter works well in a layered painting because you create echoing images that gradually sink into the background. Masking fluid allows you to build one color wash over another, protecting the colors of the former layers that will be revealed when the masking fluid is removed. Many layers can be built up creating depth and a richness of overlapping colors. In this demonstration, you will practice working with masking fluid, dropping in paint, spattering with a toothbrush, layering flat washes, negative painting, glazes and printing with Plexiglas.

MATERIALS LIST

BRUSHES

No. 8 round

3-inch (76mm) flat

No. 1 detail

WATERCOLORS

Grumbacher: Cadmium Yellow, Sap Green, Thalo Blue, Thalo Yellow Green

Winsor & Newton: Indigo

SURFACE

½ sheet (11" × 15" [28cm × 38cm]) 140-lb. (300gsm) Arches hot-pressed paper

ADDITIONAL SUPPLIES

Big gum eraser, masking fluid, Plexiglas, toothbrush

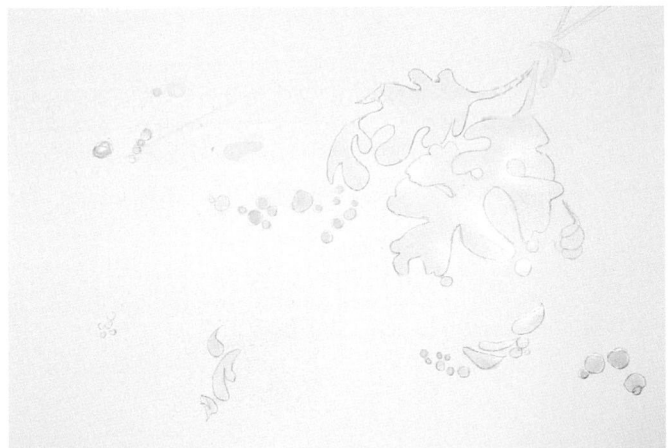

1 Get Started

Using dried oak leaves for your subject, draw one or two images that will be the focal point. This area will eventually have the whitest white next to the darkest darks. Paint these leaves with masking fluid to retain the white throughout the painting process. Spatter masking fluid with a toothbrush making tiny dots. Then, add some large drops by gently tapping the brush loaded with masking fluid. Let everything dry completely.

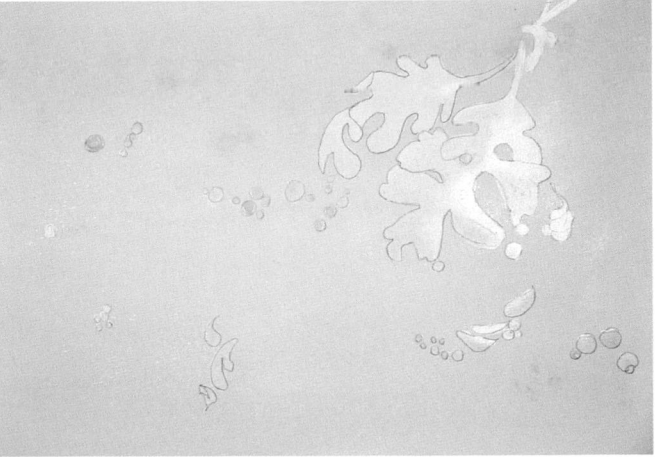

2 Layer on the First Wash

Mix a wash of Cadmium Yellow and a little Thalo Yellow Green. Using the 3-inch (76mm) flat, make a long, slow stroke from left to right at the top of the page. Tilt the paper slightly so that the paint flows to the bottom of the brushstroke. Reload your brush and make another long stroke just below the other one, overlapping slightly. Continue down the page until it is covered. Take your time. Don't rush or interrupt your brushstrokes or the wash will become uneven. Let dry. Don't worry if your first wash is not perfect. Successive washes will disguise irregularities.

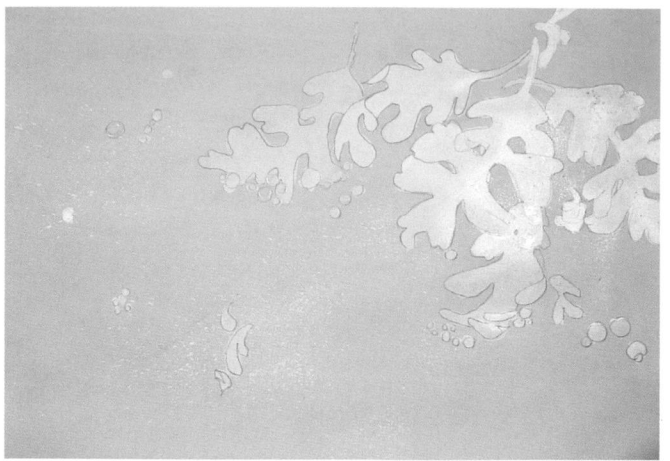 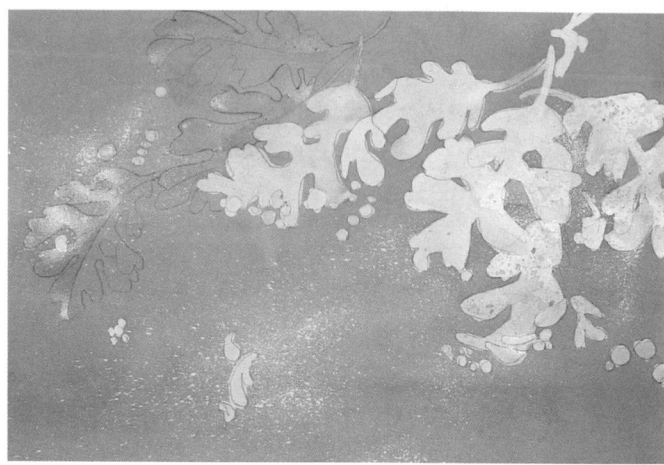

3 Create the Next Layered Flat Wash

Add a few more leaves, moving outward from the focal point. Paint over the yellow leaves with masking fluid, then do more spattering with the toothbrush. Let dry. Lay on another wash, covering the entire page with a Cadmium Yellow and Thalo Yellow Green mixture. Add more of the Thalo Yellow Green so that this wash will appear darker than the first one. Let dry.

4 Add the Next Two Layered Washes

Glide a mix of Sap Green and Thalo Yellow Green over the entire page with the 3-inch (76mm) flat. When the wash is dry, draw on more leaves and then this time paint only the top half of each leaf with masking fluid. Do more spattering with the toothbrush. Let everything dry, then lay on a wash of Sap Green mixed with Thalo Blue. Let dry.

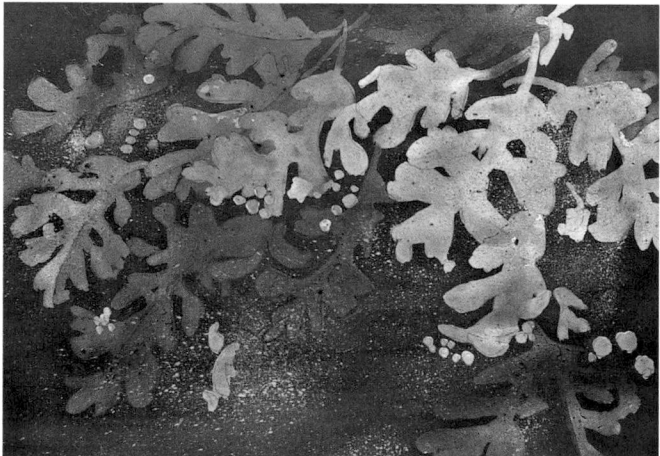

5 Draw More Layers of Leaves

Use masking fluid to paint the bottom halves of the leaves that you've just added. Draw more leaves and paint the top half with masking fluid. When dry, lay on a wash mixing Sap Green and Thalo Blue (use more blue than in the previous wash). Paint only the top or bottom halves of leaves to give each leaf a light and dark half for variety. Repeat this series of steps for several layers, adding more leaves and gradually getting darker with each successive wash.

Helpful Hint NUMBER 27

Rub soap suds into your brush before dipping it into masking fluid for easier cleanup. Be sure to wash your brushes immediately, before the masking fluid dries. This also applies to any other material you use with your brush, such as gesso, and acrylic gel medium.

6 Fill the Painting With Leaves

Draw more leaves behind the existing ones, letting them peek out from behind. Continue until most of the page is covered with leaves. Add acorns for shape variety and to help fill in areas that need more substance to create a pleasing composition. Paint these new shapes with masking fluid. When dry, lay on the final flat wash of darkest Thalo Blue, using more paint and less water.

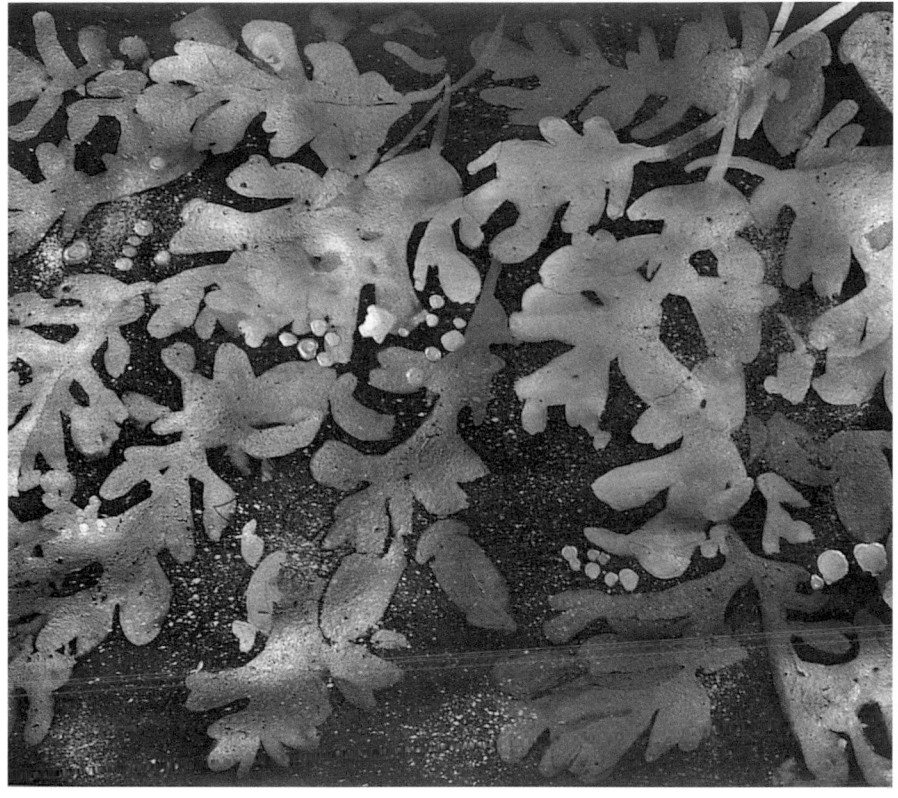

7 Reveal the Underlying Colors

Remove all of the masking fluid with a gum eraser to reveal the leaves in various receding shades of blue and green. This can be tedious, so be patient. The longer you wait, the harder it will be to remove the masking fluid. Leave on bits of masking fluid in some places. Glaze over them, let dry, and then remove them to reveal a textured pattern on the leaf surface. The white leaves of the focal point in the top right corner are an example. In the end, be sure to remove all of the masking fluid because it will damage the paper over time if left on.

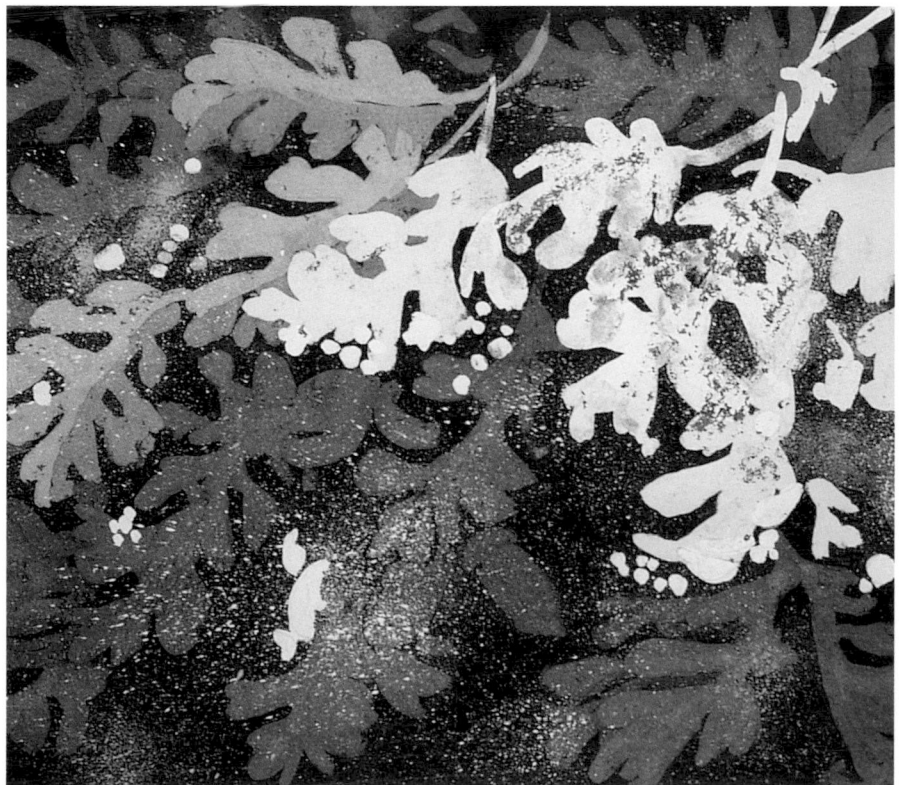

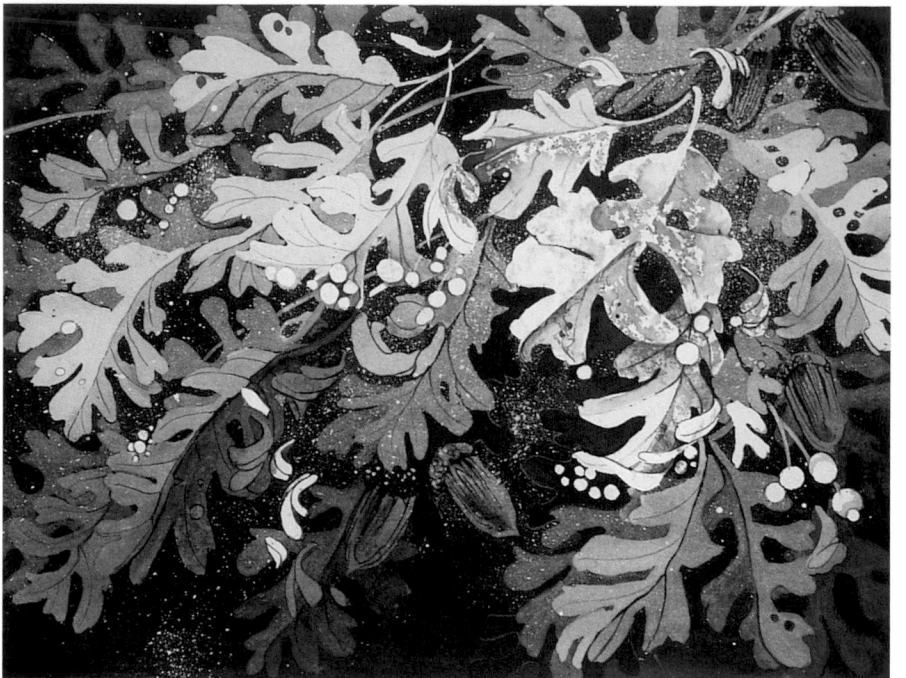

8 Add Textures and Glaze

Continue to add texture to the leaves by painting over masking fluid residue. If you want to add a different kind of texture, paint a small piece of Plexiglas with blue or green and then press it onto the surface of the leaves. Begin to glaze over various sections of some leaves to give them form. Sink some areas of leaves into the background to create a feeling of depth and tiers of leaves moving from the foreground into the distance. Add dark lines with the no. 1 detail to represent stems, leaves and veins.

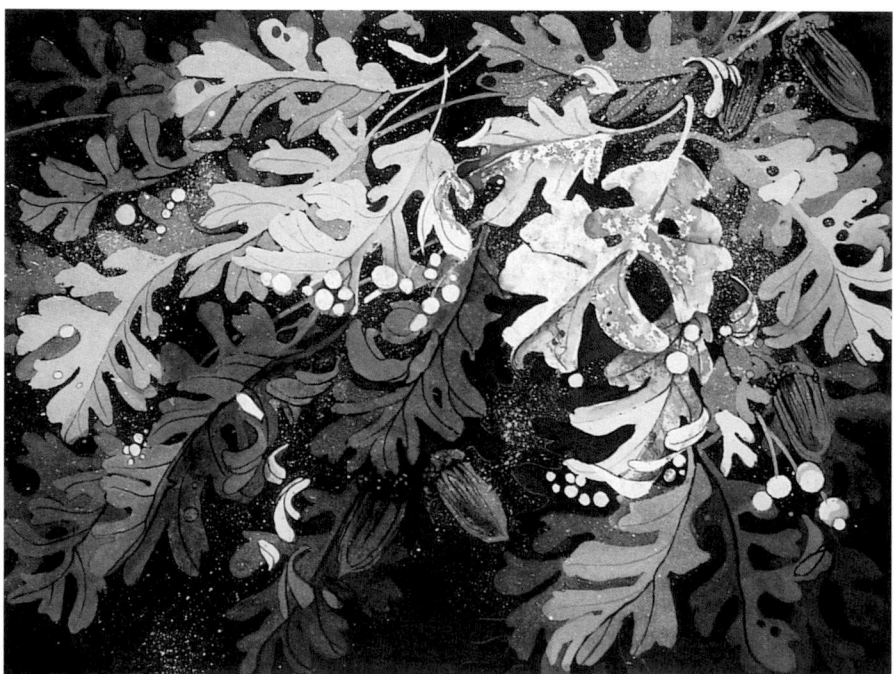

9 Finish the Details

Continue to make adjustments by glazing some areas even darker to push them into the background. This gives the effect of other areas popping into the foreground, especially the focal point. Also, this helps the flow of shapes across the page, as well as provides dimension. Tidy up and clarify leaf edges, and improve the shapes of some edges that have become lost in the layering process. Add the darkest darks with Indigo in the background around the focal point.

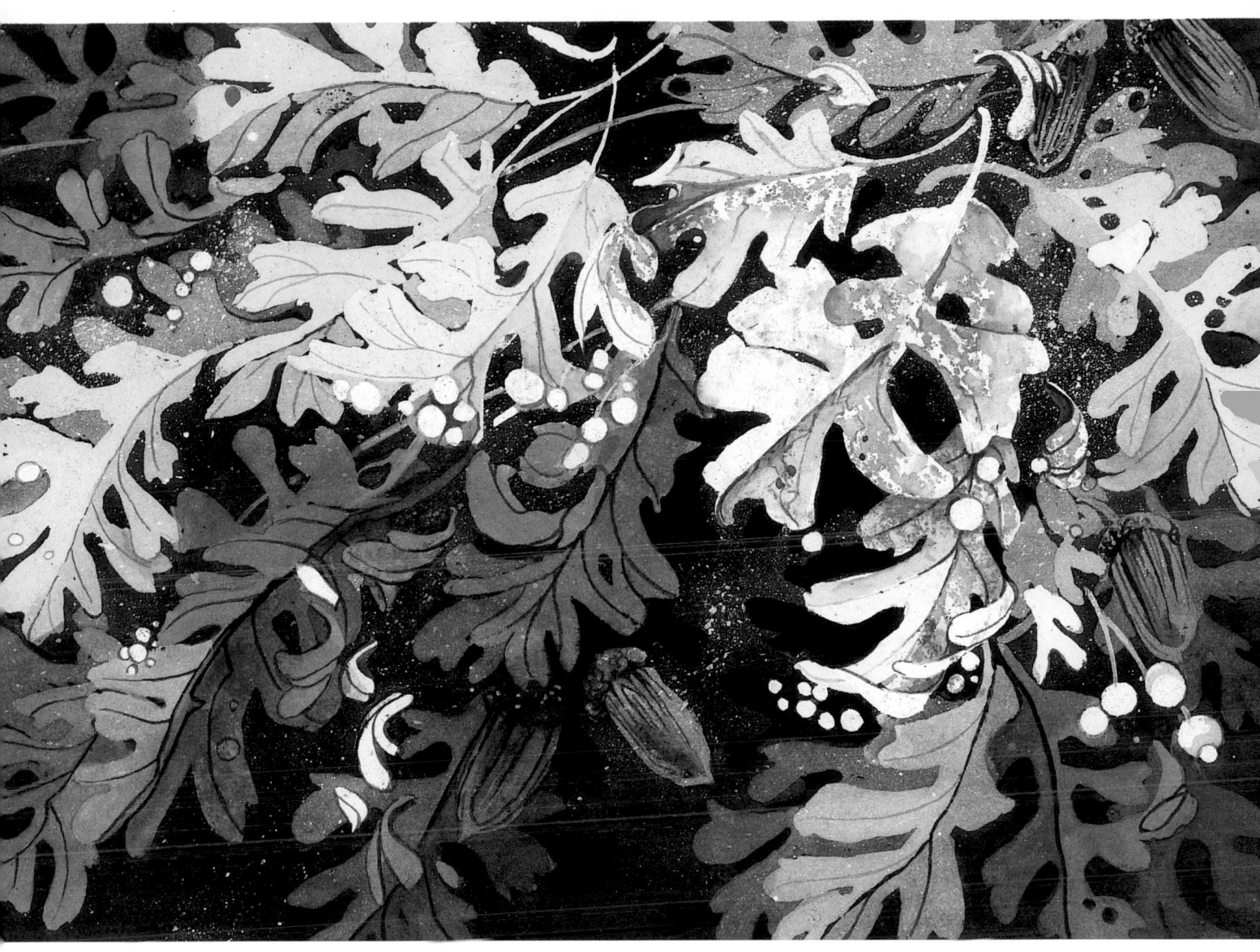

10 The Final Painting

Winterberry
11" × 15" (28cm × 38cm)

Helpful Hint NUMBER 28

Be sure to step back from your painting early and often. Look at your painting in a mirror to help locate possible flaws. When finished, put your painting away for a week or two. Then take another look at it. This will prevent you from making any rush decisions.

making the painting your own

Now that you have mastered the fundamentals of putting paint to paper and have become adroit at the craftsmanship of the painting process, it is time to make your paintings reflect what is uniquely you. As the individual artist, no one else will approach a painting in exactly the same way. The most successful paintings require a blending of spirit, mind and body, along with creativity and composition and design fundamentals, to lead the painter to the next level of expression. Step outside the box and paint beyond the lines. Look for other options and explore new paths. Ask "What if I try this?" Challenge yourself and soon you will be on the path to innovative and dynamic painting statements. You alone can bring something new to your painting process, moving beyond the ordinary via personal style, imagination, interpretation of the subject or a combination of different subject matter to match your intention.

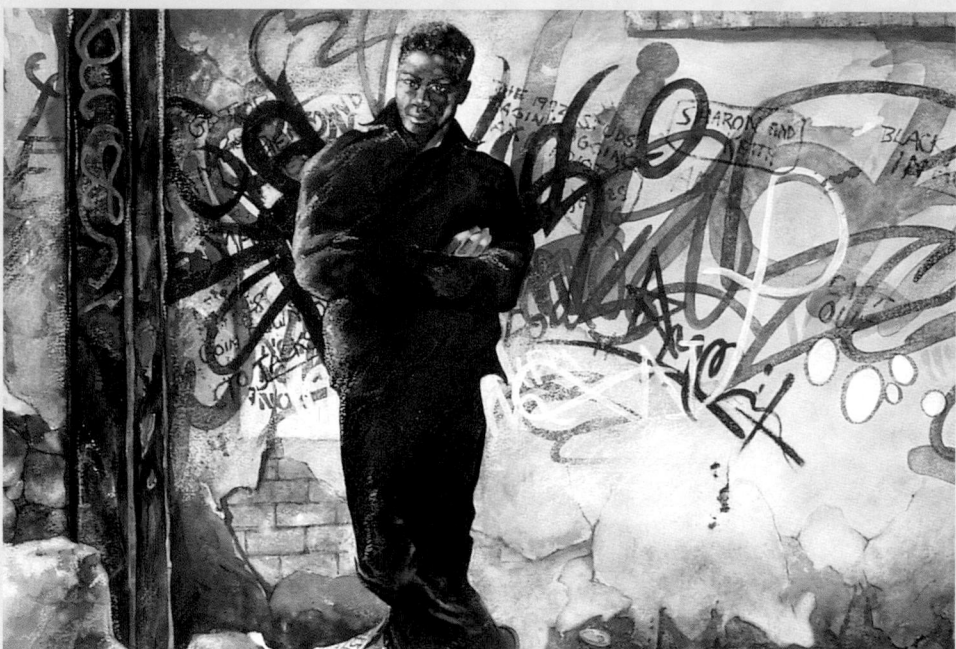

Painting Something Unique or Uncommon

Think of something that is not usually noticed or isn't thought of as beautiful by others, but appeals to you because it's unique or uncommon subject matter. A rusty old truck or a dilapidated country barn might not appeal to some people, but there are aspects of each that can be translated into dynamic, eye-catching paintings. Most people regard graffiti as nothing more than destructive vandalism, but I think it's beautiful. It always attracts my eye. In *But Is It Art?* I ask the viewer to decide. This painting is a compilation of ideas taken from different photos of graffiti that I have accumulated from several cities.

But Is It Art?
22" × 30" (56cm × 76cm)

Painting the Adjective

A pot of geraniums on a windowsill is a common subject, but what is it about that particular subject that is especially alluring to you? Is it the brilliant red of the flowers? The shadow cast upon the wall? Paint the adjective that describes your subject and compelled you to paint, and then exaggerate it. In *Patio Chairs*, the late afternoon sun cast long, purple shadows across the concrete patio. The main interest behind this painting was to capture the intriguing shadow pattern, not the chairs themselves.

Patio Chairs
22" × 30" (56cm × 76cm)

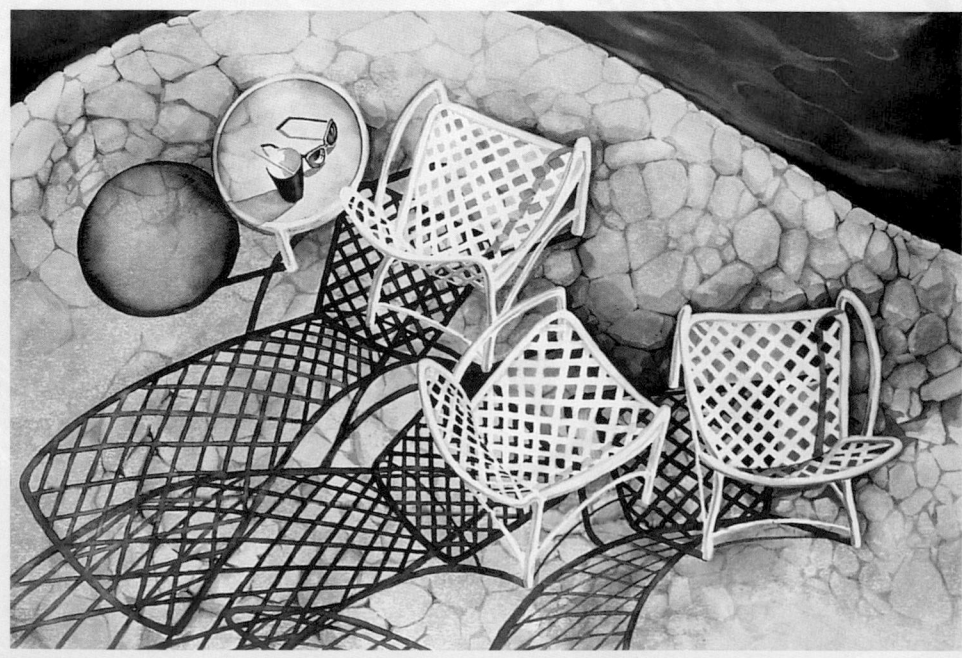

Painting a Different Perspective

Using a different perspective can make ordinary subjects new, exciting and original. An interesting vantage point can change the emphasis and create an entirely new way of looking at and appreciating commonly painted subjects. In *Orange Pekoe*, the viewer looks directly down upon the still life, with the objects placed at an angle for further interest. This adds a unique perspective that is rarely used and is a little more exciting.

Orange Pekoe
22" × 30" (56cm × 76cm)

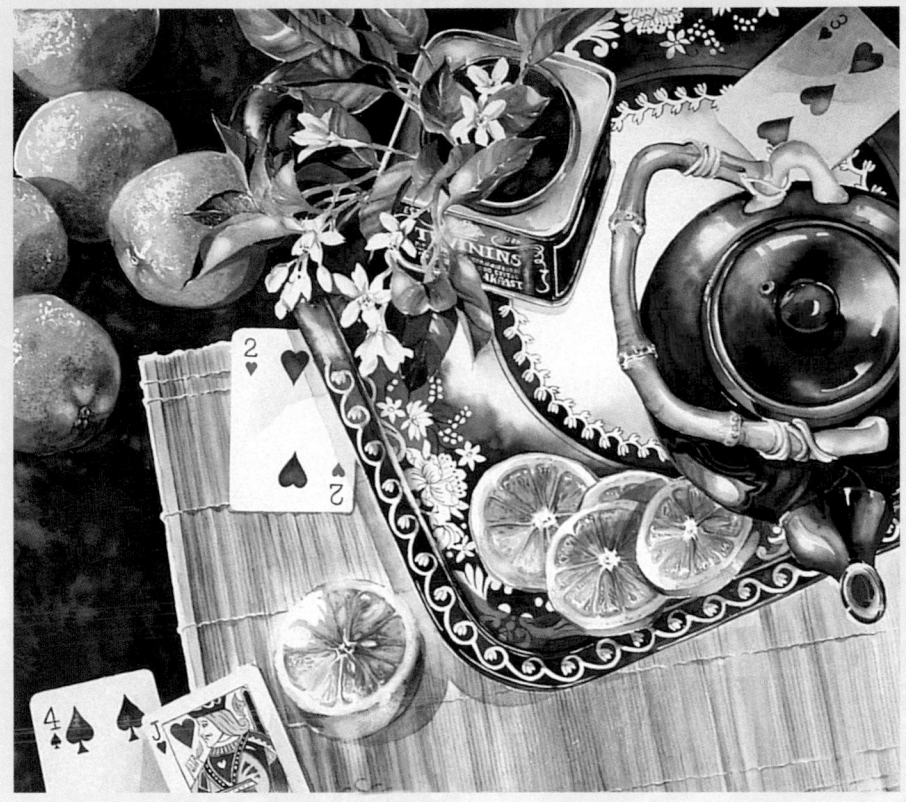

Painting a Unique Combination

A unique combination of ordinary things can intrigue the viewer. The objects you choose may have special significance to you personally, or they might just make you feel good. Try entirely unrelated pictorial content, or completely different and contrasting colors and shapes, and place them in unusual combinations. In *Enigma*, I used unrelated objects such as fish, flowers, clocks and geometrics—everything just for fun. There is a conflicting dichotomy between man-made and natural things. Interwoven, the objects become harmonious yet retain their individual attraction.

Enigma
22" × 30" (56cm × 76cm)

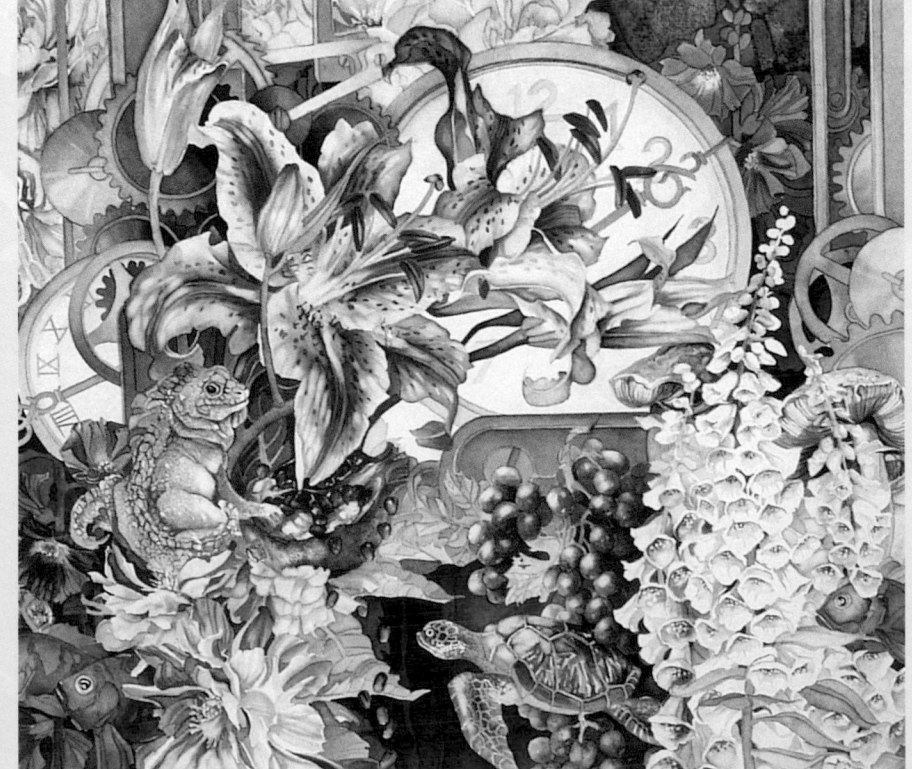

Painting With Humor

Try using humor in your paintings to amuse the viewer in a subtle way. In A *Joker in Every Pack*, a goat has joined the herd of Herefords and is very proud to be associated with the burly beasts.

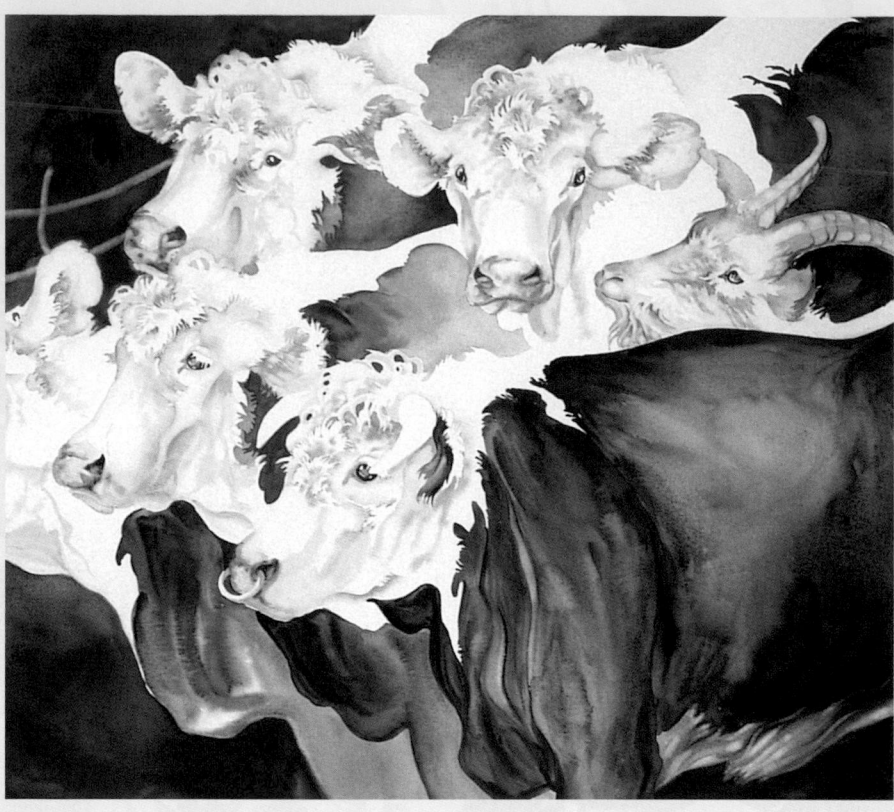

A Joker in Every Pack
22" × 30" (56cm × 76cm)

Painting With Combined Mediums

As you've learned from earlier in the book, combining mediums will open up uncharted domains in your paintings. Try putting pastel on top of watercolor. Use acrylics and watercolor together or crayon under watercolor. The choices are nearly limitless, as are the resulting effects. *Mondegreen Pools* combines watercolor with colored pencil on top for a softening effect and a blending of elements. Create the watercolor painting first, then after it dries add colored pencil to soften and blend certain areas. You can continue to build up layers of watercolor on top of colored pencil and colored pencil on top of watercolor until you are satisfied with the result.

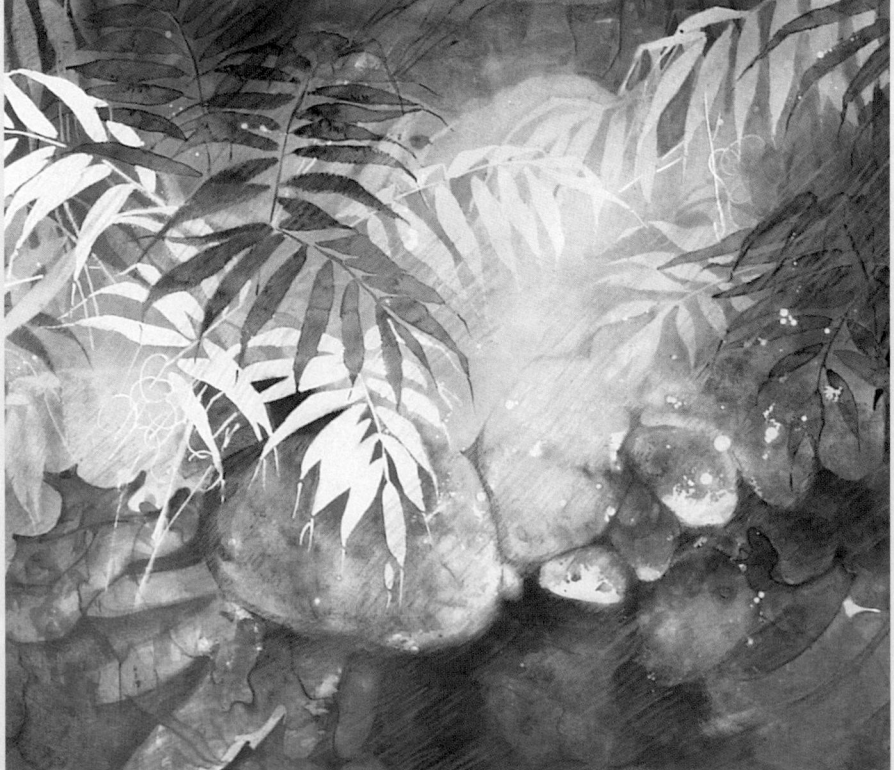

Mondegreen Pools
22" × 30" (56cm × 76cm)

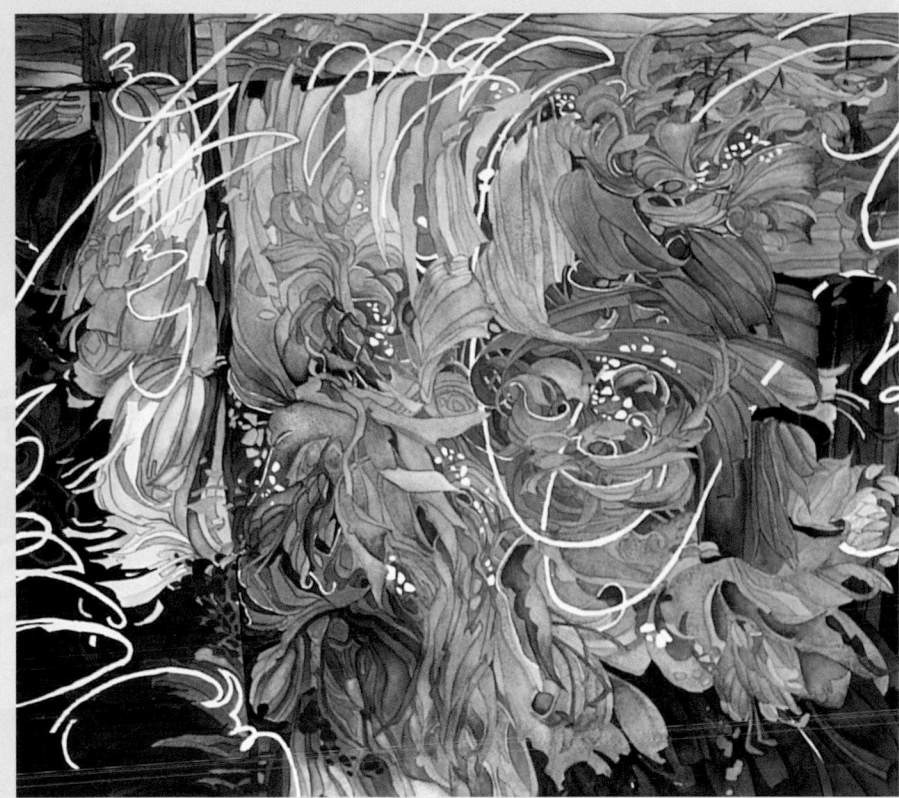

Painting Abstract Subjects

Move to the next level by abstracting the subject matter. Try to decide what aspects of the painting's content appeal the most to you, and then emphasize them. In *Wisteria*, the vigorous and wayward spreading of vines and long flower clusters of the blossoms are controlled by the verticals and horizontals of the framework. The rich color, as well as the curvilinear shapes, are stylized rather than realistic. The challenge was to control the rich color and convoluted blossom forms entwined with vines in complex patterns to create a pleasing design.

Wisteria
22" × 30" (56cm × 76cm)

Painting Nonconceptually

Move to another level by painting nonconceptually. You won't be painting in relation to realistic pictorial content, but rather emphasizing different design elements such as color, shape and line. Notice that *Gracenotes* focuses on expressions of design elements, not an interpretation of realistic subject matter. The emphasis is on geometrics rather than natural subject matter. This is a great approach to practice all aspects of composition and design without the extra complication of pictorial content.

Gracenotes
22" × 30" (56cm × 76cm)

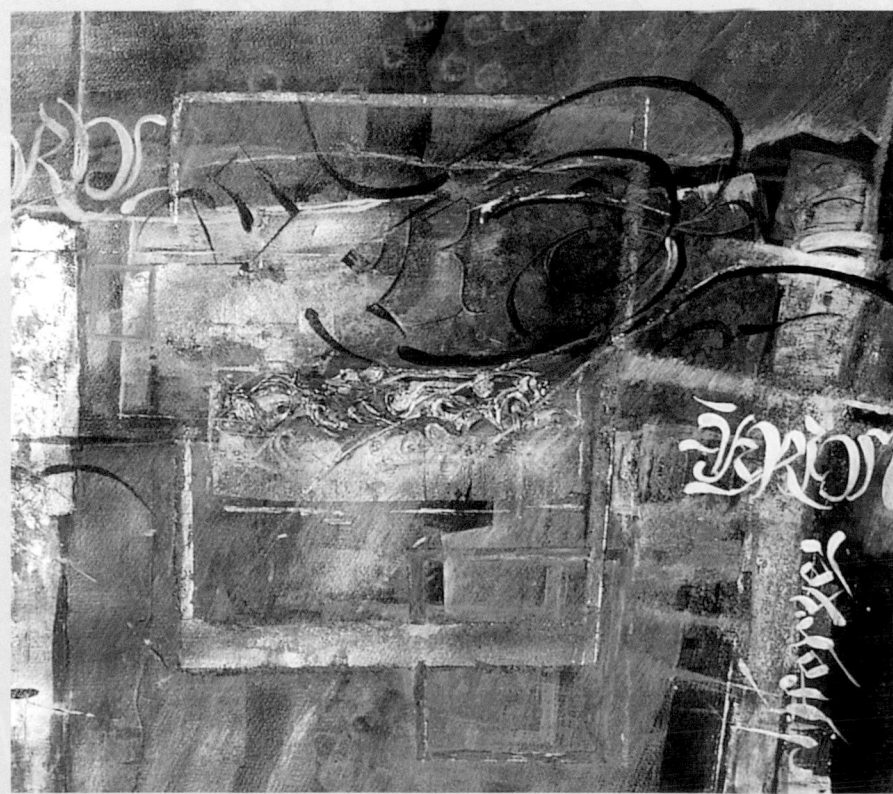

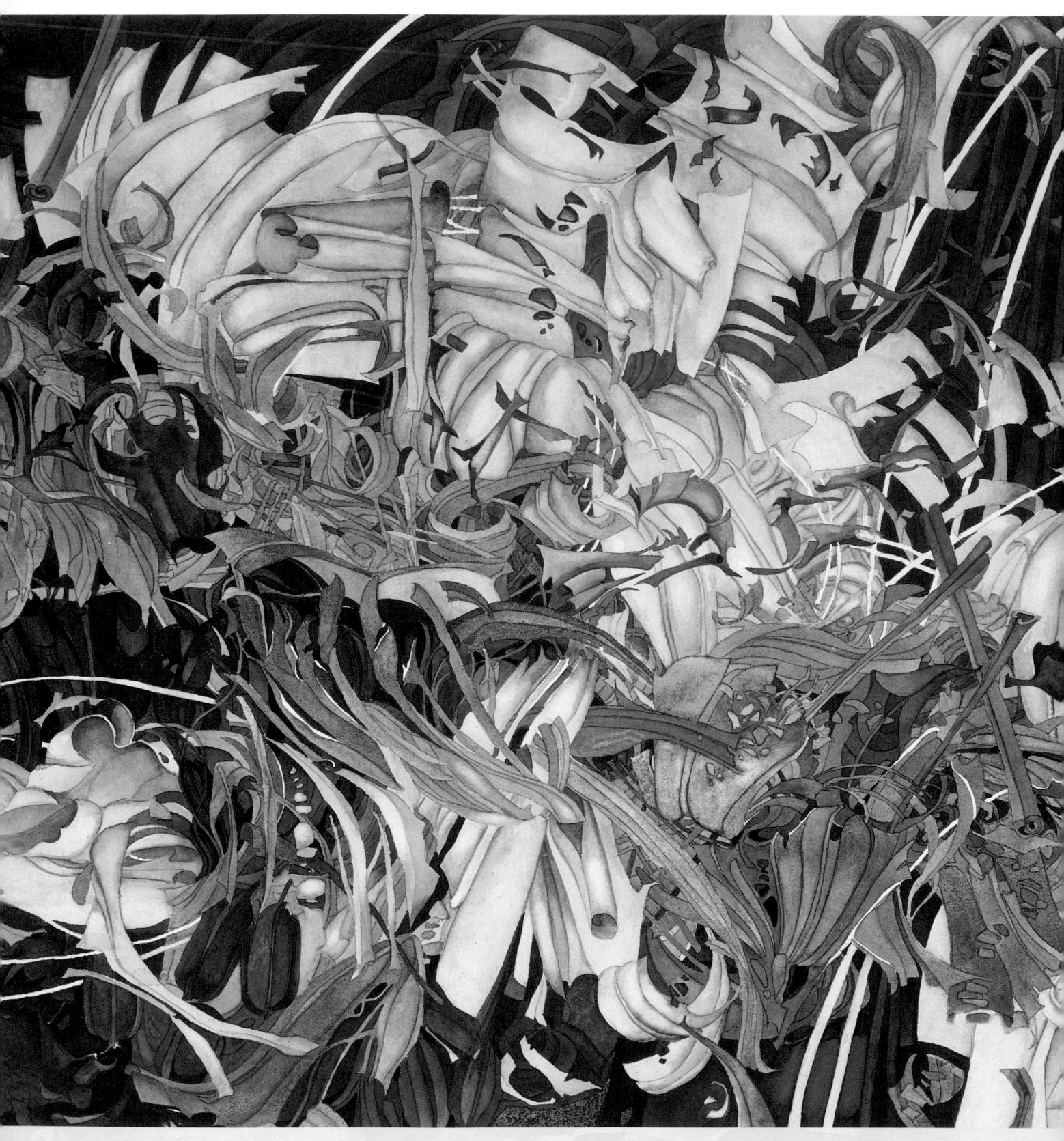

conclusion

The watercolor experience is just plain exciting! It is so versatile and colorful that you will always discover a great deal of joy by simply putting paint on paper. When you're lucky enough, you will find yourself in the "zone"—when time seems to drift away and you and the process become one. Painting is an excellent outlet for expressing a feeling or idea in such a way that others can share your unique vision.

I hope the explanations, exercises and demonstrations in this book provide the inspiration and encouragement for you to continue in your own artistic pursuits. Regardless of how you choose to paint, don't wait until an idea comes to your mind before you paint. Begin by splashing beautiful color on your paper and see where it takes you. Trust me, the muse will take notice and whisper in your ear, and that's when the magic begins.

The best advice I can give aspiring artists is to paint what you love in a way that is most true for you. The personal integrity of your work is paramount. Project your own consciousness into your painting and become emotionally involved. Perseverance, dedication and hard work will always win over talent or waiting for inspiration. Pushing boundaries and trying new approaches might create a lot of failed paintings, but never anything common, repetitive or unmemorable. Why paint yellow sunflowers on a blue sky when you can paint blue sunflowers on a red sky? How about a curvilinear fish painting with geometrical clock shapes in it? The possibilities are limitless. Just remember to work hard, have fun and don't worry. Take chances and try new things. What's the worst that can happen? The paper always has another side.

Regardless of our skill level or how many years we've been painting, we are all perpetual students. If you have the desire, and you are willing to expend the required effort, you will succeed. Personally, I think I'll always be striving to capture this elusive thing called art. I suspect I never will, but it is a wonderful thing to try.

Through the years I've learned a lot. All of the information in this book is a distillation of the knowledge that I have gained in the last twenty years of reading, attending workshops, teaching workshops, creating demonstrations and a *lot* of painting and experimentation. I hope that from this information you are able to glean some ideas that you can incorporate into your own work. Try tackling the demonstrations and exercises in this book. Mix them up, combine one with another, and invent your own, unique ways of using this material. Consider each completed demonstration as a stepping stone along a pathway of unending discoveries. Remember, you never really "arrive" at your final painting destination because the path goes on and on as far as you wish to pursue it.

Let your own journey begin.

Elizabeth Groves

Agapanthus
22" × 30" (56cm × 76cm)

index

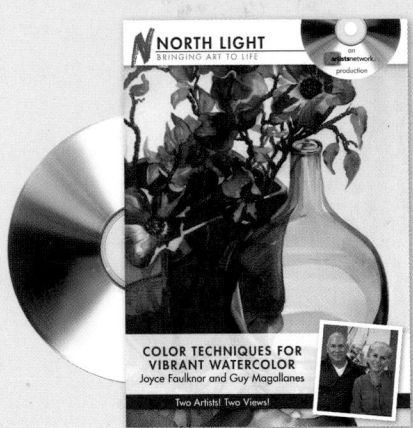
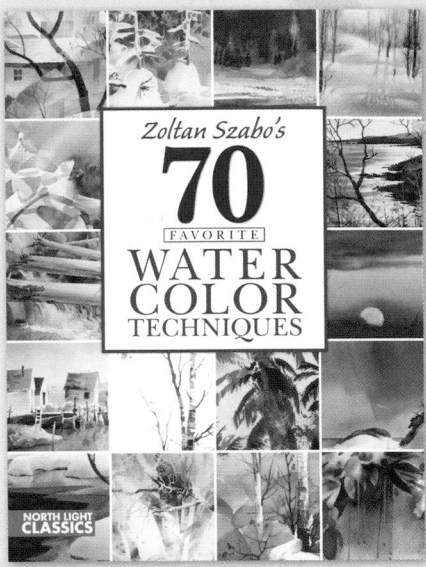
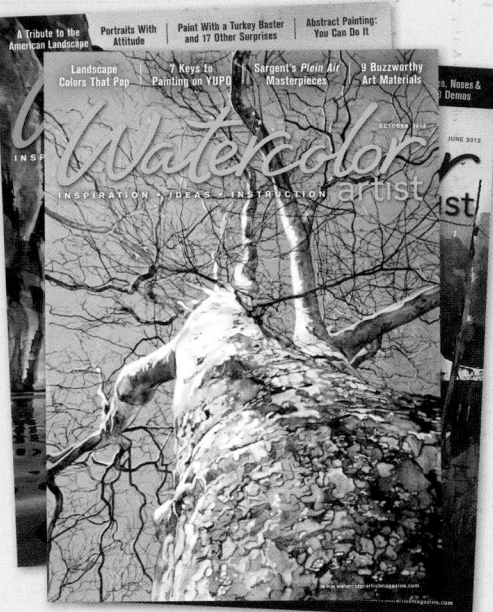

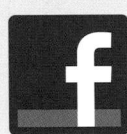
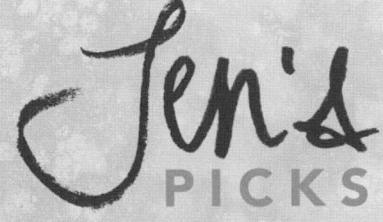
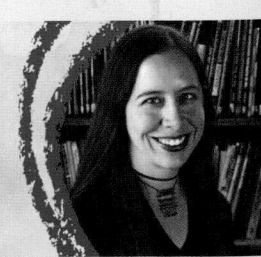
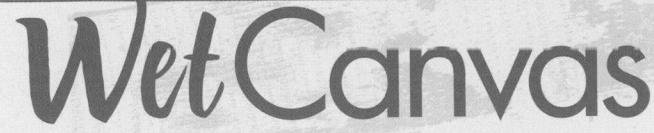